IMISCOE Research Series

AF394702

Now accepted for Scopus! Content available on the Scopus site in spring 2021.

This series is the official book series of IMISCOE, the largest network of excellence on migration and diversity in the world. It comprises publications which present empirical and theoretical research on different aspects of international migration. The authors are all specialists, and the publications a rich source of information for researchers and others involved in international migration studies. The series is published under the editorial supervision of the IMISCOE Editorial Committee which includes leading scholars from all over Europe. The series, which contains more than eighty titles already, is internationally peer reviewed which ensures that the book published in this series continue to present excellent academic standards and scholarly quality. Most of the books are available open access.

More information about this series at https://link.springer.com/bookseries/13502

Ermira Danaj

Women, Migration and Gendered Experiences

The Case of Post-1991 Albanian Migration

 Springer

Ermira Danaj
Centro de Investigaçao e Estudos de Sociologia (CIES-Iscte)
ISCTE-Instituto Universitário de Lisboa
Lisboa, Portugal

ISSN 2364-4087   ISSN 2364-4095   (electronic)
IMISCOE Research Series
ISBN 978-3-030-92094-4   ISBN 978-3-030-92092-0   (eBook)
https://doi.org/10.1007/978-3-030-92092-0

© The Editor(s) (if applicable) and The Author(s) 2022. This book is an open access publication.

Open Access   This book is licensed under the terms of the Creative Commons Attribution 4.0 International License (http://creativecommons.org/licenses/by/4.0/), which permits use, sharing, adaptation, distribution and reproduction in any medium or format, as long as you give appropriate credit to the original author(s) and the source, provide a link to the Creative Commons license and indicate if changes were made.

The images or other third party material in this book are included in the book's Creative Commons license, unless indicated otherwise in a credit line to the material. If material is not included in the book's Creative Commons license and your intended use is not permitted by statutory regulation or exceeds the permitted use, you will need to obtain permission directly from the copyright holder.

The use of general descriptive names, registered names, trademarks, service marks, etc. in this publication does not imply, even in the absence of a specific statement, that such names are exempt from the relevant protective laws and regulations and therefore free for general use.

The publisher, the authors and the editors are safe to assume that the advice and information in this book are believed to be true and accurate at the date of publication. Neither the publisher nor the authors or the editors give a warranty, expressed or implied, with respect to the material contained herein or for any errors or omissions that may have been made. The publisher remains neutral with regard to jurisdictional claims in published maps and institutional affiliations.

This Springer imprint is published by the registered company Springer Nature Switzerland AG
The registered company address is: Gewerbestrasse 11, 6330 Cham, Switzerland

Acknowledgements

This book is the result of the work I did during my doctoral studies at the MAPS (Maison d'analyse des processus sociaux), University of Neuchâtel. I wrote my PhD dissertation across different cities, starting it in Tirana, developing it in New York and Lisbon, and completing it in Paris – an appropriate trajectory for a book about migration and gender. I would like to thank Elzbieta Matynia at the New School in New York and Maria das Dores Guerreiro at the Centre for Research and Studies in Sociology (CIES-Iscte) in Lisbon who have supported me through our constant intellectual exchanges, and through their suggestions and constructive criticism at several points over the course of my research and writing. Maria das Dores Guerreiro made my integration to Lisbon easier and gave me the opportunity to present my work on various occasions. Special thanks go also to Joana Patricio, my friend and colleague, for our long discussions over coffee in sunny Lisbon, for the academic recommendations and our on-going support and friendship. I would like to express my gratitude to Ilda Petri Nina and Genta Kulari, who helped me both enjoy and get down to work in New York and Lisbon, respectively, and Fjolla Cakuli and Andris Stastoli, who lent me their support and courage as I laboured on my dissertation.

I am also grateful for my friends and colleagues, Ani Plaku, Monika Kocaqi and Daniela Kalaja, who were a great encouragement during this journey and provided highly useful references and information. Sincere thanks go to Mirjana Morokvasic and Julie Vullnetari who enabled me to improve my work through their valuable and constructive comments and suggestions.

I would like to thank the two anonymous reviewers of this book, the staff of Springer, and Irina Isaakyan and Anna Triandafyllidou of IMISCOE Books for ensuring a smooth process as I prepared my work for publication. Barbara Halla, thank you for editing my English and for all the fantastic suggestions and advice.

The Fulbright Visiting Scholar programme allowed me to conduct part of this research at the New School. I would like to express my gratitude for this experience to all Fulbright and Institute of International Education (IIE) advisors as well as to the US State Department officers and the staff of the US Embassy in Albania. I am grateful to the Gulbenkian Library of Arts in Lisbon, where I wrote a significant part of my dissertation, for the inspiration afforded by this place and for the kindness of its staff. I am thankful as well to the Equal Opportunities Office at the University of Neuchâtel for their financial support.

Patrick Festy and Ann Snitow inspired me from the very first day we met in Tirana and throughout our encounters in Paris and New York. I especially appreciate their open-mindedness that fortunately motivated me and helped me to get out of my box and see things differently.

I would also like to express my appreciation to all the women whom I interviewed. They made it possible for me to write this book and contribute to our knowledge about migration in Albania. I wish them all the best of luck wherever they may be now. I cannot adequately express my thanks and gratitude to Ajkuna Hoppe, my dear friend and colleague who was a critical companion throughout the writing of this work. She patiently listened to many of my ideas, helped me organize and investigate them further, and attentively read my chapters.

Taulant, my best friend and partner, who has stood by my side all this time, listening to my nervous ramblings and my research dilemmas, and who never stopped encouraging me regardless. He and my daughter, Noa, endured many of my long days on my laptop and my ever-changing moods, and yet still managed to make my life brighter. Tasha and Koço, my mother and father, believed in me even when I didn't and supported me in every decision I made, even the difficult ones that increased the physical distance between us. They always were there for me, regardless of the cities that keep us apart, and their support has been a constant source of happiness for me. I can simply say that I love these four people with all my heart.

I want to conclude this section by expressing my utmost gratitude to my doctoral research supervisor, Janine Dahinden. She has supported me throughout this journey, from the very first moment when this research project was nothing but a vague idea in my mind. She helped me through my most difficult moments when I lacked the confidence to accomplish this undertaking. She has my most profound gratitude not only for the time and energy she dedicated to guiding me through the ups and downs of this process, but also for the support, understanding and patience she provided throughout. It was her on-going encouragement that pushed me to finalize this publication.

Faleminderit të gjithë/ave!
Thank you all!
Obrigada a todas!
Merci à tous/tes!

Contents

Chapter 1
Introduction

1.1 Motivations Behind This Research

International and internal migration have characterised Albania since 1990, when the communist regime established in the aftermath of the Second World War was on its last legs[1]. While the number of studies on Albanian migration, both national and transnational, has grown, only a few adopt the perspective of gender. Employing a gender perspective on migration is not only about using sex-disaggregated statistics but also explaining the processes and discourses in migration involving women and men, their relations to each other (Erel et al., 2003) and among women themselves (Parreñas, 2009)

In the early 2000s, while working at the Albanian National Institute of Statistics (INSTAT), I was part of a research group on Gender and Migration, whose primary output was the publication of *Gender Perspectives in Albania*, (Ekonomi et al., 2004), an essay that focused on the 2001 Albanian Census from a gender perspective, and that marked the first serious attempt to analyse gender and internal migration in Albania. I benefited greatly from this work, firstly because, as a recent sociology graduate, I was thrown straightaway into the vast universe of gender and migration studies. Secondly, this particular project helped me evaluate the many gaps in knowledge concerning the relationship between gender and migration in Albania. As I worked with census data, I realised the pressing need for qualitative research to grasp the dynamics of migration processes from a gender perspective.

---

[1] Albania was called the People's Republic of Albania from 1946 until 1976 and the People's Socialist Republic of Albania from 1976 until 1991. Nevertheless, the literature, both Albanian and foreign, frequently refers to the 1944–1991 period and the state during that period as the communist regime, the communist period, totalitarianism, the socialist state, socialism and monism. This terminology applies not only to Albania but also to Central and Eastern European countries more generally, which are often called the Communist Bloc, the socialist states and similar terms. Therefore, when referring to Albania, I use the terms socialist period, socialist regime, communist period and communist regime interchangeably.

© The Author(s) 2022

E. Danaj, *Women, Migration and Gendered Experiences*, IMISCOE Research Series, https://doi.org/10.1007/978-3-030-92092 0_1

This experience magnified further my goal to pursue an in-depth analysis of gender and migration in Albania. Over the ensuing years, I worked on other projects related to gender issues in the country, but as I embarked on my doctoral research, this initial idea persisted in my mind.

The reason behind this project, however, is rooted also in something more personal: internal and international migration have characterised my life. I was born in Shkodër, a large city in northern Albania, while my parents, both from the south, were transferred there for work. My family's experience represents the primary pattern of internal Albanian migration during the communist period: the state stationed you wherever there was need. After Shkodër, my father was next assigned to Tirana, and later Saranda, a coastal city in southern Albania. In 1990, I moved back to Tirana, and in 1994, after finishing high school, I went to Switzerland. The eight years I spent in Switzerland represented the longest period of stillness I had ever experienced, at the time. Upon my return to Albania in 2002, I went through another period of relative motionlessness for another ten years, before returning, in 2012, to back-to-back international relocations. Personal experiences with migration, whether internally or internationally, are not in themselves reason enough to pursue research on gender and migration in Albania. However, these experiences did give me an extra push, a more personal motivation, to choose this topic for my doctoral research, which is the basis of the present book.

1.2   Research Context

The feminist and the constructivist approaches provide the epistemological lenses of this research. The feminist standpoint adopted here aims to critically analyse women's experiences and voices, while taking into account the differences between them. This book focuses on Albanian migrant women's experiences and starts with the assumption that gender is a social construct and an organising principle of society. Within the framework of these two epistemological lenses, I seek to understand how gender relates to the migration process. In particular, I will look into how gender shapes migration and the construction of the migrant woman, on the one hand, and how different migration processes influence gender relations, on the other.

Until the mid-1980s, women were mostly invisible in migration studies, except as the family members in charge of the domestic sphere and childrearing. When their experiences were addressed, studies treated women as the dependents of men, who were considered to be the leading providers of household resources. These views started to change once scholars such as Morokvasic (1984b) introduced a gender perspective into migration studies, and thus began to examine women's particular experiences at large[2]. Studies have shown that gender informs migration

---

[2] In this book, I refer extensively to the work of Mirjana Morokvasic, not only for the analyses she has provided on gender in migration studies but also her contributions on the topics of circular migration, the transnational presence of mothers, patterns of south-eastern European female

processes by influencing migrants' projects, trajectories, work opportunities, family relations and social networks (Boyd & Grieco, 2003; Dahinden et al., 2007)

Scholars have demonstrated that many women migrate on their own to help their families economically, in contrast to the image of women as passive dependent subjects that is often presented in the literature on migration (Kofman & Raghuram, 2015; Oso Casas, 2006; Schmoll, 2006; Vianello, 2009). Women participate in the decision-making process regarding migration, receive and send remittances and support the migration of other family members and themselves (Dahinden et al., 2007). Additionally, analyses of migration have also considered the intersection of gender with class and race (Dahinden 2010b; Silvey 2004; Parreñas, 2001). Studies have also shown that it is challenging to draw universal conclusions regarding the interrelation of gender and migration. According to Dahinden et al. (2007), migration influences gender relations in various ways; it may reinforce gender inequalities or question and transform them. Migration can be either exploitative or liberating: it might lead to new opportunities and better economic situations but also new gender constraints and precarity (Morokvasic, 2003; Moujoud, 2008).

Migration was long studied mainly in terms of immigration, and only from the perspective of the destination country (Morokvasic 1984a, 17). Studies on transnationalism and the diversity of migration trajectories (Morokvasic 1984a, Morokvasic, 2003; Dahinden, 2010a, b; Vianello, 2011; Vullnetari, 2012; Mai & Paladini, 2013), however, have demonstrated that looking solely at the destination country limits how we analyse migratory processes. The realities of migration cannot be understood when considered only in binary terms of emigration and immigration, integration and return, temporary and permanent migration, and when the migration process is understood as a one-way, unidirectional affair (Morokvasic, 1984a). Other forms of migration, such as pendular movement, might not be statistically visible, as in the case of Albanian migration, but they do exist. Moreover, the reasons for engaging in migration, whatever trajectory migration may take, are always gendered. In putting forth its analysis, this research project employs the concept of migration as a process, not a unidirectional movement. Migration as a process encompasses various migration trajectories, including internal, international, circular and return trajectories, all shaped by and interrelated with gender.

1.3   The Albanian Context

Women's emancipation was among the state's central policies during the socialist era. The government followed a model similar to that of other socialist countries that Moghadam (1995) calls the "Women's Emancipation Model." This model

---

migration, among others. Another scholar quoted significantly is Janine Dahinden, in particular for her studies on transnationalism and pendular migration. For Albania more specifically, I refer widely to the work of Juli Vullnetari and Russell King. Vullnetari has also analysed Albanian migration from a gender perspective; hence her work is valuable to my own analysis.

included policies to support women's participation in the productive labour force, as well as new laws to promote the equality between men and women. A reconfiguration of gender roles and the gender division of labour occurred in socialist countries (Verdery, 1996). However, women's increased participation in education, employment, and even in the Albanian Labour Party and high-level bureaucracy did not translate into an equal division of roles and responsibilities within the household. Traditional gender roles, with women remaining the sole responsible for reproductive labour, persisted in the domestic space.

Women's situation in the aftermath of the fall of the communist regime is proof of this persistence of traditional family roles (Gal & Kligman, 2000; Verdery, 1996; Brunnbauer, 2000). Former socialist countries, each in its own way, experienced a period of retraditionalisation[3]—a return to so-called traditional values and family life that relegated women to the home once again (Kligman, 1994, 256; Verdery, 1996, 79). Following this pan-East European trend (Bonfiglioli, 2014; Gal & Kligman, 2000; Heyns, 1995; Morokvasic, 2003; Rosenberg, 1991), women in Albania, too, retired to the domestic space and reproductive work. This state of affairs has changed over the ensuing years, as Albanian women have increasingly re-entered the formal labour market, politics and become active members in civil society organisations. Other, less visible phenomena have accompanied these changes, however, including women's engagement in the informal labour market, working long hours for low pay and no social security protection. Albania has also seen a rising numbers of female university students, and a falling fertility rate.

Uniquely among former communist countries, Albania entirely forbade migration from the country during the socialist era. Consequently, after the fall of Communism in 1991, many Albanians felt the pull of freedom of movement, regardless of whether they were allowed to cross other countries' borders. Since the fall of socialism and the accompanying erosion of the state infrastructure that strictly regulated internal and international migration, an estimated 1.5 million people have left Albania, more than half of the resident population in 2017 (GoA, 2018). The first decade of post-socialism witnessed mostly male migration, but data gathered in 2001 point to a shift: the gap between male and female migrants leaving Albania has become increasingly insignificant (Galanxhi et al., 2004; INSTAT, 2002; King & Vullnetari, 2012; Vullnetari, 2012). The ratio of women and men involved in international migration rose from 1:5 in 1991 to 3:5 in 2001 (Azzarri & Carletto, 2009, 7). Although women migrate abroad primarily for family reunification, the two primary exceptions are 'professional women and students moving to obtain a

---

[3] When talking about *retraditionalisation*, we should be cautious considering also that during communism gender roles were not free from 'traditional' traits. Women's emancipation during communism was meant principally in relation to the productive sphere, not the reproductive one; it did not mean an individual liberation. Women's engagement in the productive sphere did not result in the equal participation of men in the reproductive sphere; women remained in charge of the caregiver role. They were asked to re-model patriarchal traits to mirror an ideal socialist family: they were now part of the productive sphere, but in the domestic sphere they remained mainly within the borders of the patriarchal system, subordinated to husband and/or in-laws (Danaj, 2020)

high-status qualification or job that brings prestige to the family' (King & Vullnetari, 2012, 213). Additionally, data (Ekonomi et al., 2004; Galanxhi et al., 2004; INSTAT, 2002) on internal Albanian migration reveal that it is not men but rather women who are more likely to migrate internally. According to the 2011 census (Galanxhi et al., 2014), women made up 59 per cent of internal migrants in the 2001–2011 period. Put differently, the sex ratio for internal migration during this period was 100 women to 69 men.

Numerous studies on Albanian migration, primarily to Greece and Italy, were conducted during the 1990s (e.g. Barjaba, 2000; Barjaba et al., 1992; Bërxholi & Doka, 1996; Tarifa, 1995) and have been enriched by a proliferation of research on Albanian migration since 2001. A significant reason for this proliferation was that the publication of the Albanian Population and Housing Census of 2001 gave the first overall picture of the dramatic magnitude of internal and international migration in Albania. The 2002 and 2005 Albanian Living Standards Measurement Surveys (ALSMS) followed. This research stream focused precisely on internal and international migration and initially drew mostly from the statistical data generated by the 2001 census and the 2002 ALSMS. Other INSTAT publications based on the 2001 census data shared insightful analysis of internal migration (Galanxhi et al., 2004) from a gender perspective (Ekonomi et al., 2004) and built an overall picture of the scope of international migration (INSTAT, 2002). Since the early 2000s, Albanian migration has become an attractive case study for domestic and foreign scholars, who treat the country as a laboratory for the research of migration (King 2005). Scholars have also analysed the ALSMS 2002 data to capture statistical insights about internal and international movement (Azzarri & Carletto, 2009; Stecklov et al., 2010; Zezza et al., 2005). Topics of analysis have included remittances (King & Vullnetari, 2010; Uruci & Gëdeshi, 2003), high-skilled migration (EMA, 2010; Gërmenji & Gëdeshi, 2008; Gërmenji & Milo, 2011; Orgocka, 2005; Trimçev et al., 2005; Zenelaga & Sotirofski, 2011) and the link between internal and international migration (King et al., 2008; Vullnetari, 2012). There is valuable research on Albanian migrants abroad from the perspective of receiving countries (Vathi, 2011; Olsson, 2014; Mai & Paladini, 2013; Maroukis & Gemi, 2011; Vaiou, 2002; Lyberaki 2011; Gemi, 2015).

More research on migrants' experiences incorporating a gender perspective followed (Çaro 2011; Vullnetari, 2012; Gjermeni, 2004; Vullnetari, 2009; Vullnetari & King, 2016) and promoted the visibility of women in the internal and international processes of migration in AlbaniaOn the other hand, some studies have shown that statistical analysis of migration often obscures or does not examine the experiences of women migrants. Analyses from migrants' perspective (Vullnetari, 2012; Çaro 2011; Gjermeni, 2004; Olsson, 2014) have demonstrated that the dynamics are far more complex than what numbers can show us, as is the position of women in the migratory processes. Thus, there still remains space for research and studies that will enable us to understand the experiences of Albanian migrant women and the broader interrelations between migration and gender.

Although figures (Ekonomi et al., 2004; INSTAT, 2002; Stecklov et al., 2010; World Bank, 2007) at the national level reveal a predominance of men in international migration and women in internal movements, women's participation in migration processes in Albania is more multifaceted. Amid the numerous studies on Albanian migration, few focus specifically on the entanglement of gender and migration and even fewer on the experiences of migrant women. Furthermore, an in-depth investigation of the migration trajectories of Albanian women that is not be limited only to internal and international migration can produce profound insights. As I show throughout this book, these migratory trajectories undoubtedly influence gender relations, either by reinforcing the inequalities between women and men or by challenging gender norms and transforming gender relations.

1.4   Research Objectives and Question(s)

International migration in Albania has been considered to be a male-dominated phenomenon, particularly in the decade between 1990 and 2000 when men migrated for economic reasons, and women remained in Albania or moved internally to care for their families. Various scholars (Vullnetari, 2009; King & Vullnetari, 2012; Çaro 2011), however, have shown that women's participation in Albanian migration processes is many-sided, much more so than it may first appear in macro-level studies. Researchers have called for additional studies that provide a more comprehensive understanding of women's experiences and roles in migration in Albania.

This project is situated in this context, and the primary objective of my research is: *To explore and understand the interrelation of gender and migration in Albania and, more specifically, to examine how gender influences the process of migration for women and how the effects of migration transform gender relations.* This study follows a qualitative methodology aimed at answering a general question and several sub-questions guiding the research process. The central research question explored in this research is: *How can we understand the interrelation of gender and migration in Albania?*

The central research question is broken into three main sub-questions, further refined into the main points on which this research focuses, *(1) What tactics and strategies do Albanian migrant women employ during the migration process? (2) How can the migration trajectories of Albanian women be characterised? (3) How can the lives of female migrants in Tirana be understood and characterised?*

This research focuses on the narratives told by women living in Tirana after experiencing trajectories of internal and international migration and, therefore, cannot give answers about what happens next in their lives. The moment when I conducted the interviews may be only a step in their migratory journeys before they move again. However, these women's experiences, up until the time this research was conducted and when they all lived in Tirana, help deepen our understanding of Albanian migration and the interrelation of gender and migration in the Albanian context.

1.5   Research Design and Methods

Neither observer nor observed come to a scene untouched by the world.
Kathy Charmaz (2006, 15)

This research follows a qualitative approach, as such an approach is best suited to the exploration of gender relations and migration in Albania. To engage in qualitative research means 'to step beyond the known and enter the worlds of participants, to see the world from their perspective' (Corbin & Strauss, 2008, 16). Qualitative research allows the researcher to grasp the inner experience of the participants, to determine the formation of meanings through and in culture and to discover, instead of simply testing variables. Besides, qualitative research helps better explain migrant livelihoods because it enables an in-depth understanding of the participants' experiences (Çaro 2011, 55). Thus, given that quantitative-only approaches have been shown to be limited when exploring the gendered aspect of migration, and the need to grasp the complexity of migrant women's experiences, a qualitative feminist approach is justified in this case.

Qualitative research focused on women's experiences has become a precious tool for feminist studies. Thirty years ago, Maria Mies (Mies, 1983) outlined the reasons why feminist analysis is more linked to qualitative than quantitative studies. According to Mies (Mies, 1983), quantitative research often ignores the voices of women, turns them into objects and analyses them in a value-neutral way rather than specifically as women. Qualitative research, in contrast, listens to women's perspectives and engages with their lived experiences. However, feminist scholars and researchers have argued that feminist research should not be limited to qualitative methods, and methodological pluralism has become more popular among gender researchers (Walby, 2011).

In addition to qualitative research and a feminist social constructivist approach, I also chose to apply some elements of the grounded theory method. This theory holds that both researchers and participants interpret meanings and actions and that both analysis and data are social constructions that mirror the production process involved (Charmaz, 2006). Charmaz (2005) furthermore highlights that research focussed on social justice topics can use grounded theory methodology. The ability to do so is crucial for my research because as a feminist scholar, my aim is not only to study and understand migrant women's experiences but also to identify and highlight present gender inequalities in order to contribute to some measure of change in women's situations.

Throughout this research project, with regards to methodology, I rely mostly on the works of Flick (2009), Hesse-Biber (2007a), Bryant and Charmaz (2007), Charmaz (2005) and Olesen (2007). Other sources, such as Glaser and Strauss (2012), Mason (2002), Denzin and Lincoln (2005), provide a broad understanding and thoughtful example of the uses of the research methods employed in qualitative and grounded theory. I follow Bryant and Charmaz's (2007) method which is considered to be a more constructivist approach to grounded theory research. According to Charmaz (2006, 10), data and theories are not discovered but rather are 'part of the world we study and the data we collect'. It is of great importance to mention here that the constructivist approach to grounded theory fits very well with feminist research, as both recognise the role of the researcher in the construction and interpretation of data (Olesen, 2007, 422).

1.5.1 Research Methods and Analysis

Following a feminist perspective, I decided to work only with women. Doing so does not hinder my analysing of the interrelation of gender and migration (Erel et al., 2003; Parreñas, 2009). As Parreñas (2001) states, when we speak about women's gendered experiences, we are always implicitly referring to men also. Likewise, gender relations imply relations not only between men and women, but also among men and women (Connell, 2002). In the same vein, Erel, Morokvasic and Shinozaki (2003) contend that even if we take only female migrants as our direct subject of inquiry, their experiences shed light on gendered migration, gendered institutional settings and social arrangements as a whole.

I started my research in the neighbourhood of Don Bosko in 2011, and after conducting a first small set of interviews, I expanded into the area of Komuna e Parisit. Both sites were developed mainly due to internal migration, as explained in Chap. 3. I did not set an exact number of women to interview beforehand, as I had decided to construct the sample based on my analysis of the first set of interviews.

I had three key informants, one in Don Bosko and two in Komuna e Parisit, who shared their knowledge of the neighbourhoods, informed me about the geographical distribution of migrants in the area and helped me map the economic conditions within the research sites[4]. When conducting qualitative research, participants are selected according to their significance to the research topic, and not to construct a statistical sample that is representative of the general population. The goal is to increase complexity by bringing in context, as opposed to reducing complexity by dissolving it into variables (Flick, 2009, 91). For my research, I followed a purposive sampling, selecting the participants based on their specific characteristics according to the main objective of the study. However, I did not develop the sample beforehand but based it on the on-going analysis of the data. I applied several criteria (Morse, 1998) while sampling participants: they had to have knowledge and experience of the issue to provide useful insights through their narratives, as well as time to participate in the research (by doing interviews in this case). I approached a few women using my key informants' information and then developed the sample through the snowballing technique. When using this nonprobability sampling

---

[4] I had no limits or preferences regarding the city or village of origin, whether north or south. Likewise, I had no specific age limitations for the participants, other than no younger than 18 years old and no older than 60 years old. The lower limit of 18 years old respected the Albanian Civil Code's ban on marriage among those younger than 18 years old. The upper limit of 60 years old excluded female old-age pensioners.

method, each person interviewed may be asked to suggest additional people for interviewing (Babbie, 2013, 129).

I started interviews in Don Bosko with migrant women who had arrived in Tirana after 1991. During this early exploratory phase, while conducting the first interviews and consulting the relevant literature, however, I noted other themes coming to the fore, such as educational migration. I modified and expanded the sampling accordingly to reflect on, complicate and do justice to the vast experiences of female migration in Albania. During the sampling process—through a constant process of data analysing and observations, identification of interesting themes and statements and writing of memos —it became clear that focusing only on internal migration would limit the answers to the main research question about the interrelation of gender and migration. At the same time, internal migration in Albania is very rarely unconnected to international migration. Consequently, I decided to modify the sample by also including women who had migrated internationally. This modification was also in response to an additional research question that developed gradually as I researched the migratory trajectories of Albanian migrant women. The distinction between internal and international migration is necessary as, despite overlapping patterns of internal and international migration, crossing country borders entails significant challenges for Albanian citizens. Whereas they can freely move internally, Albanian citizens have to comply with visa regimes and migration policies if they intend to enter other countries. Therefore, I first separated the sample into two broad groups: women who migrated only internally and women who engaged in international, internal, circular and return migration.

The number of single women migrating on their own to Tirana as students has been on the rise the last two decades. However, they still remain an under-researched group in the context of Albanian migration. For this reason, I opted to include educational migration as a further point of distinction regarding both internal and international migration. Thus, four groups began to take a more precise shape, and included women who migrated internally for reasons other than education; internal student migrants; women who migrated internationally for reasons other than education; international student migrants.

The common feature of all the thirty-two participating women is that they had undergone internal or multiple migratory trajectories. Still, at the time I conducted my fieldwork, all lived in Tirana. I did not divide the sample into these four groups to draw comparisons between them. Instead, I highlight the idiosyncrasies of Albanian female migrants to see what their specific experiences reveal about the social processes in regards to migration and gender.

The final sample includes thirty-two women of different ages involved in various migratory processes. One of my aims while doing the sampling was to have women from various regions of the country, including villages, small towns and big cities. The majority of the women interviewed come from small towns, and four from villages. Only three women lived in extended families at the time of their first migration project, while the rest lived in nuclear families. The low number of extended families reflects their decline in the Albanian context, as I explain in Chap. 3. The economic situation of the participants' families (or families of origin for the women who migrated on their own) is diverse. Educational attainment was another criterion for sampling—I deliberately set out to interview women who had migrated for educational purposes. In this case, I sought to diversify the sample by region of origin (northern-southern city—town—village). The women who did not migrate for educational purposes have various educational backgrounds (lower secondary—upper secondary—university).

My research objectives began to crystallise during the interviewing and analysis processes, which allowed me to refine my sample configuration. Through the ongoing examination of the conducted interviews, I polished my objectives and turned them into research questions. For example, when starting this research, I had no clear goals, such as investigating the migration trajectories of women (as mentioned above).

Table 1.1 gives some brief general information about the research participants. I include more details about these women at the beginning of each analysis chapter.

The participants' anonymity was a critical point of concern respected throughout this research. To preserve anonymity, the names used in this table and throughout the text are not the participants' real names but suitable equivalents.

To conduct the interviews, I drew on Charmaz (2006) and Hesse-Biber (2007b), who describe the process of feminist interviewing. Charmaz (2006, 26) calls this 'intensive interviewing'; however, I refer to it as 'in-depth' interviewing. 'Intensive interviewing permits an in-depth exploration of a particular topic or experience and, thus, is a useful method for interpretive inquiry' (Charmaz, 2006, 26). In-depth interviews are a valuable tool for feminist research in order to better understand the world of the respondents (Hesse-Biber, 2007b, 114). Feminist scholars must capture the experiences under the surface. In-depth interviewing allows researchers to listen to women's voices and to get a better sense of their hidden experiences. It gives researchers access to the participants' ideas, thoughts and memories in their own words rather than the researcher's terms. This latter is essential to studies centred on women, as 'in this way learning from women is an antidote to centuries of ignoring women's ideas altogether or having men speak for women' (Reinharz, 1992, 17).

In-depth interviews are not interrogations but exploration tools. The interview process resembles a conversation where the interviewer talks less and listens more in order to explore and understand the respective issues and topics of interest of the interviewee and to discover others. An in-depth interview may be unstructured (or a loosely guided exploration of issues) (Charmaz, 2006, 26), semi-structured or structured (Hesse-Biber, 2007b, 116) depending on the themes chosen and the methods picked to explore them.

For this research, I conducted interviews that fell somewhere between the semi-structured and unstructured models. I had an interview guide, a list of written topics that I needed to cover to respond to the primary research objective and questions. I selected this interview style as I wanted to thoroughly explore the women's experiences but also guide the interview back to my questions, in case it deviated from the main topic. However, I was also open to asking new questions based on the information revealed by the participants. The interview schedule was not tightly fixed and allowed time and space for spontaneity, as recommended by Hesse-Biber (2007b).

Table 1.1 Research participants – brief presentation

Name	Age (years)	City or village of origin	Civil status	Migration type	Economic activity: current/previous	Tirana neighbourhood
Drita	42	Village in Lezhë	Married	Internal	Cleaning lady/unemployed/agriculture	Don Bosko
Eleni	47	Town of Tepelenë	Married	Internal	Domestic worker/unemployed/agriculture	Don Bosko
Eli	39	Village in Fier	Married	Internal	Housewife	Don Bosko
Silvana	58	Town of Lezhë	Married	Internal	Civil servant	Don Bosko
Arjana	51	City of Fier	Married	Internal	Kindergarten teacher/teacher	Komuna e Parisit
Zhani	50	City of Fier	Married	Internal	Business owner—small shop	Komuna e Parisit
Manjola	40	City of Vlorë	Married	Internal	Business owner—small shop/unemployed	Komuna e Parisit
Flutura	55	City of Shkodër	Married	Internal	Civil servant	Komuna e Parisit
Eriola	28	Town of Pogradec	Single	Internal	Journalist at a private television	Komuna e Parisit
Kiara	27	City of Fier	Single	Internal	Psychologist, nongovernmental organisation	Komuna e Parisit
Olisa	28	City of Fier	Single	Internal	Call centre	Don Bosko
Iris	27	Town of Librazhd	Single	Internal	Private television	Don Bosko
Erida	30	Town of Lezhe	Single	Internal	Call centre	Don Bosko
Alba	28	Town of Rrëshen	Single	Internal	Nongovernmental organisation	Don Bosko
Erjona	26	Village in Gjirokastër	Single	Internal	Law firm	Komuna e Parisit
Marjola	26	City of Fier	Single	Internal	Information technology in a project managament office	Komuna e Parisit
Artemisa	30	City of Vlorë	Single	International	Journalist/research assistant	Komuna e Parisit
Beti	31	Town of Diber	Single	International	Lecturer	Don Bosko
Fiona	28	Town of Kukës	Single	International	Lecturer/consultant	Don Bosko
Egesta	35	Town of Lezhë	Single	International	Private television psychologist/travel agent/social worker	Komuna e Parisit
Monika	28	City of Fier	Single	International	Nongovernmental organisation	Don Bosko
Rovena	42	City of Fier	Single	International	Nurse/domestic worker	Don Bosko

(continued)

Table 1.1 (continued)

Name	Age (years)	City or village of origin	Civil status	Migration type	Economic activity: current/previous	Tirana neighbourhood
Lindita	28	City of Vlora	Single	International	Consultant in a project office	Komuna e Parisit
Irida	36	City of Shkodër	Single	International	Business owner, hairdresser/domestic worker/ factory worker	Komuna e Parisit
Marta	34	City of Fier	Divorced	International	Self-employed, tailor	Don Bosko
Elida	38	Town of Dibër	Married	International	Lecturer	Komuna e Parisit
Migena	40	Town of Pogradec	Married	International	Private bank/babysitter and domestic worker	Don Bosko
Elona	39	Town of Lezhë	Married	International	Business owner, bakery/cleaner and domestic worker	Komuna e Parisit
Juli	38	village near the town of Tepelenë	Divorced	International	Business owner, hairdresser/cleaner and domestic worker	Komuna e Parisit
Denisa	45	City of Gjirokastër	Married	International	Domestic worker	Komuna e Parisit
Arlinda	46	Town of Kukës	Married	International	Unemployed/domestic worker	Don Bosko
Mimoza	41	Town of Saranda	Married	International	Business owner, dry cleaning/cleaning and domestic worker	Komuna e Parisit

However, I followed the principle that interviewing requires some narrowing of the interview topics in order to gather specific data for developing theoretical frameworks (Charmaz, 2006, 29.) I designed my interview guide so that I would be able to capture a broad view of the participants' experiences, but also so that the questions are narrow enough for me to gather sufficient data to construct my theoretical framework.

Only the preliminary questions concerning all participants' general background information—such as their age, civil status and city or village of origin—expected specific answers. At the start of the interview, I asked the participants to share this information briefly. Next, I had a list of topics that I needed to cover while still leaving room for the participants' stories. My main concern was to occasionally narrow the interview without abruptly interrupting the narrative, while still directing it so as to cover the area of interest. Based on Charmaz's (2006) guidelines, I also tried to leave enough space for the participants to speak but was careful not to display a lack of interest, which can be an issue during in-depth interviews.

To conclude this section, I want to recall Denzin and Lincoln's (2005, 643) idea that the interview 'is not a neutral tool, for at least two people create the reality of the interview situation. In this situation, answers are given. Thus, the interview produces situated understandings grounded in specific interactional episodes. This method is influenced by the personal characteristics of the interviewer, including race, class, ethnicity, and gender'. The relation between the researcher and the participant then is of paramount importance. Feminist researchers have concluded that it is impossible for there to be an equal balance of power between the researcher and the participant. This imbalance can be solved by the researcher exercising reflexivity throughout the interview and the research in general and by following all the ethical principles of conducting interviews. Reflexivity entails the constant examination of the 'unthought categories of thought which delimit the thinkable and predetermine the thought' (Bourdieu, 1982, 10). The researcher should continuously reflect on biases that may affect the construction of the object and 'scrutinise and neutralise… the collective scientific unconscious embedded in theories, problems, and [especially national] categories of scholarly judgment' (Bourdieu & Wacquant, 1992, 40). Moreover, reflexivity is a critical element in feminist research (Hesse-Biber, 2007a, b; Olesen, 2007).

> Reflexivity begins with an understanding of the importance of one's values and attitudes within the research process, and this begins prior to entering the field. Reflexivity means taking a critical look inward—a reflection on one's own lived reality and experiences, a self-reflection or journey. How does your own biography impact the research process? What shapes the questions you chose to study and your approach to studying them? How does the specific social, economic, and political context in which you reside impact the research process at all levels?' (Hesse-Biber, 2007b, 129)

The reflexivity process has been one of my biggest concerns as my work as a woman's rights activist in Albania likely influenced the data collection and analysis at some point during my research. Given that the social conditions, social location and social biography of both the observer and the observed affect knowledge (Hesse-Biber, 2007b, 131), I sought to minimise the influence of my biases and background on the research as much as possible. Through consultations with colleagues and their comments, I attempted to get a good description of how I handled my study and reflect on my background, how it was influencing my research and my emotions, worries and feelings—the three levels of reflections according to Olesen (2007, 423). These consultations and discussions often brought me face to face with the 'unthought categories' (Bourdieu, 1982, 10) expressed in my writing and analysis and encouraged me to scrutinise them, reflect upon them and rewrite.

1.6 Book Structure

This book is divided into two main parts. The first part serves to set the context by including the theoretical framework and chapters on the Albanian context. The second part includes four chapters where I analyse the interviews and results. Chapter 2 of Part 1 discusses the theoretical framework, presents the primary lenses used in this research (feminist and constructionist epistemologies) and develops the concepts of gender and migration that are central to this study. The introduction of gender to migration studies and the main patterns identified in these many studies provides another analytical framework. Chapter 3 on the Albanian context is longer and includes at first a brief overview of social, economic and political background in Albania and the migratory processes in the nation during the twentieth and twenty-first centuries. Next, the chapter discusses Tirana, the capital of Albania and the primary research site. Finally, this chapter covers women's situation in Albania, setting the context for the investigation and the analysis of the interviews that will follow.

The four remaining chapters present an analysis of the four categories of migrant women living in Tirana that I interviewed at the time of the research. First, I focus on studying the experiences of those migrants that migrated for reasons other than education, and secondly, on the experiences of internal and international student migrants. The final and concluding chapter presents the main analytical findings concerning the research question and highlights points for further research and analysis.

References

Azzarri, C., & Carletto, C. (2009, May). Modeling migration dynamics in Albania. *Policy Research Working Paper, 4945*.

Babbie, E. (2013). *The practice of social research*. Wadsworth.

Barjaba, K. (2000). Contemporary patterns in Albanian emigration. *South-East Europe Review for Labour and Social Affairs, 3*, 57–64.

Barjaba, K., Dervishi, Z., & Perrone, L. (1992). L'Emigrazione Albanese: Spazi, Tempi e Cause. *Studi Emigrazione, 107*, 513–538.

Bërxholi, A., & Doka, D. (1996). Migrimi dhe proceset social-ekonomike në periudhën e tranzicionit në Shqipëri. *Studime Gjeografike, 10*, 36–38.

Bonfiglioli, C. (2014). Gendered citizenship in the global European periphery: Textile workers in post-Yugoslav states. *Women's Studies International Forum, 29*, 57–65.

Bourdieu, P. (1982). *Leçon sur la leçon*. Editions de Minuit.

Bourdieu, P., & Wacquant, L. J. (1992). *An invitation to reflexive sociology*. Polity Press.

Boyd, M., & Grieco, E. (2003). *Women and migration: Incorporating gender into international migration theory*. Washington D.C.

Brunnbauer, U. (2000). From equality without democracy to democracy without equality? Women and transition in southeast Europe. SEER. *Journal for Labour and Social Affairs in Eastern Europe, 3*(3), 151–168. http://www.jstor.org/stable/44627816

Bryant, A., & Charmaz, K. (2007). *The SAGE handbook of grounded theory*. Sage Publications.

Çaro, E. (2011). *From the village to the city: The adjustment process of internal migrants in Albania*. Rozenberg Publishers.

Charmaz, K. (2005). Grounded theory in the 21st century: Applications for advancing social justice studies. In N. K. Denzin & Y. S. Lincoln (Eds.), *Sage handbook of qualitative research* (pp. 507–535). Sage Publications.

Charmaz, K. (2006). *Constructing grounded theory: A practical guide through qualitative analysis*. Sage Publications.

Connell, R. W. (2002). *Gender*. Polity.

Corbin, J., & Strauss, A. (2008). *Basics of Qualitative Research: Techniques and Procedures for Developing Grounded Theory* (3rd ed.). Sage Publications.

Dahinden, J. (2010a). Are you who you know? A network perspective on ethnicity, gender and transnationalism: Albanian-speaking migrants in Switzerland and returnees in Kosovo. In C. Westin, J. Bastos, J. Dahinden, & P. Góis (Eds.), *Identity processes and dynamics in multi-ethnic Europe* (pp. 127–148). Amsterdam University Press.

Dahinden, J. (2010b). Cabaret dancers: "settle down in order to stay Mobile? "bridging theoretical orientations within transnational migration studies. *Social Policies, 17*(3), 323–348.

Dahinden, J., Rosende, M., Benelli, N., Hanselmann, M., & Lempen, K. (2007). Migrations: genre et frontieres – frontieres de genre. *Nouvelles Questions Féministes, 26*(1), 4–14.

Danaj, E. (2020). How tradition and patriarchy impact on violence against women in the Western Balkans. In *Balkan perspectives* (Vol. 8, pp. 13–18). Stiftung.

Denzin, N., & Lincoln, Y. S. (2005). *The Sage Handbool on qualitative research* (3rd ed.). Sage Publications.

Ekonomi, M., Danaj, E., Dakli, E., Gjermeni, E., Budowski, M., & Schweizer, M. (2004). *Gender perspectives in Albania*. INSTAT.

EMA. (2010). *Brain gain policies and their impact on the European integration process of Albania*. European Movement in Albania.

Erel, U., Morokvasic, M., & Shinozaki, K. (2003). Introduction. Bringing gender into migration. In M. Morokvasic, U. Erel, & K. Shinozaki (Eds.), *Crossing borders and shifting boundaries: Gender on the move* (Vol. I, pp. 9–22). Springer.

Flick, U. (2009). *An introduction to qualitative research* (4th ed.). Sage Publications.

Gal, S., & Kligman, G. (2000). *The politics of gender after socialism: A comparative — historical essay*. Princeton University Press.

Galanxhi, E., Misja, E., Lameborshi, D., Lerch, M., Wanner, P., & Dahinden, J. (2004). *Migration in Albania*. INSTAT.

Galanxhi, E., Nesturi, M., & Hoxha, R. (2014). *Shqipëri, Popullsia dhe Dinamikat e Saj - Horizonte te Reja Demografike? [Albania, population and its dynamics - new demographic horizons?]*. INSTAT.

Gemi, E. (2015). The incomplete trajectory of Albanian migration in Greece. *Athens: Hellenic Foundation for European and Foreign Policy (ELIAMEP)*.

Gërmenji, E., & Gëdeshi, I. (2008). *Highly skilled migration from Albania: An assessment of current trends and the ways ahead.* Development Research Centre on Migration, Globalisation and Poverty.

Gërmenji, E., & Milo, L. (2011). Migration of the skilled from Albania: Brain drain or brain gain? *Journal of Balkan and Near Eastern Studies, 13*(3), 339–356.

Gjermeni, E. (2004). *Ardhja në Tiranë: Migrimi femëror në Shqipëri [Coming to Tirana: Female migration in Albania].* Doctoral Dissertation (Unpublished).

Glaser, B. G., & Strauss, A. L. (2012). *The discovery of grounded theory: Strategies for qualitative research.* New Brunswick and London.

GoA. (2018). *The National Strategy on migration governance and action plan 2019–2022.* Government of Albania.

Hesse-Biber, S. N. (2007a). Teaching grounded theory. In A. Bryant & K. Charmaz (Eds.), *SAGE handbook of grounded theory* (pp. 311–339). Sage Publications.

Hesse-Biber, S. N. (2007b). The practice of feminist in-depth interviewing. In S. N. Hesse-Biber & P. L. Leavy (Eds.), *Feminist research practice: A primer* (pp. 111–148). Sage Publications.

Heyns, B. (1995). Review of Cinderella goes to market: Citizenship, gender, and Women's movements in east Central Europe. By Barbara Einhorn. *American Journal of Sociology, 100*(5), 1343–1345.

INSTAT. (2002). *Albania population and housing census 2001.* INSTAT.

King, R. (2005). Albania as a laboratory for the study of migration and development. *Journal of Southern Europe and the Balkans, 7*(2), 133–155. https://doi.org/10.1080/14613190500132880

King, R., & Vullnetari, J. (2010). Gender and remittances in Albania: Or, why 'are women better remitters than men?' Is not the right question. In *Trans-Atlantic perspectives on international migration: Cross border impacts, border security, and socio-political responses.* University of Texas San.

King, R., & Vullnetari, J. (2012). A population on the move: Migration and gender relations in Albania. *Cambridge Journal of Regions, Economy and Society, 5,* 207–220.

King, R., Skeldon, R., & Vullnetari, J. (2008). Internal and international migration: Bridging the theoretical divide. *Working Paper, 52.*

Kligman, G. (1994). The social legacy of communism: Women, children and the feminization of poverty. In J. R. Millar & S. L. Wolchik (Eds.), *The social legacy of communism* (pp. 252–169). Cambridge University Press.

Kofman, E., & Raghuram, P. (2015). Gendered migrations and global social reproduction: An introduction. In E. Kofman & P. Raghuram (Eds.), *Gendered migrations and global social reproduction* (pp. 1–10). Palgrave Macmillan.

Lyberaki, A. (2011). Migrant Women Care Work and Women's Employment in Greece. *Feminist Economics, 17*(3), 103–131. https://doi.org/10.1080/13545701.2011.583201

Mai, N., & Paladini, C. (2013). Flexible circularities: Integration, return, and socio-economic instability within Albanian migration to Italy. In A. Triandafyllidou (Ed.), *Circular migration between Europe and its Neighborhood, choice or necessity?* (pp. 42–67). Oxford University Press.

Maroukis, T., & Gemi, E. (2011). *Circular migration between Albania and Greece: A case study.* Technical Reprt METOIKOS, European University Institute.

Mason, J. (2002). *Qualitative researching.* Sage.

Mies, M. (1983). Towards a methodology for feminist research. In G. Bowles & R. D. Klein (Eds.), *Theories of women's studies* (pp. 117–140). Routledge and Kegan Paul.

Moghadam, V. M. (1995). Gender and revolutionary transformation. *Gender & Society, 9*(3), 328–358. https://doi.org/10.1177/089124395009003005

Morokvasic, M. (1984a). Introduction. In M. Morokvasic (Ed.), *Current Sociology: Special Edition "Tendances de recherche et approche sociologique des migrations en Europe: perspectives des pays de départ et des pays d'arrivée 1960–1983"* (pp. 17–40). Sage Publications.

Morokvasic, M. (1984b). Birds of passage are also women…. *The International Migration Review, 18*(4), 886–907.

Morokvasic, M. (2003). Transnational mobility and gender: A view from post-wall Europe. In M. Morokvasic, U. Erel, & K. Shinozaki (Eds.), *Crossing Borders and shifting boundaries* (pp. 101–136). Springer.

Morse, J. M. (1998). Designing funded qualitative research. In N. K. Denzin & Y. S. Lincoln (Eds.), *Strategies of qualitative research* (pp. 56–85). Sage Publications.

Moujoud, N. (2008). Effets de la migration sur les femmes et sur les rapports sociaux de sexe: au-delà des visions binaires. *Cahiers du CEDREF*, 57–79.

Olesen, V. (2007). Feminist qualitative research and grounded theory: Complexities, criticisms, and opportunities. In A. Bryant & K. Charmaz (Eds.), *SAGE handbook of grounded theory* (pp. 417–436). Sage Publications.

Olsson, F. (2014). *Between dreams of papers and a house: Everyday life of Albanian undocumented migrant women in Greece.* University of Lund.

Orgocka, A. (2005). Albanian high skilled migrant women in the US: The ignored experience. In R. King, N. Mai, & S. Schwander-Sievers (Eds.), *The new Albanian migration* (pp. 139–152). Sussex Academic Press.

Oso Casas, L. (2006). Prostitution et immigration des femmes latino-américaines en Espagne. *Cahiers du Genre, 40*(1), 91–113.

Parreñas, R. S. (2001). *Servants of globalization: Women, migration and domestic work.* Stanford University Press.

Parreñas, R. S. (2009). Inserting Feminism in Transnational Migration Studies. *migrationonline.cz.*

Reinharz, S. (1992). *Feminist methods in social research.* Oxford University Press.

Rosenberg, D. J. (1991). Shock therapy: GDR women in transition from a socialist welfare state to a social market economy. *Signs, 17*(1), 129–151.

Schmoll, C. (2006). *Moving "on their own"? Mobility strategies and social networks of migrant women from Maghreb in Italy.* IIIS Discussion Paper 154.

Silvey, R. (2004). Power difference and mobility: Feminist advances in migration studies. *Progress in Human Geography, 28*(4), 490–506. https://doi.org/10.1191/0309132504ph490oa

Stecklov, G., Carletto, C., Azzarri, C., & Davis, B. (2010). Gender and migration from Albania. *Demography, 47*(4), 935–961.

Tarifa, F. (1995). Albania's road from communism: Political and social change, 1990-1993. *Development and Change, 26*, 133–162.

Trimçev, E., Dakli, E., & Ymeri, S. (2005). *Albanian brain drain: Turning the tide.* Albanian Institute for International Studies.

Uruci, E., & Gëdeshi, I. (2003). Remittances Management in Albania. *Working Papers 05.*

Vaiou, D. (2002). In the interstices of the City: Albanian women in Athens. *Espaces, Populations, Societes, 3*, 373–385.

Vathi, Z. (2011). *The children of Albanian migrants in Europe: Ethnic identity, transnational ties and pathways of integration.* University of Sussex.

Verdery, K. (1996). *What was socialism, and what comes next.* Princeton University Press.

Vianello, F. A. (2009). *Migrando Sole; Legami transnazionali tra Ucraina e Italia.* Franco Angeli.

Vianello, F. A. (2011). Suspended migrants. Return migration to Ukraine. In M. Nowak & M. Nowosielski (Eds.), *(Post)transformational migration inequalities, welfare state, and horizontal mobility* (pp. 251–272). Peter Lang.

Vullnetari, J. (2009). Women and migration in Albania: A view from the village. *International Migration, 50*(5), 169–188.

Vullnetari, J. (2012). *Albania on the move: Links between internal and international migration.* Amsterdam University Press.

Vullnetari, J., & King, R. (2016). 'Washing men's feet': Gender, care and migration in Albania during and after communism. *Gender, Place & Culture: A Journal of Feminist Geography, 23*(2), 198–215.

Walby, S. (2011). The impact of feminism on sociology. *Sociological Research Online, 16*, 1–17.

World Bank. (2007). *Albania: Urban growth, migration and poverty reduction*. World Bank.
Zenelaga, B., & Sotirofski, K. (2011). *The `brain gain hypotheses` of transition countries elites and socioeconomic development in their home country (Albanian emigrants in Italy sample)*. Alma Laurea Working Papers.
Zezza, A., Carletto, G., & Davis, B. (2005). Moving away from poverty a spatial analysis of poverty and migration in Albania. *ESA Working Paper No. 05–02*.

Open Access This chapter is licensed under the terms of the Creative Commons Attribution 4.0 International License (http://creativecommons.org/licenses/by/4.0/), which permits use, sharing, adaptation, distribution and reproduction in any medium or format, as long as you give appropriate credit to the original author(s) and the source, provide a link to the Creative Commons license and indicate if changes were made.

The images or other third party material in this chapter are included in the chapter's Creative Commons license, unless indicated otherwise in a credit line to the material. If material is not included in the chapter's Creative Commons license and your intended use is not permitted by statutory regulation or exceeds the permitted use, you will need to obtain permission directly from the copyright holder.

Chapter 2
Theoretical Framework

This chapter sets out the epistemological lenses and the central theoretical concepts guiding this research. Given the many theories and models regarding the intersection of gender and migration, it is important to highlight those that inspire this research and help to investigate and better understand how gender affects migration processes and, vice versa, how migration impacts gender relations. The first section of this chapter presents the main perspectives adopted here: feminist and constructivist epistemology. The next section discusses patterns of various migration trajectories. The third section gives a brief historical overview of the debate on gender in migration studies and clarifies the theorisation of gender and migration in this book. The analytical Chaps. 4, 5, 6 and 7 include other essential concepts and findings.

2.1 Epistemological Position: Feminist Standpoint and Constructivist Approaches

This research builds on a feminist standpoint epistemology. Various approaches and debates fall under this label, so the aim in the following is to highlight the main elements guiding this research. The origins of the epistemological and methodological focus of feminist research lie in the understandings and struggles of authors such as Virginia Woolf and Simone de Beauvoir, who 'express their deep feelings of exclusion from the dominant avenues of knowledge building, seeing their experiences, concerns, and worth diminished and invalidated by the dominant powers of their society' (Hesse-Biber, 2012, 3).

The primary target of feminist scholars during 1960s, 70s and 80s was the androcentric bias in science. To correct this bias and to make women's experiences visible, scholars added women to research samples, which allowed them to hear and learn about the experiences and perspectives of women that were relevant to new research questions (Hesse-Biber, 2012; Jackson & Scott, 2002). This attempt to

© The Author(s) 2022

E. Danaj, *Women, Migration and Gendered Experiences*, IMISCOE Research Series, https://doi.org/10.1007/978-3-030-92092-0_2

eradicate sexist dispositions in research permeated many disciplines, such as psychology, philosophy, history, sociology, education and anthropology, and the fields of law, medicine, language and communication. This period saw the publication of many 'ground-breaking anthologies critical of androcentric research' (Hesse-Biber, 2012, 5). It marked a defining moment shaking the traditional, taken-for-granted, male-biased knowledge frameworks (Hesse-Biber, 2012) from which 'women were largely excluded' (Smith, 1987, 281). Moreover, this period lead to a proliferation of challenges by feminist researchers and scholars to knowledge building (Hesse-Biber, 2012, 8). A second significant contribution of feminist standpoint epistemology is its focus on the experiences of marginalised women (Harding, 2009). Women's position as an oppressed class gives them a richer view of society (Hesse-Biber, 2014), and 'the experience and lives of marginalised people, as they understand them, provide the most significant agendas for the feminist research process' (Harding, 1993, 54).

Throughout its extensive use and development, feminist standpoint theory has also been subject to debate and critiques. Early critics argued that standpoint epistemology assumes that all women's experiences match a single defining experience and neglects the diversity of women's lives, especially the differences of race, class and sexual preference (Hesse-Biber, 2012, 11). Authors such as Patricia Hill Collins (1990) and bell hooks (1984) extended the initial feminist standpoint epistemology, claiming that we cannot talk about a single woman's experience or standpoint as both experience and standpoint differ because of and intersect with age, sex, race and class. The concept of intersectionality (Crenshaw, 1989, 1994) highlights the interaction of different types of oppression and discrimination, such as race, gender, sexuality, ethnicity and class. Authors including Mohanty (1991), Spivak (1988) and Kandiyoti (1999) introduced geographical and cultural placement as a critical dimension of feminist analysis related to the significance of women's experiences in the global context of post-colonialism, imperialism and national identity. In the first decade of the twenty-first century, feminists focused on issues of sexual preference and disability, along with nationality and geographical region (Connell, 2015; Hesse-Biber, 2012). In summary, 'feminists should not merely describe women's situations, but consider how race, class, gender, sexual orientation, age, and material circumstances in multiple contexts render the taken for granted problematic in ways that move toward social justice' (Olesen, 2007, 426).

Feminist research, in its many variations, places women's diverse experiences and the social institutions framing them on centre stage (Olesen, 2007). This focus on the experiences of women is foundational to most scholars working from the approach of feminist standpoint theory. One central premise of feminist research is to 'begin with experience since it is only from such a vantage point that it is possible to see the extent to which women's worlds are organised in ways that differ from those of men' (Maynard, 1994, 12). This research is based on this first element of the feminist standpoint epistemology, starting with women's daily lives, voices and experiences.

Second, the feminist standpoint has the goal of 'studying up' meaning to critically analyse 'what's wrong and what's still useful or otherwise valuable in the dominant institutions of society, their cultures, and practices' (Harding, 2009, 195). This activity entails a political stance and a normative commitment to gender equality (Chafetz, 2006; Hesse-Biber, 2014). Third, the feminist standpoint takes into account the differences among women and applies an intersectional approach to social inequality. Harding (2009) urges that standpoint work should be persistently intersectional. Fourth, the feminist perspective is an achievement, not an ascription, and requires scientific work to see beyond 'the ideological surface of [the] social relations that we all come to accept as natural' (Harding, 2009, 195). Accordingly, I based this research on migrant women's experiences, starting with the assumption that gender is a social construct and an organising principle of society.

In this book, feminist epistemology is considered in connection to the social constructivist approach. Constructivist epistemology includes a variety of elements and developments that, because of spatial constraints, this chapter will not be able to address in an exhaustive manner; as a perspective, it implies that knowledge is socially constructed (Alvesson & Sköldberg, 2009) or, in the words of Smith (1987, 72), that it 'is a social accomplishment'. Constructivism

> assumes that people create social reality(ies) through individual and collective actions. Rather than seeing the world as given, constructionists ask, how is it accomplished? Thus, instead of assuming realities in an external world—including global structures and local cultures—social constructionists study what people at a particular time and place take as real, how they construct their views and actions, when different constructions arise, whose constructions become taken as definitive, and how that process ensues. (Charmaz 2006, 189)

Constructivism assumes that people create the realities in which they participate and that the researcher's interpretation of the studied facts, too, is a construction. The constructivist viewpoint shifts the question from '*what* social reality is in the perspective of actors' to '*how* this reality is produced or accomplished in these actors' everyday practice' (i.e. where practice means action and talk, but also presentation and argumentation) (Bohnsack, 2010, 102).

Constructivism goes hand in hand with the feminist standpoint that sees the object of knowledge as socially constructed. For something to be socially constructed, it does not mean that it is not real but, rather, that it is the product of human activity (Sprague & Kobrynowicz, 2006). Constructivism thus reveals that the 'natural' in what may be 'commonly regarded as self-evident and natural' is socially constructed (Alvesson & Sköldberg, 2009, 35). The lens of constructivism is particularly useful here given that gender is a social construction rather than a natural given, and I will explain the implications of this distinction in my research in the following subsection.

Knowledge theories are embedded in particular positions, perspectives and experiences with entrenched notions of gender, race, class and ethnicity. Combining feminist and constructivist epistemology helps this research avoid the trap of "discovering" universal and unique truths. Consequently, this research aims at understanding how gender is related to the migration process, significantly how the social construction of gender shapes migration and how different migration processes influence gender relations.

2.1.1 A Feminist and Constructivist Perspective on Gender

I believe gender is a social construct (i.e. it is continuously produced and reproduced through social practices and interactions and experienced through multiple
social institutions, such as the family, labour market and state) (Mahler & Pessar,
2001; West & Fenstermaker, 1995). Gender is an analytical concept that enables
understanding of social roles, relations and processes; it is distinct from the constructed meaning of sex as a biological inevitability (Glenn, 2000) and the idea of
an immutable social structure. The notion of gender refers to socially created meanings, relationships and identities organised around reproductive differences
(Connell, 2002; Scott, 1986). Gender represents social status and an organising
principle of social institutions that extends beyond reproductive differences
(Connell, 2002; Lorber, 2007) and is an on-going product of everyday social practice (West & Zimmerman, 1987). Thus, gender is 'much more than a role or an
individual characteristic: it is a mechanism whereby situated social action contributes to the reproduction of social structure' (West & Fenstermaker, 1995, 21). This
formulation highlights how gender operates to produce and maintain asymmetrical
relations, inequalities in social life and systems of domination and subordination
(Lutz, 2010; West & Fenstermaker, 1995). 'Gender hierarchies are inscribed in the
division of labour, in social representations, ascriptions, behavioural expectations
and, in general, in the social status attributed to the categories of "men" and
"women"'(Höpflinger, et al. 2012, 620).
    We can look at the historical, cultural and situational variability in the definitions
of womanhood and manhood, the meanings of masculinity and femininity, the relationships between and within gender categories and the extent of their relative
power and political status (Glenn, 2000, 3). The constructivist feminist approach
views gender not merely as an individual human production and an identity, but
more broadly as an organising principle of collectivities, social institutions, historical processes and social practices—including sexuality, family, education, the economy and the state (Glenn, 2000, 5). From the feminist perspective, gender shapes
the social in every aspect.
    This point of view allows analysing how migration and gender intersect to see
how constructed gender roles and the meanings of femininity and masculinity influence the migration process of women and how migration impacts gender relations
and roles. The construction of the definitions of masculinity and femininity, the different meanings of private and public workplaces, the gender-specific evaluation of
migration experiences and the various consequences of migration for male and
female migrants as couples, singles, parents and children then become of critical
interest (Lutz, 2010, 1650–1651). This feminist, constructivist and intersectional
approach enables seeing beyond the dichotomy of men and women. It permits to
identify asymmetrical relations among men and women, including class, race and
ethnicity (Connell, 2002; Parreñas, 2010). This asymmetrical relation among
women is shown, for example, in the case of international care chains and migrant

domestic workers who enable their female employers to 'undo' their gendered obligations of care work (Lutz, 2010, 1651).

This research regards gender relations as changeable social products and processes subject to resistance as well as conformity, contestation as well as acceptance—therefore, they are open to change (Pilcher & Whelehan, 2004). Gender relations are not static, and change is inherent, but the direction of change has a range of possibilities (Connell, 2002). Consequently, migration is a gendered process in which the experiences of men and women reflect gender constructed representations, roles and social institutions. Therefore, it is crucial to identify and analyse the experiences of women during migratory processes and the entanglement of gender and migration.

2.2 Gender and Migration

The interrelations among various types of migration reflect the multiple and overlapping motivations arising from individual and structural/institutional conditions. The links at the family and the individual levels reflect constructed gender roles and relations. Gender shapes the entire process of migration at both the family and the personal scale.

The intersections of internal, international, return, and circular migratory practices are beneficial for analysing the experiences of the women participants in this research and reveal the complexity of their migration processes. This approach is crucial as Albanian migration has very often been seen only as internal or international, obscuring other migratory practices (except for a few authors such as Vullnetari, 2012; Mai & Paladini, 2013; Maroukis & Gemi, 2011; Labrianidis & Hatziprokopiou, 2010). Existing research does not focus sufficiently on the experiences of migrant women.

My aim in this research, therefore, is to explore the migratory experiences of Albanian women without limiting migration to a one-way movement but viewing it as including various paths.

2.2.1 Migration as a Process: International, Internal and Circulatory Migration

In this research, migration is understood not as a unidirectional movement but as a process that can take different forms, whether international, internal or circulatory movement. Often, international migration is defined as the movement of persons who take up residence in foreign countries. Still, this definition renders short-term forms of migration, such as circular migration, tourism and business travel, invisible (Morokvasic 2003), and neglects the practices of return migration. Unfortunately, often, as Skeldon (2008, 31) explains, the word *migration* seems to mean only international migration, with internal migration classified as 'urbanisation' or 'population redistribution'.

Studies (Morokvasic 1984; Tarrius, 1993; Kofman, 2004; Dahinden, 2009, 2014; Wihtol de Wenden, 2015) have shown that migration should not be considered to be a single movement but rather a diversity of movements. I, therefore, base this research on such an integrative approach, viewing migration as a process that includes one-way internal and international migration, return migration and combinations of internal and international, and circular migratory practices. The integrative approach views migrants as social actors and agents, not as passive victims, and simultaneously takes into account the social, political and economic structures limiting their agency (Sri Tharan, 2010). Analysis of internal and international migration only partly explains the migratory process of Albanian women; consequently, this book also analyses circular and return migration, two migration trajectories increasingly present and visible in Albanian migration. A migration trajectory is understood not only as a physical movement but as a place of social relations and exchanges (Tarrius, 1993).

In this book, I argue that the case of Albanian migration demands an analysis of more than just the interrelations of international and internal movements with gender. Other trajectories, such as circular and return migration, are also interrelated with gender and, in most cases, entwined with each other. Often, transnational relations too are part of these various migration experiences. An integrated approach to the process of migration helps improve understanding of its interrelation with gender by recognising the multitude of strategies used by women and men during migration.

2.2.1.1 International and Internal Migration

Scholars have already shown a significant link between internal and international migration that is very relevant to this research on Albanian migration (Vullnetari, 2012; Skeldon, 2008; King, Skeldon and Vullnetari 2008). According to Ravenstein's (1885, 198) first 'law' of migration, 'the great body of our migrants only proceed a short distance' and mostly perform internal migration. Unfortunately, in most research on migration, internal migration is rarely represented, and the relationship between internal and international migration is a 'remarkably neglected topic' (King, Skeldon and Vullnetari 2008, 34).

Nation-state building processes have profoundly shaped the perception and reception of migration and the development of the studies on migration (Wimmer & Glick Schiller, 2002). The literature and studies on migration have focused mainly on migration by non-citizens and made cross-national migration their primary object. Wimmer and Glick Schiller (2002) opine that internal migration is approached primarily as part of urbanisation studies rather than migration. The nation-state is an internally flexible but externally enclosed space, and this logic underlies the invisibility of internal migration and the taken-for-granted reference of *migration* to international migration (Brubaker, 2010). Population movement within nation-states is often expected, even desirable, contributing to cultural homogenisation and the smooth functioning of labour and housing markets (Brubaker, 2010). 'Cross-border migration, by contrast, appears as an anomaly, a problematic exception to the rule of people staying where they "belong", that is, to "their" nation-state. Post-war migration studies thus naturalised this belonging, moving it into the background of social science reasoning and transforming it into one of its incontestable axioms' (Wimmer & Glick Schiller, 2002, 311).

In this context, the role of the nation-state in shaping how migrants organise their migration process is crucial, both through the 'creat[ion of] barriers' via migration regimes and visa policies and through employment and labour market structures (Mazzucato, 2008, 72). The logic of the nation-state and nation-state border crossing through various visa regimes is what lies behind the construction of illegal, undocumented and irregular migrants. 'Irregular, illegal, undocumented, unauthorised, clandestine: all these are adjectives applied to the words "migration" and "migrants" to imply that something is "wrong" and needs to be "controlled" or "fixed" (King & DeBono, 2013, 3). Among these numerous adjectives, I prefer to use the term *illegalised* to stress the political construction of the illegal or irregular migrant. When using other adjectives in this book, I always imply the political dimension behind them.

While the main difference between internal and international migration is the crossing of national borders, two other crucial differences regulate migration streams: distance and culture (Zohry, 2005). King and Skeldon (2010) highlight that space and culture often blur the distinction between internal and international migration. First, the distance between the two countries might be smaller than distances within the same country. Second, cultural differences may well exist within one country, not only between countries. Furthermore, the reasons and motivations for internal and international migration are not clear-cut and often overlap. For example, women may engage both in internal and international migration trajectories to escape from gender constraints in their place of origin. However, we should not forget the cost difference between international and internal migration. The very act of crossing a border controlled by a state, often in illegalised ways, directly increases the costs of international migration relative to internal migration. Crossing borders requires significant preparation involving documents and social networks (which might include not only friends and relatives but also smugglers). Thus, the higher travel costs of international migration compared to internal migration present an obstacle, especially for the poor. However, expectations for higher incomes and savings in the country of destination compensate for the higher costs of international migration.

An integrated approach to internal and international migration trajectories from a gender perspective does not assume that both these trajectories are the same; to the contrary, the aim is to see how gender informs migration, both internal and international. In the case of Albania, families and individuals alike use both migration processes as strategies for survival and improved wellbeing (Vullnetari, 2012, 36). In Albania, it is more often the rule than the exception that members of a family have migrated internally and internationally, and very often, the same persons engage in various types of migration during their lives. Furthermore, the link between internal and international migration in Albania has significant relevance as neither migration type was allowed during the four and a half decades of communist governance, as further explained in Chap. 3 on the Albanian context.

2.2.1.2 Return Migration

Return migration is part of the moving process but, unfortunately, is 'the great unwritten chapter in the history of migration', as Russell King puts it (2000, 7). In this book, the analysis of return migration is highly essential as some of the participants are return migrants. In the context of this research, return migration is defined as 'the process whereby people return to their country or place of origin after a significant period in another country or region' (King 2000, 8). Here, I define this period as having spent at least three months abroad. Additionally, return migration is neither permanent nor the end of the migration cycle (Black & King, 2004; Cassarino, 2013; Ley & Kobayashi, 2009).

The neoclassical and new economics of labour theories explain that financial and economic factors determine the motivations for return. These theories view migration in the context of economic development processes and emphasise the economic logic of migratory decisions at the macro and micro levels but do not consider how the social, economic and political environments of the home country may affect the return experience (Cassarino, 2004; Lang et al., 2016). The structuralist theory makes up for this shortcoming. The structuralist approach expands research to investigate more explanatory variables, particularly the structural elements that frame migratory decisions, such as the political, economic, demographic and social situations in both the origin and the possible destination country (Lang et al., 2016).

Social network theories and transnational approaches concerned with the maintenance of migratory processes are quite relevant to the analysis of return migration (Lang et al., 2016). These approaches focus on how the sustained links between receiving and sending countries enable migrants to return at a point when enough financial and non-financial resources are mobilised and when conditions in the home country are favourable (Cassarino, 2004). In social network theory, embeddedness in transnational social networks is a crucial factor in successful reintegration upon return. Additionally, institutionalised networks can play an important role and contribute significantly to resolving any bureaucratic problems that might arise during return migration, such as labour market integration, housing and schooling. A transnational conceptualisation of return migration views this latter as part of an on-going itinerary, not a permanent move detached from earlier migratory experiences. We should see return migration not as the end of a process but as another stage in a continuing itinerary (Ley & Kobayashi, 2009).

This research draws upon social network theory and transnational approach in research on return migration. Return migration is not solely an economic endeavour but also a socio-cultural process driven by a mix of economic, social, cultural and gendered motives. Return migration decisions do not constitute purely rational, individual decisions; they are socially formed decisions made within a household, a family and a broader cultural context (Lang et al., 2016). Returnees differ significantly in their return motivation, and often their reasons overlap and are ambivalent (Sri Tharan, 2010). Like other phases of the migration process, a single cause can hardly explain return migration as a whole (Castles & Miller, 1998). Furthermore, the factor of gender influences the decisions to return, as well as the readjustment process. Female migrants have different motivations for deciding whether to return that, for example, range from the everyday experiences they live through to how much access do they have to a male-dominated labour market in the home country (King & Kılınç, 2016; Sondhi & King, 2017).

The readjustment process is complex and varies depending on migrants' experience and agency and on institutional, political and economic conditions. Return migrants often engage in other migratory processes, making return an impermanent settlement (Black & King, 2004; Cassarino, 2004). A return does not constitute the end of the migration cycle as it is part of a circular system of social and economic relationships and exchanges facilitating the reintegration of migrants and transmitting knowledge, information and membership (Cassarino, 2004; Ley & Kobayashi, 2009). Return migration is not a sufficient description of the diversity of the current movement trajectories. The life cycle of return migrants is characterised by a constant openness to further movement during distinctive phases of said cycle (Ley & Kobayashi, 2009). Thus, the concept of permanent return is becoming less relevant. Besides, migrants keep themselves mobile to maintain their international professional and social networks, thus engaging in circulatory practices (Black & King, 2004).

Taking into account an assortment of reasons and motivations to return and not considering return migration to be the end of the migratory process enables a better analysis of the experiences of Albanian migrant women. Furthermore, the feminist constructivist perspective allows examining return migration starting from the experiences of migrants to identify the various reasons and motivations for return that go beyond simple economical and financial considerations and to explore their experiences in Albania after returning. This approach permits seeing how gender influences both the readjustment process and reasons for return.

2.2.1.3 Circulatory Migration

As mentioned at the beginning of this subsection, this book approaches migration as a process with multiple trajectories, including circular migration. In this study, I consider circular migration as temporary, repeated international migration for reasons such as economic, education, family and legal issues (e.g. residency permit regulations in a destination country). Beyond a simple binary movement between the country of origin and the country of destination, circular migration may also include multiple trajectories in various countries (Cassarino, 2013; Triandafyllidou, 2013).

The visibility of this pattern in studies on migration has grown (Morokvasic, 2003; Dahinden 2010; Triandafyllidou, 2013; Parreñas, 2010). The concept of circular migration is essential to understanding migration as a process and not as a unilinear movement in which settling in the destination country demands all the attention of those engaged in migratory processes. As Morokvasic (2003, 113) emphasises, 'migration processes can take many forms and do not necessarily lead to settlement—integration and assimilation in only one place'. Circular migration demonstrates the complexity of migratory processes as migrants settle in mobility (Dahinden, 2010; Morokvasic, 2003) rather than a single destination country.

Another pattern of the circular movement is what Morokvasic (2003) calls pendular migration, or trans-border and short-term movements, regular and undocumented, for work and trade. In this back–and–forth motion, the migrant spends several months per year in each country (Fokkema et al., 2016). This migration process entails a lifestyle of leaving home and going away and, paradoxically, a strategy of staying at home and an alternative to emigration. In this sense, Tarrius (1993) speaks of the new nomads who, by creating circular territories *(territoires circulatoires)*, simultaneously belong both here and there. This type of migration again emphasises the inadequacy of unilinear or permanent settling frameworks of migration.

Circular migration arises from personal and structural reasons in both the country of origin and the country of destination. First, the mobility capital related to adequate visa regimes is an element in circular migration. The possibility of complying with visa regimes and border-crossing policies and possessing residency permits in a foreign country increases engagement in circular migration, as highlighted in the case of Albanian migration to Italy (Mai & Paladini, 2013). Nevertheless, when free movement turns out to be impossible, people often engage in pendular migration with a neighbour country by crossing the borders in illegalised ways. Such an example is found in those Albanian migrants who split the year between Greece and Albania (Maroukis and Gemi 2011). Another case of circular migration is short-term work permits, also called 'temporal segregation' by Parreñas (2010, 312) who uses the term to describe Filipino female entertainers in Japan. Parreñas also explains that circular migrants may not fit the transnational migrant figure who, according to Basch, Schiller and Blanc (1994), balances allegiance to both home and host society. Analysing the case of Filipino entertainers in Japan, Parreñas (2010) finds that these circular migrants maintain stronger relations with the sending countries.

Second, Mai and Paladini (2013) show that we may relate circular migration to conditions in both the sending and the destination country (e.g., adaptation difficulties and marginalisation in the destination country and a lack of economic security and detachment from cultural practices in the land of origin). Parreñas (2010, 320), therefore, suggests that research should look 'not at the extent of migrants' integration but instead at their segregation in the host society'. Additionally, she stresses the need for more research from the perspective of sending countries to identify the intertwinement of return and circular migration and the reasons and conditions for the frequent engagement of return migrants in other circular migratory practices.

Third, the proximity of countries is significant in circular, primarily pendular, migration, allowing migrants to follow pendular trajectories between the two countries. Proximity is an important factor, as the main reason for this pattern is to work but not settle in a neighbouring country (Morokvasic, 2003). Women, in particular, have high engagement in circular migration. Their involvement in this process is shaped by gender as it is driven by their role as mothers, gender representations and the division of household labour. Under the constructed gender roles that cast men as breadwinners and women as caregivers, circular migration appears to optimise the opportunities and minimise the obstacles to women's reproductive and productive work by combining them (Dahinden, 2010; Morokvasic, 2003). Schmoll (2006, 10) provides a similar account of Tunisian circular migrants to Italy who gain an opportunity to migrate and support their families while 'reduc[ing] the social and family costs that would be generated by the neglect of their family responsibilities'.

2.2.1.4 Transnationalism

The brief preceding presentation of return and circular migration stresses that we should view migration as more than a simple, linear, unidirectional movement. Migrants are increasingly able to construct their lives across borders, creating economic, social, political and cultural activities that allow them to maintain membership in both their destination and their home countries. Migrants can hardly be uprooted from their home countries as they simultaneously maintain multiple linkages to their homelands, bringing together their societies of origin and settlement. Hence, the usefulness of the concept of transnationalism, defined by Glick Schiller, Basch and Blanc-Szanton (1992, 1) as 'the process by which immigrants build social fields that link together their country of origin and their country of settlement'. The notion of transnationalism has become fundamental to understanding the contemporary practices taking place across national borders. Especially when speaking of migration (Dahinden, 2010b), transnationalism challenges the assumed linearity of the migration process as a one-way journey and acknowledges the 'fluid relationships between two or more countries' (Zontini, 2004, 1114).

Transnationalism, which emerged as a new approach in the 1990s, 'accents the attachments migrants maintain to families, communities, traditions and causes outside the boundaries of the nation-state to which they have moved' (Vertovec, 2001, 574). As stressed by Faist (2010, 12), the transnational turn in the early 1990s 'brought migrants "back in" as important social agents.' Transnationalism connotes migrants' everyday practices in various activities, including small-scale cross-border entrepreneurship, reciprocity and solidarity within kinship networks, political participation in the countries of both emigration and immigration and the transfer and re-transfer of cultural customs and practices (Faist, 2010).

An issue of interest in this book is migrants' two-fold transnational relations with their home country and with their destination country after their return (Black & King, 2004; Dahinden, 2010a). Transnational linkages have been often viewed from only one perspective: migrants' relationships to their home countries. However, as Dahinden (2010a) argues, analysing these linkages from a different perspective—i.e., transnational relations and their role after migrants' return—is also very fruitful. As mentioned, scholars have examined return not as the end of a movement but as a new phase in the migratory process that often involves maintenance of transnational relations with the destination country (Black & King, 2004; Dahinden, 2010a). Dahinden (2010a) reveals that returnees' transnational networks remain highly relevant, both emotionally and economically, and have substantial effects on the lives of the return migrants. For instance, returned Albanian women in Kosovo develop a kind of 'transnational belonging', identifying with a European 'femininity' in contrast to the 'traditional Albanian woman' (Dahinden, 2010a, 143, 144). Another point of interest is women's engagement in transnational families and transnational mothering (Hondagneu-Sotelo & Avila, 1997; Hochschild, 2000; Parreñas 2000; Zontini, 2004; Vianello, 2009), which highlights the shifting gender relations and caring roles within transnational networks.

Finally, transnational practices and formations do not develop independently of the constraints and opportunities imposed by specific contexts. Who migrates and where they migrate, are shaped by the social, economic, political and legal contexts in the home and the destination countries. In particular, immigration policies are a significant factor in mobility (Dahinden, 2010b; Mazzucato, 2008). Nation-state barriers, such as migration regimes and labour market structures, remain crucial influences on migration. As Dahinden (2017, 1481) contends, 'nation-states may be losing sovereignty concerning their ability to regulate socio-economic realities in general, but when it comes to migration issues, the nation-state, its institutions and its inherent logic remain strong, impacting and shaping transnational fields in multiple ways'.

2.2.1.5 Student Migration

The study of student migration, particularly internal migration, from a gender perspective, remains a domain open to further development (King & Raghuram, 2013; Sondhi & King, 2017). The number of female migrant students is growing and, in many cases, exceeding that of male students (Kim, 2012; Moskal, 2016).

Findlay et al. (2012, 127) argue that student migration is not 'discrete and disconnected from other mobilities' but that it is part of an individual's life-course planning. Education migration is often an early phase in stepwise migration, such that youth may first migrate internally to obtain education and skills, and later to other domestic or international destinations providing more and better opportunities (King & Skeldon, 2010). However, this individual life-course planning is shaped by gender and is not individual but embedded within social relationships, particularly with parents and friends (Brooks & Waters, 2010; Kajanus, 2014; Oluwaseun, 2016).

Female student migrants do not migrate only in search of better future career opportunities. Through educational migration, they seek more freedom and independence by associating destination places with ideals of 'modernity', freedom and opportunities (Kajanus, 2014). A binary configuration remains behind these geographic gendered imaginaries: gender constraints and freedom, tradition and modernity, social control or independence, hardship or luxury (Kajanus, 2014; Appadurai 1996). Gendered geographical imaginaries are a powerful force shaping human action (Appadurai 1996) and various migration trajectories. Furthermore, research has emphasised that student migrants are not only students but also daughters, mothers, wives. Their decisions and negotiations about their migration project, therefore, reflect these other roles (Oluwaseun, 2016).

In this research, I often blur the lines between high-skilled and student migration. The term 'highly skilled' commonly assumes these people have a tertiary educational qualification or its equivalent (Moskal, 2016). However, we need to be cautious about the value of different forms of knowledge and skills. Sandoz (Sandoz, 2019, p. 14) alerts that as academics, we should be conscious that universities do not have a monopoly in providing expertise and their importance is socially, geographically, and historically situated.

University-based definition of skills does (Moskal, 2016) not take into account other forms of knowledge that are practised and valued in various places. The notion of skills as dependent on a university degree is culturally and socially marked since it favours people who have a particular social background or who live in places where this model of education is both valued and available' (Sandoz, 2019, 15).

This complexity also appears in this research where high skilled migrants might include those having finished tertiary education but also those who upon international migration gain new skills that allow them to establish their enterprises, etc.

Additionally, almost half the sample of this research includes women who have migrated for educational purposes. However, they are also highly skilled migrants, they have completed their degrees, and most of them are probably engaged in various migratory trajectories. I mostly refer to them as student migrants, as education was their (almost) primary migration motivation. The analysis of their migration experiences encompasses both statuses, starting from their experiences as students and going to them as high skilled migrants. Research on student and high skilled migration have shown how these migrants engage in various experiences – return migration, circular migration, transnational relations (Black & King, 2004; Ghosh & Wang, 2003; Sondhi & King, 2017). Thus, student migration needs to be analysed through an integrated approach, encompassing various migration trajectories, as well as an intersectional one, including gender, social and economic background, race age, sexual orientation, civil status, ethnicity.

2.2.2 Gender in Migration Studies

'Woman is a greater migrant than man'.
Ravenstein (1885, 196)

This research builds on the premise that migration patterns and processes, migrants' experiences and the social, political, economic and cultural impacts of migration are gendered, and at the same time, migration influences gender relations (Erel et al., 2003) in various social institutions. I argue that migrant women manifest and employ their agency in various forms through various phases of the migration process. Agency is the ability to define one's own goals and act upon them; it is a form of bargaining and negotiation, deception and manipulation and subversion and resistance, as well as the cognitive processes of reflection and analysis (Kabeer, 1999, 438). Agency is 'exercised within the "gendered structures of constraint": the limits imposed by the structural distribution of rules, norms, resources and responsibilities that served to position different groups of women and men within the broader social hierarchies of their societies' (Kabeer, 2013, 3). Discussing the tactics and strategies used by individuals to achieve their goals, De Certeau (1984, 37) labels tactics 'the art of the weak' who move in the hostile terrain of 'gender structures of constraint'. This concept is useful to identify and understand the agency of women, even in situations when the outcome is not a change of the dominant structure or order. This perspective helps avoid the trap of victimising women and precluding their agency.

Since the pioneering work of Ernest Ravenstein, it took about another century before women's role and agency through the migration processes was analysed. Indeed, the social geographer Ernest Ravenstein published the first work on the importance of migrant women in 1885 in *The Laws of Migration*. He clearly stated that women are more significant migrants than men, despite the prevailing view associating women with 'domestic life' (1885, 196). He also explained how women are more engaged in short-distance migration to 'some other county of the same kingdom', whereas men more often migrate to another 'kingdom' (Ravenstein, 1885, 197).

In 1984, in a special edition of *International Migration Journal*, Mirjana Morokvasic (1984) criticised the persistent male bias in migration studies. Until that moment, studies on migration had been blind to gender differences as the prototype migrant was considered to be male as analysed by Dahinden et al. (2007), Donato et al. (2006), Lutz (2010). These scholars examine how classical theories of migration started from the idea that migration is triggered mostly by economic reasons, and economic activity is primarily associated with men; consequently, women were assumed not to migrate.

Several research streams on gender and migration proved useful for this research. First, a critical development in migration studies is the practice, mostly by feminist scholars, of analysis that permits envisaging women as actors and protagonists in migration. In contrast to the image of women migrants as passive, dependent subjects, scholars have shown that women migrate on their own to help their families economically (Vianello, 2009; Schmoll, 2006; Parreñas 2000; Oso Casas, 2006; Dahinden et al., 2007; Dahinden, 2010; Erel et al., 2003). To investigate the agency of migrant women, scholars have applied the concepts of *tactics* (De Certeau, 1984) in migration studies (Kihato, 2009; Lévy, 2015). Kihato (2009) reports that women employ specific tactics to engage with dominant structures, and their practices sometimes challenge these dominant structures (e.g., the family, labour market and community), allowing women to escape the prevailing order without leaving it.

Scholarly attention thus has shifted from the male individual to the family and social networks (Boyd, 1989). Research on gender and migration now considers the consequences of the migration process not only for migrants themselves but also for their family members and views migration decisions as the result of negotiation between various peoples (Dahinden et al., 2007). This shift constitutes a second significant development for my research.

A third development relevant to the framework of the research is the introduction of an intersectional approach to migration studies. Amid socio-economic and political changes in recent years, the analysis of migration has expanded to include the intersection of gender with class, race and other factors (Dahinden, 2010; Silvey, 2004). These recent changes have seen increased participation by women in paid, productive work in northern countries and simultaneous shrinking and restructuring of the welfare state. These developments have led to higher demand for migrant women among domestic and care workers. Gender and migration studies analyse the growing numbers and geographical variety of household care and work migrants in research on global care chains (Hochschild, 2000a), and the international division of reproductive labour (Parreñas 2000) has elaborated the relationship between gender and migration.

> A typical global care chain might work something like this: An older daughter from a low-income family in a third world country cares for her siblings (the first link in the chain) while her mother works as a nanny caring for the children of a nanny migrating to a first world country (the second link) who, in turn, cares for the child of a family in a rich country (the final link). Each kind of chain expresses an invisible human ecology of care, one care worker depending on another and so on. A global care chain might start in a poor country and end in a rich one, or might link rural and urban areas within the same poor country. More complex versions start in one poor country and extend to another slightly less poor country and then link to a rich country (Hochschild, 2000a, 33).

These complex care chains reveal the intertwinement of political and economic changes at the national and global levels with the gendered constructed roles of women as caregivers. This international division of reproductive labour also is visible in Southern Europe as migrants from former socialist countries (Vianello, 2009; Lyberaki 2011; Vaiou 2002) fill the care gaps left by women engaged in paid work. The international division of reproductive labour also highlights rising social inequalities among women themselves and contradictory patterns of mobility (Parreñas 2001).

A fourth useful frame for this research comes from gender and migration studies that break from the unidirectional conception of migration. The transformation of the former Communist Bloc states has led to new migration processes enabling increased mobility by women from these countries (Dahinden, 2010; Morokvasic, 2003). Analysis of these migration flows illustrates the diverse characteristics of migration that demand reconsideration of conventional models. As mentioned, Morokvasic (2003) describes the situation of Eastern Europe women involved in circular migration as pendular migration. Dahinden (2010) gives another illustration of pendular/circular migration in a study of cabaret dancers in Switzerland who mostly come from former socialist countries in Eastern Europe.

Fifthly, I rely on studies showing that migrant women do not move only for economic reasons and do not take only low-skilled jobs. Very complex mixtures of economic and non-economic reasons lead women to emigrate (Morokvasic, 1984; Vianello, 2009; Kihato, 2009; Riaño & Baghdadi, 2007). Migration permits escape from the dominant gender constraints and patriarchal practices and customs in the country of origin (Kihato, 2009; Morokvasic, 1984; Vianello, 2009). Furthermore, the profile of the migrant is no longer that of the poor or less-skilled woman (and man). Studies on migration have shown that both women and men migrate for educational purposes or are highly skilled and migrate in search of better-paid jobs and career opportunities (Kofman & Raghuram, 2009; Kofman & Parvati, 2015; Brooks & Waters, 2010; King & Raghuram, 2013).

Finally, when considering migration as a process, return migration emerges as a distinct, gendered phase. Although gender affects the reasons for returning and the post-return experience (Vianello 2011; Sri Tharan, 2010), research analysing gender and return migration is lacking (Sri Tharan, 2010). Studies on gender and migration concentrate on the reasons and ways of migration and the receiving countries. Still, very little research has been done on their experiences of women after they return to their country of origin. Research has not considered the effects of migration on their positions, roles, being, wellbeing, everyday life and relationships with their families, households and community.

In this research, I see the intersection of gender and migration as going beyond the dichotomous evolutionist perspective of tradition/modernity that associates each with the place of origin and the place of destination, respectively. This intersection is not so simple because migration does not automatically move women from subordination to liberation (Dahinden et al., 2007; Parreñas 2009; Vianello, 2009). 'Crossing borders can be empowering, and established gender norms may be challenged. However, it can also lead to new dependencies and reinforce existing gender boundaries and hierarchies' (Morokvasic 2008, 2).

The empowerment and the agency of migrant women are enhanced and displayed not only in the place of destination but also in the location of origin. Women manifest already their agency in the very act of engaging in migratory projects (Erel, 2009; Lévy, 2015; Moujoud, 2008). Empowerment is a process, not a single move from point A to point B, which makes it difficult to jump to simplistic conclusions regarding the question of whether migration empowers. These concepts aid in understanding the experiences of women during migration and the empowering dimension of migration (or lack thereof). I use Kabeer's (1999) concept of empowerment as an on-going process. Kabeer (1999) defines women's empowerment as the process by which those denied the ability to make strategic life choices acquire that ability. This conceptualisation by Kabeer (1999) implies the use of resources and gives space for agency throughout the process of empowerment. Kabeer (1999) also suggests the employment of everyday discursive alternatives and practices (similar to De Certeau's, 1984 tactics) that enable women to act in spaces they do not own but can use for their own goals.

References

Alvesson, M., & Sköldberg, K. (2009). (Post)positivism, social constructionism, critical realism: Three reference points in the philosophy of science. In M. Alvesson & K. Sköldberg (Eds.), *Reflexive methodology new vistas for qualitative research* (pp. 15–51). Sage Publications.

Appadurai, A. (1996). *Modernity at large: Cultural dimensions of globalization*. University of Minnesota Press.

Black, R., & King, R. (2004). Editorial introduction: Migration, return and development in West Africa. *Population, Space and Place, 10*, 75–83.

Bohnsack, R. (2010). Documentary method and group discussions. In R. Bohnsack, N. Pfaff, & W. Weller (Eds.), *Qualitative analysis and documentary method in international educational research* (pp. 99–124). Opladen: Barbara Budrich Publishers.

Boyd, M. (1989). Family and personal networks in international migration: Recent developments and new agendas. *International Migration Review, 23*(3), 638–670.

Brooks, R., & Waters, J. (2010). Social networks and educational mobility: The experiences of UK students. *Globalisation Societies and Education, 8*(1), 143–157. https://doi.org/10.1080/14767720903574132

Brubaker, R. (2010). Migration, membership and the nation-state. *Journal of Interdisciplinary History, XLI*(1), 61–78.

Cassarino, J.-P. (2013). The drive for securitized temporariness. In A. Triandafyllidou (Ed.), *Circular migration between Europe and its neighbourhood: Choice or necessity?* (pp. 22–40). Oxford University Press.

Cassarino, J.-P. (2014). A case for return preparedness. In G. Battistella (Ed.), *Global migration issues: Global and Asian perspectives on international migration* (pp. 135–165). Springer International Publishing Switzerland.

Castles, S., & Miller, M. J. (1998). *The age of migration, international population movements in the modern world*. Palgrave Macmillan.

Chafetz, J. S. (2006). The varieties of gender theory in sociology. In J. S. Chafetz (Ed.), *Handbook of the sociology of gender* (pp. 3–24). Springer.

Charmaz, K. (2006). *Constructing grounded theory: A practical guide through qualitative analysis*. Sage.

Collins, P. H. (1990). *Black feminist thought: knowledge, consciousness and the politics of empowerment*. Routledge.

Connell, R. W. (2002). *Gender*. Polity.

Connell, R. (2015). Meeting at the edge of fear: Theory on a world scale. *Feminist Theory, 16*(1), 49–66.

Crenshaw, K. (1989). Demarginalizing the intersection of race and sex: A Black feminist critique of antidiscrimination doctrine, Feminist theory, and antiracist politics. *The University of Chicago Legal Forum*, 139–168.

Crenshaw, K. (1994). Mapping the margins: Intersectionality, identity politics, and violence against women of color. *Stanford Law Review, 43*, 1241–1299.

Dahinden, J. (2009). *Migration and mobility: Universality and resulting tensions* (pp. 359–376). Universality - From Theory to Practice.

Dahinden, J. (2010). Cabaret dancers: "Settle down in order to stay Mobile?" bridging theoretical orientations within transnational migration studies. *Social Policies, 17*(3), 323–348.

Dahinden, J. (2010a). Are you who you know? A network perspective on ethnicity, gender and transnationalism: Albanian-speaking migrants in Switzerland and returnees in Kosovo. In C. Westin, J. Bastos, J. Dahinden, & P. Góis (Eds.), *Identity processes and dynamics in multi-ethnic Europe* (pp. 127–148). Amsterdam University Press.

Dahinden, J. (2010b). The dynamics of migrants' transnational formations: Between mobility and locality. In R. Bauböck & T. Faist (Eds.), *Diaspora and transnationalism: Concepts, theories and methods* (pp. 51–72). Amsterdam University Press.

Dahinden, J. (2014). The circulation of people. Understanding the dynamics of transnational formations among Albanian-speaking migrants in Switzerland by bringing in theories of mobility, social inequality and ethnicity. *Working Paper, 6.*

Dahinden, J. (2017). Transnationalism reloaded: The historical trajectory of a concept. *Ethnic and Racial Studies, 40*(9), 1474–1485.

Dahinden, J., Rosende, M., Benelli, N., Hanselmann, M., & Lempen, K. (2007). Migrations: genre et frontieres – frontieres de genre. *Nouvelles Questions Féministes, 26*(1), 4–14.

De Certeau, M. (1984). *The practice of everyday life.* University of California Press.

Donato, K. M., Gabaccia, D., Holdaway, J., Manalansan, M., & Pessar, P. R. (2006). A glass half full? Gender in migration studies. *International Migration Review, 40*(1), 3–26. https://doi.org/10.1111/j.1747-7379.2006.00001.x

Erel, U. (2009). *Migrant women transforming citizenship: Life-stories from Britain and Germany.* Ashgate.

Erel, U., Morokvasic, M., & Shinozaki, K. (2003). Introduction. Bringing gender into migration. In M. Morokvasic, U. Erel, & K. Shinozaki (Eds.), *Crossing borders and shifting boundaries: Gender on the move* (Vol. I, pp. 9–22). Springer.

Faist, T. (2010). Diaspora and transnationalism: What kind of dance partners? In R. Bauböck & T. Faist (Eds.), *Diaspora and transnationalism: Concepts, theories and methods* (pp. 9–34). Amsterdam University Press.

Findlay, A. M., King, R., Smith, F. M., Geddes, A., & Skeldon, R. (2012). World class? An investigation of globalization, difference and international student mobility. *Transactions of the Institute of British Geographers, 37*(1), 118–131.

Fokkema, T., Cela, E., & Witter, Y. (2016). Pendular migration of the older first generations in Europe: Misconceptions and nuances. In V. Horn & C. Schweppe (Eds.), *Transnational aging: Current insights and future challenges* (pp. 141–162). Routledge.

Ghosh, S., & Wang, L. (2003). Transnationalism and identity: A tale of two faces and multiple lives. *Canadian Geographer, 47*(3), 269–283.

Glenn, E. N. (2000). The social construction and institutionalization of gender and race: An integrative framework. In M. M. Ferree, J. Lorber, & B. B. Hess (Eds.), *Revisioning gender* (pp. 3–43). Alta Mira Press.

Harding, S. (1993). Rethinking standpoint epistemology: What is "strong objectivity"? In L. Alcoff & E. Potter (Eds.), *Feminist epistemologies* (pp. 49–82). Routledge.

Harding, S. (2009). Standpoint theories: Productively controversial. *Hypatia, 24*(4), 192–200.

Hesse-Biber, S. N. (2012). Feminist research: Exploring, interrogating, and transforming the interconnections of epistemology, methodology, and method. In S. N. Hesse-Biber (Ed.), *Handbook of feminist research: Theory and praxis* (pp. 2–26). Sage Publications.

Hesse-Biber, S. N. (2014). A re-invitation to Feminist research. In S. N. Hesse-Biber (Ed.), *Feminist research practice – A primer* (2nd ed., pp. 1–14). Sage Publications.

Hochschild, A. R. (2000). Global care chains and emotional surplus value. In W. Hutton & A. Giddens (Eds.), *On the edge: Living with global capitalism* (pp. 130–146). Jonathan Cape.

Hochschild, A. R. (2000a). The nanny chain. *The American Prospect, 11*(4), 32–36.

Hondagneu-Sotelo, P., & Avila, E. (1997). "I'm here, but I'm there": The meanings of Latina transnational motherhood. *Gender and Society*, 548–571.

Höpflinger, A-K, Lavanchy, A., & Dahinden, J. (2012). Introduction: Linking gender and religion. *Women's Studies, 41*(6), 615–638. https://doi.org/10.1080/00497878.2012.691401

Jackson, S., & Scott, S. (2002). Introduction: The gendering of sociology. In S. Jackson & S. Scott (Eds.), *Gender. A sociological reader* (pp. 1–26). Routledge.

Kabeer, N. (1999). Resources, agency, achievements: Reflections on the measurement of women's empowerment. *Development and Change, 30*, 435–464.

Kabeer, N. (2013). *Paid work, women's empowerment and inclusive growth: Transforming the structures of constraint.* UN Women.

Kajanus, A. (2014). *Journey of the Phoenix: Overseas study and women's changing position in China.* University of Helsinki.

Kandiyoti, D. (1999). Islam and patriarchy: A comparative perspective. In S. Hesse-Biber, C. Gilmartin, & R. Lydenberg (Eds.), *Feminist approaches to theory and methodology: An interdisciplinary reader* (pp. 236–256). Oxford University Press.

Kihato, C. W. (2009). *Migration*. University of South Africa.

Kim, Y. (2012). Female individualization? Transnational mobility and media consumption of Asian women. In Y. Kim (Ed.), *Women and the media in Asia the precarious self* (pp. 31–53). Palgrave Macmillan.

King, R. (2000). Generalizations from the history of return migration. In Ghosh, Bimal (Ed.) *Return migration: Journey of hope or despair?* (pp. 7–55). United Nations and the International Organization for Migration. ISBN 9789290680963.

King, R., & DeBono, D. (2013). Irregular migration and the "Southern European model" of migration. *Journal of Mediterranean Studies, 22*(1), 1–31. ISSN 1016-3476.

King, R., & Kılınç, N. (2016). The counter-diasporic migration of Turkish-Germans to Turkey: Gendered narratives of home and belonging. In R. Nadler, Z. Kovács, B. Glorius, & T. Lang (Eds.), *Return migration and regional development in Europe: Mobility against the stream* (pp. 167–194). Palgrave Macmillan.

King, R., & Raghuram, P. (2013). International student migration: Mapping the field and new research agendas. *Population, Space and Place, 19*(2), 127–137.

King, R., & Skeldon, R. (2010). 'Mind the gap!' integrating approaches to internal and international migration. *Journal of Ethnic and Migration Studies, 36*(10), 1619–1646.

King, R., Skeldon, R., & Vullnetari, J. (2008). *Internal and international migration: Bridging the theoretical divide (Sussex Centre for Migration Research Working Papers, 52)*. University of Sussex.

Kofman, E. (2004). Gendered global migrations. *International Feminist Journal of Politics, 6*(4), 643–665.

Kofman, E., & Raghuram, P. (2009). Skilled female labour migration. *Focus migration: Policy brief, No 13*. http://focus-migration.hwwi.de/index.php?id=6029&L=1

Kofman, E., & Parvati, R. (2015). Gendered migrations and global social reproduction: An introduction. In: *Gendered migrations and global social reproduction*. Migration, Diasporas and Citizenship Series. Palgrave Macmillan. https://doi.org/10.1057/9781137510143_1

Labrianidis, L., & Hatziprokopiou, P. (2010). *Albanian return migration: Migrants tend to return to their country of origin after all*. European Commission.

Lang, T., Glorius, B., Nadler, R., & Kovács, Z. (2016). Introduction: Mobility against the stream? New concepts, methodological approaches and regional perspectives on return migration in Europe. In R. Nadler, Z. Kovács, B. Glorius, & T. Lang (Eds.), *Return migration and regional development in Europe: mobility against the stream* (pp. 1–22). Palgrave Macmillan.

Lévy, F. (2015). *Entre contraintes et interstices, l'évolution des projets migratoires dans l'espace transnational: Une ethnographie des migrants de Chine du Nord à Paris*. EHESS.

Ley, D., & Kobayashi, A. (2009). Back to Hong Kong: Return migration or transnational sojourn? In D. Conway & R. B. Potter (Eds.), *Return migration of the next generations: 21st century transnational mobility* (pp. 119–138). Ashgate.

Lorber, J. (2007). 'Night to his day': The social construction of gender. The paradoxes of gender. In P. S. Rothenberg (Ed.), *Race, class, and gender in the United States: An integrated study* (pp. 54–68). Worth Publishers.

Lutz, H. (2010). Gender in the migratory process. *Journal of Ethnic and Migration Studies, 36*(10), 1647–1663.

Lyberaki, A. (2011). Migrant women care work and women's employment in Greece. *Feminist Economics, 17*(3), 103–131. https://doi.org/10.1080/13545701.2011.583201

Mahler, S. J., & Pessar, P. R. (2001). Gendered geographies of power: Analyzing gender across transnational spaces. *Identities, 7*(4), 441–459.

Mai, N., & Paladini, C. (2013). Flexible circularities: Integration, return, and socio-economic instability within Albanian migration to Italy. In A. Triandafyllidou (Ed.), *Circular migration between Europe and its neighborhood, choice or necessity?* (pp. 42–67). Oxford University Press.

Maroukis, T., & Gemi, E. (2011). *Circular migration between Albania and Greece: A case study. METOIKOS Project*. European University Institute.

Morokvasic, M. (2008). *Crossing borders and shifting boundaries of belonging in Post-Wall Europe. A Gender Lens*. migrationonline.cz.

Maynard, M. (1994). Methods, practice and epistemology: The debate about feminism and research. In M. Maynard & J. Purvis (Eds.), *Researching Women's lives from a feminist perspective* (pp. 10–26). Taylor and Francis.

Mazzucato, V. (2008). Simultaneity and networks in transnational migration: Lessons learned from an SMS methodology. In J. DeWind & J. Holdaway (Eds.), *Migration and development within and across borders: Research and policy perspectives on internal and international migration* (pp. 69–100). IOM and SSRC.

Mohanty, C. T. (1991). Under Western eyes: Feminist scholarship and colonial discourses. In C. T. Mohanty, A. Russo, & L. Torres (Eds.), *Third world women and the politics of feminism* (pp. 51–80). Indiana University Press.

Morokvasic, M. (1984). Birds of passage are also women. *The International Migration Review, 18*(4), 886–907.

Morokvasic, M. (2003). Transnational mobility and gender: A view from post-wall Europe. In M. Morokvasic, U. Erel, & K. Shinozaki (Eds.), *Crossing borders and shifting boundaries* (pp. 101–136). Springer.

Moskal, M. (2016). International students' mobility, gender dimension and crisis. In A. Triandafyllidou & I. Isaakyan (Eds.), *High-skill migration and recession-gendered perspectives* (pp. 193–214). Palgrave Macmillan.

Moujoud, N. (2008). Effets de la migration sur les femmes et sur les rapports sociaux de sexe: au-delà des visions binaires. *Cahiers du CEDREF*, 57–79.

Olesen, V. (2007). Feminist qualitative research and grounded theory: Complexities, criticisms, and opportunities. In A. Bryant & K. Charmaz (Eds.), *SAGE handbook of grounded theory* (pp. 417–436). Sage.

Oluwaseun, S. (2016). *Understanding international student migration: The case of Nigerian Christian women students engaged inpostgraduate studies in UK higher education*. PhD thesis. University of Nottingham.

Oso Casas, L. (2006). Prostitution et immigration des femmes latino-américaines en Espagne. *Cahiers du Genre, 40*(1), 91–113.

Parreñas, R. S. (2000). Migrant filipina domestic workers and the international division of reproductive labor. *Gender & Society, 14*(4), 560–580. https://doi.org/10.1177/089124300014004005

Parreñas, R. S. (2001). *Servants of globalization: Women, migration and domestic work*. Stanford University Press.

Parreñas, R. S. (2009). *Inserting feminism in transnational migration studies*. migrationonline.cz,

Parreñas, R. S. (2010). Homeward bound: The circular migration of entertainers between Japan and the Philippines. *Global Networks, 10*(3).

Pilcher, J., & Whelehan, I. (2004). *Fifty key concepts in gender studies*. Sage Publications.

Ravenstein, E. G. (1885). The Laws of migration. *Journal of the Statistical Society of London, 48*(2), 167–235.

Riaño, Y., & Baghdadi, N. (2007). "Je pensais que je pourrais avoir une relation plus égalitaire avec un Européen". Le rôle du genre et de l'imaginaire géographique dans la migration des femmes. *Nouvelles Questions Féministes, 26*(1), 38–53.

Sandoz, L. (2019). *Mobilities of the highly skilled towards Switzerland: The role of intermediaries in defining "wanted immigrants"* (IMISCOE Research Series). Springer Open.

Schiller, N. G., Basch, L., & Blanc-Szanton, C. (1992). Transnationalism: A new analytic framework for understanding migration. *Annals of the New York Academy of Sciences, 645*, 1–24. https://doi.org/10.1111/j.1749-6632.1992.tb33484.x

Schmoll, C. (2006). *Moving "on their own"? Mobility strategies and social networks of migrant women from Maghreb in Italy*. IIIS Discussion Paper 154.

Scott, J. W. (1986). Gender: A useful category of historical analysis. *The American Historical Review, 91*(5), 1053–1075.

Silvey, R. (2004). Power, difference and mobility: Feminist advances in migration studies. *Progress in Human Geography, 28*(4), 1–17.

Skeldon, R. (2008). Linkages between internal and international migration. In J. DeWind & J. Holdaway (Eds.), *Migration and development within and across borders - research and policy perspectives on internal and international migration* (pp. 27–36). IOM and SSRC.

Smith, D. E. (1987). *The everyday world as problematic: A feminist sociology.* University of Toronto Press.

Sondhi, G., & King, R. (2017). Gendering international student migration: An Indian case-study. *Journal of Ethnic and Migration Studies, 43*(8), 1308–1324.

Spivak, G. C. (1988). *In other worlds: Essays in cultural politics.* Routledge.

Sprague, J., & Kobrynowicz, D. (2006). A feminist epistemology. In J. S. Chafetz (Ed.), *Handbook of the sociology of gender* (pp. 25–44). Springer.

Sri Tharan, C. T. (2010). *Gender, migration, and social change: The return of Filipino women migrant workers.* University of Sussex.

Tarrius, A. (1993). Territoires Circulatoires et Espaces Urbaine. *Annales de la Recherche Urbain,* 59–60.

Triandafyllidou, A. (2013). Circular migration: Introductory remarks. In A. Triandafyllidou (Ed.), *Circular migration between Europe and its neighborhood: Choice or necessity?* (pp. 1–21). Oxford University Press.

Vaiou, D. (2002). In the interstices of the city: Albanian women in Athens. *Espaces, populations, societes (Persee), 3,* 373–385.

Vertovec, S. (2001). Transnationalism and identity. *Journal of Ethnic and Migration Studies, 27*(4), 573–582.

Vianello, F. A. (2009). *Migrando Sole; Legami transnazionali tra Ucraina e Italia.* Franco Angeli.

Vianello, F. A. (2011). Suspended migrants. Return migration to Ukraine. In M. Nowak & M. Nowosielski (Eds.), *(Post)transformational migration inequalities, welfare state, and horizontal mobility* (pp. 251–272). Peter Lang.

Vullnetari, J. (2012). *Albania on the move: Links between internal and international migration.* Amsterdam University Press.

West, C., & Fenstermaker, S. (1995). Doing difference. *Gender and Society, 9*(1), 8–37.

West, C., & Zimmerman, D. H. (1987). Doing gender. *Gender and Society, 1*(2), 125–151.

Wihtol de Wenden, C. (2015). Faut-il ouvrir les frontières? *Forum 2015.* La conference socio-politique de Caritas: Immigration. Berne: Caritas Suisse.

Wimmer, A., & Glick Schiller, N. (2002). Methodological nationalism and beyond; nation- state building, migration and social sciences. *Global Networks, 2*(4), 391–334.

Zohry, A. (2005). Interrelationships between internal and international migration in Egypt: A pilot study. In *Development research Centre on migration, globalisation and poverty.* University of Sussex.

Zontini, E. (2004). Immigrant women in Barcelona: Coping with the consequences of transnational lives. *Journal of Ethnic and Migration Studies, 30*(6), 1113–1144.

Open Access This chapter is licensed under the terms of the Creative Commons Attribution 4.0 International License (http://creativecommons.org/licenses/by/4.0/), which permits use, sharing, adaptation, distribution and reproduction in any medium or format, as long as you give appropriate credit to the original author(s) and the source, provide a link to the Creative Commons license and indicate if changes were made.

The images or other third party material in this chapter are included in the chapter's Creative Commons license, unless indicated otherwise in a credit line to the material. If material is not included in the chapter's Creative Commons license and your intended use is not permitted by statutory regulation or exceeds the permitted use, you will need to obtain permission directly from the copyright holder.

Chapter 3
Albanian Context

This chapter aims to present the migration framework and the situation of women in Albania. The first section briefly reviews the socio-economic conditions of Albania during the twentieth and twenty-first centuries, which I separate into two main periods: before and after 1991. I take the year 1991 as the official end of the mono-party political system, also known as the communist era or regime, as it is also the year when the country's first multiparty elections happened. I explain how, in this context, migration became one of the leading forces transforming Albanian society. The second section of this chapter focuses on the history of migration in Albania, limited to the twentieth and twenty-first centuries. Here, I also discuss the research site, the city of Tirana. The third section presents the situation of women in Albania, focusing on some central matters that support the analysis in this research.

3.1 Albania: Some Historical Markers

The scope of this chapter precludes exploring the history of Albania in detail. However, it is necessary to highlight some turning points and prevailing circumstances to understand the issue of migration in Albania.

3.1.1 Pre-1991 Period—A Country Weakened by Wars and Isolation

Albania became an independent state on November 28, 1912, under a provisional government. However, after independence, political instability and social and economic upheaval gripped Albania, the neighbouring Balkan countries and beyond. Before World War II, Albania had practically no industry, and its agriculture system

© The Author(s) 2022
E. Danaj, *Women, Migration and Gendered Experiences*, IMISCOE Research
Series, https://doi.org/10.1007/978-3-030-92092-0_3

was fragile. The transportation system had been built mostly by wartime occupiers: Austrian forces constructed 400 miles of strategic road during World War I, and the Italian military did the same during WWII (Keefe et al., 1971, 45). On November 29, 1944, the country was liberated from the Nazi-Fascist occupation that had started on April 7, 1939. The Communist Party, founded on November 8, 1941, led the Antifascist National Liberation War and consequently came to power after the liberation (Keefe et al., 1971). The establishment of a socialist state regime via a liberation war from the occupying forces of Fascist Italy put Albanian on a different trajectory than the other socialist countries, except for former Yugoslavia, with which Albania maintained close ties in the early post-WWII era (Ramet & Wagner, 2010).

The new regime, which called itself a 'dictatorship of the proletariat' (Keefe et al., 1971, 1) established a one-party system. International migration was banned (unlike in neighbouring Yugoslavia) (Bonifazi & Manolo, 2004), and the state controlled the internal migration of the population through an internal passport system, as explained later in this chapter. Any opposition to the party, first called the Communist Party and later the Albanian Party of Labour, was forbidden. The state put all media and information sources under its tight control and banned religion from 1969 until 1991 (Keefe et al., 1971; Woodcock, 2016).

Like other countries in the region and beyond, Albania entered the post-WWII era in a very adverse economic situation and with an infrastructure in dire need of reconstruction. Along with its transformation of the country's political framework, the communist government also reformed the national economic structure essentially from scratch, using two pillars as its foundation: agrarian reform (and more notably, the collectivisation of land into cooperatives) and the nationalisation of industry. The agricultural reform of 1945 redistributed all privately-owned land exceeding certain limits to landless peasants (Vickers, 1999). With regards to industrialisation, Albania adopted a Stalinist model, establishing a strongly centralised economy with an emphasis on self-sufficiency through reliance on heavy industry (Vickers, 1999, 176), similarly to Romania, which underwent the same strict post-1944 reforms (Stan, 2010). The constitution of 1976 banned all private ownership of land and immovable property (Çaro, 2011). Two significant achievements during this period were the electrification of the country and the construction and improvement of infrastructure. Until the mid-1970s, the Albanian government succeeded in industrialising the economy and increasing per capita income at an average rate of more than 8.2 per cent a year. By 1985, the 'relatively modern' multi-branched industrial sector generated 43.3 per cent of the total national income (Gjonca et al., 2008, 262).

Economic improvement spurred also the development of a national social and health care system, including through the establishment and construction of services and infrastructure intended to cover the entire country. In the immediate aftermath of WWII, life expectancy at birth was no more than 50 years for both sexes. Infant mortality was the highest in the region, at 148 infant deaths per 1000 live births. However, by the end of the 1990s, life expectancy at birth had improved, shooting to 70.7 years, and the infant mortality rate had fallen to 45.4 deaths per 1000 live births (Gjonca et al., 2008, 263).

By the early 1970s, countrywide literacy campaigns and the overhauling of the national education system had eradicated illiteracy among those younger than 40 years old. By 1989, the illiteracy rate was less than 8 per cent (INSTAT, 2002). The communist regime had some undeniable achievements: it diversified the country's economy and society through its five-year industrialisation plans, it 'raised the standard of living, [and] reduced the impact of divisive factors on Albanian society, such as regional and clan loyalties, [and] the traditional north-south division' (Fischer, 2010, 421). However, despite the economic progress achieved during the early decades, a very harsh financial crisis hit the last years of the communist regime. Over the years, the regime broke off all ties with the Communist Bloc, ending its relationship with the Soviet Union in 1961 and with China in 1978, which led to a worsening of the economic conditions of the country and deepened its isolation. Albania emerged from its communist years as the poorest country in Europe, with an annual gross national product per capita of approximately US$380 (Gjonca et al., 2008; World Bank, 1996).

At the political level, after its break with Yugoslavia, Albania allied with the Soviet Union beginning in 1948. Still, that alliance was also broken in 1961, when Enver Hoxha, First Secretary of the Party of Labour and head of state of Albania from 1944 to 1985, expelled Soviet advisers and aligned the country with China. After China ceased sending aid in 1978, Albania, like Romania under Nicolae Ceausescu, entered a period of economic recession and severe isolation not only from the Soviet Union but also other East European countries. While civil society grew and put pressure on communist governments in other countries—including Hungary, Czechoslovakia and Poland—no such developments occurred in neither Albania, nor Romania. Instead, any signs of opposition and dissidence were rapidly suppressed (Fischer, 2010; Ramet & Wagner, 2010; Woodcock, 2016). The communist regime in Albania, like Ceausescu's regime in Romania, has been criticized for its extreme harshness, as it ignored human rights, controlled the population through the secret police and crushed any resistance or criticism to the party line (Stan, 2010). Fischer (2010, 421) summarises some of the most challenging aspects of the communist regime in Albania: 'its state-of-siege isolation, its political murders, its prisons, its forced labour camps, and the hardships of long internal exile'.

3.1.2 Post-1991—The Long Transition

The Albanian communist regime fell in 1991, part of a wave of regime-topping revolutions that swept Eastern Europe. The fall of communism in Albania differed from what happened, for instance, in Poland, Hungary and Czechoslovakia, where socialism was ended from above. Albania also deviated from the widespread violent riots that exploded in Romania, leading to the execution of its leader, Ceausescu (Ramet & Wagner, 2010). In Albania, the 'collapse' (Ramet & Wagner, 2010, 18) of the communist regime started in 1990 and was completed in 1992 with the electoral victory of the anti-communist opposition party, founded in December 1990.

In the early 1990s, Albania was the poorest country in Europe, and the troubled political crises of 1990, 1991 and 1992 were accompanied by a difficult economic situation (Gëdeshi & Jorgoni, 2012). It was in this context, and precisely during this period, that Albania began experiencing international and internal migration. These years saw the so-called 'boat exodus' to Italy and the 'mass migration' to Greece (Vullnetari, 2007, 32), with migrants travelled along the pathways through the southern mountains to reach Albania's southern neighbour.

> Law and order broke down; unemployment was rampant; anarchy, crime and violence in the streets reached frightening proportions. … Hundreds of schools, hospitals, health and day-care centres, shops, post offices, collective farms, and industrial plants were either looted or destroyed, causing further damage to an economy which was already in virtual ruins. The public transportation system broke down, and disorder prevailed. (Tarifa, 1995, 148).

Uncontrolled demographic movement and a degree of government laissez-faire that was hard to distinguish from 'economic and judicial anarchy' followed suit (De Waal 2005, 5). The new (anti-communist) government that came to power in 1992 'began to implement a fully-fledged neoliberal programme based on economic liberalisation, monetarist policies, massive and rapid privatisation, and the opening up of the local market to foreign capital, often referred to as shock therapy. During the 1992–1996 period, Albania became the "shining star; of the IMF and the World Bank, the 'success story of the Balkans'" (Kajsiu, 2014, 57). This programme, however, did not produce the expected outcomes. It led to some macroeconomic stabilisations (Bezemer, 2001) but also significant declines in income and employment, a constant reduction of unemployment benefits, shrinkage of the social security system and high rates of emigration (Kajsiu, 2014, 57).

Albanian families relied mostly on remittances and returns from investments in Ponzi or pyramid schemes (Korovilas, 1999; Musaraj, 2011) that had developed from 1992 to 1997. These Ponzi schemes offered superior returns to early investors by paying them with money invested by subsequent investors, not from profits generated by the investments themselves (Musaraj, 2011, 85). In Albania, people deposited money in financial schemes run by local businesspersons and even anonymous individuals with the promise of interest rates of up to 100 per cent. Many families sold their houses and deposited the money in these schemes. Most likely, slightly more than half of the total investments came from remittances (Korovilas, 1999). Hundreds of thousands of Albanians lost their savings that were worth approximately US$2 billion, or 15 per cent of Albania's gross domestic product (GDP) (Barjaba and Barjaba 2015). Pyramid schemes were not exclusive to Albania and took place in other post-socialist countries, including Romania, Russia, the Czech Republic, Slovakia, Bulgaria and former Yugoslavia (Verdery, 1996). Caritas in Romania and the MMM in Russia (Bezemer, 2001) remain among the most well-known. Despite several similarities with other post-socialist pyramid schemes, Albania's case was unique for the reach of these Ponzi schemes had among the Albanian population. The amount of money invested and the suddenness of the collapse and its consequences, including a popular uprising in 1997 and the dissolution of state institutions for several months, were quite impressive compared to other countries.[1]

After 1997, Albania entered a period of state reconstruction, followed by political and economic stability. The European Union (EU) Stabilisation and Association Agreement with Albania was signed in 2006 and entered in force in 2009 (European Commission, 2015). Albania became a member of the North Atlantic Treaty Organization in 2009 and was granted EU candidate status in June 2014. Despite the post-1997 recovery, many economic problems persist. The agricultural sector, which accounts for more than 40 per cent of employment but less than one-quarter of the GDP, is limited to small family operations and subsistence farming due to a lack of modern equipment, unclear property rights and the prevalence of small, inefficient plots of land. Corruption, property issues, inadequate infrastructure and a weak judicial system remain significant obstacles to the development of an attractive business environment for foreign investment and returning migrants (CIA, 2015, BBC 2015, Mai & Paladini, 2013). Albania remains one of the poorest countries in Europe outside the former Soviet Union. Public debt stood at 69,9 per cent of GDP in 2018 (IMF, 2019).

Remittances,[2] mostly from Albanians residing in Greece and Italy, constitute a significant source of financial support for families and thus contribute to the improvement of their living standards amid the lack of state social policies and state solidarity (Danaj, 2014). Remittances peaked at nearly 952 million euros in 2007, accounting for 15 per cent of GDP, but have been decreasing since then, reaching 5,8 per cent of GDP in 2015 (Barjaba and Barjaba, 2015; CIA 2015). Moreover, few remittances have been invested in economic activities, and the businesses that do exist are small, have limited productivity and are often informal (Gëdeshi, 2008; King & Vullnetari, 2010).

In 2018, the Survey on Income and Living Conditions showed the share of the population at risk of poverty was 23,4 per cent (INSTAT, 2019b). Previous statistics based on the Living Standards and Measurement Survey had noted a shift of poverty from rural mountain areas to central urban areas[3] (INSTAT and World Bank 2015). Migration—internal and international—took its shape in this context and remains a vital force driving social transformation in Albania. Albania can indeed be considered to be a laboratory for the study of migration, as expressed by King (2005).

---

[1] For more information and analysis on pyramid schemes in Albania, see Musaraj (2011) and Bezemer (2001). Concerning a similar case in Romania, see Verdery (1996).

[2] I do not cover this issue in this book. For more detailed and developed research on remittances, see Uruçi and Gëdeshi (2003), World Bank (2007), Vullnetari (2012), King and Vullnetari (2010), Vullnetari and King (2011) and Korovilas (1999)

[3] When measuring poverty, the Albanian Living Standards Measurement Survey divides Albania into four regions: coastal, central, mountain and Tirana (the urban area of Tirana City).

3.2 Migration in Albania

Albania's twentieth century history before 1991 can be divided into two central eras: before the establishment of and during the communist regime. Before the founding of the communist government in 1946, internal and international movement were both present. Internal migration consisted of rural mobility to main urban centres, coinciding with the first steps towards the development of industry, communications, trade and services. By 1945, despite the growth of the urban population, 80 per cent of the population lived in rural areas (Çaro, 2011). International migration mostly took the form of labour migration and was male-dominated (Vullnetari, 2007; Dahinden 2013). Migration for study, training purposes and educational opportunities were scarce. The impact of international migrants on the country's socio-economic development can be seen in the increasing education levels in the cities with the highest migration rates (Vullnetari, 2007).

The communist government forbade international migration and placed internal migration under its tight grip. However, immediately following the immediate establishment of the new regime and until 1950, Albania saw some emigration, especially from those with political affiliations that opposed the new power. After 1950, crossing borders was forbidden with the exception of short, approved, official visits or studies. The state organised internal migration primarily to develop various urban centres according to the needs of the labour force in different industries and to improve remote mountain areas, especially in the health and education sectors (Çaro, 2011). Rural retention and minimal urbanisation started in the early 1960s onwards (Sjöberg, 1994), and the use of a domestic passport was obligatory (Vullnetari, 2014).

The system of internal passports, *pashaportizimi*[4], resembled the internal passport in the former Soviet Union and present-day Russia (Shevchenko, 2010; Wegren & Drury, 2001) and the *hukou* in China (Chan & Zhang, 1999; Lévy, 2015). The Soviet Union established a system of internal passports in 1932 to 'manage the population flows' (Wegren & Drury, 2001, 17). China formalised the *hukou* system (i.e. a family registration programme that issues domestic passports regulating population distribution and rural-to-urban migration) as a permanent system in both rural and urban areas (Chan & Zhang, 1999). Similar to the cases of Russia (and the former Soviet Union) and China, the objective of Albania's internal passport system was to control the population's internal movement, primarily from rural to urban areas, to balance rural and urban residents and to serve the two most important economic sectors, agriculture and industry. The restriction of internal movement was aimed primarily at rural-urban migration, especially to Tirana. Still, people found ways to bypass these restrictions by, for example, moving to the rural areas neighbouring the forbidden cities and by marrying urban dwellers. A more concrete

---

[4] *Pashaportizim* refers to the use of domestic passport/identity card as a condition in the process of internal movement (Vullnetari, 2014, 49).

example is diverted migration (Sjöberg, 1992) to Tirana, as presented later in this chapter.

3.2.1   Post-1991 Migration—The Entanglement of Internal and International Migration

However, with the breakdown of the communist regime, migration became a foremost issue in Albania. Indeed, we might say that migration has been one of the most significant developments in post-communist Albania. Although migration, both internal and international, started in 1990, when people understood that the regime might soon fall, only in 1993 was the internal and international movement of Albanian citizens liberalised. Article 22 of the Law on Amendments to the Constitutional Provisions, drafted in 1993, recognised the right of all Albanian citizens to choose their place of residence, move freely within the state's territory and emigrate abroad (Vullnetari, 2007). The Constitution of 1998—which remained in effect until 2016—states that 'everyone has the right to choose its inhabitancy and move freely in every part of the state territory and nobody should be impeded to move freely out of the state' (Ikonomi, 2009, 109).

Ikonomi (2009) points out that the Albanian constitution uses the expression 'nobody should be impeded to move freely out of the country', not 'everybody has the right to move out of the country', as other countries limit Albanians' right to entry. As Wihtol de Wenden (2015, 2) explains, recognition of the right to move out of the country was not followed by the right to enter another country. This contradicts the essence of several international documents, such as the Universal Declaration of the Rights of 1948 and the 1990 United Nations Convention on the Rights of All Migrant Workers and Their Families. More concretely, in order to move from Albania, Albanian citizens could enter another country only after complying with its visa regime. The EU and other developed nations put in place strict visa regimes that made it difficult for Albanian citizens to leave the country through legalised ways. Visas were mostly issued for official visits, students and tourism purposes, with particular restrictions based on the applicants' financial situation and employment status in Albania. Albanian citizens could also migrate for work purpose on regular work visas if they fulfilled all the requirements placed by the foreign destination country, and if this latter accepted their application. That is why visa liberalisation for tourist visits to the Schengen area in 2010 represented a significant moment in the history of Albanian citizens' freedom of movement.

Lacking the right to freely enter other countries and given the criminalisation of irregular border crossings (Wihtol de Wenden 2015), smuggling and human trafficking became highly profitable businesses for organised crime and mafia in Albania. Speed-boat smuggling of migrants to Italy through the coastal city of Vlora (Mai, 2004) continued at a significant pace until the late 2000s despite numerous drownings and deaths. In south-eastern Albania, the border with Greece became a hotspot of activities, generating resources for the villagers living along the border. Villagers would offer accommodations for the 'candidate migrants' preparing to cross the border, provide collective transportation and guides and work with the Greek collaborators that helped migrants cross the Greek border—all these undertakings helped the social and economic life of these villages (De Rapper & Sintès, 2006, 262).

In the following sections, I explore more in detail the dynamics of Albanians' migration processes since 1990. First, I will briefly discuss the development of international migration before delving into the details of internal population movements and return migration—remaining conscious that these processes are entangled and that migrants may engage in one or more such processes at any given time. These diverse migratory movements have important gendered aspects which warrant consideration. Most studies dealing with these gendered aspects are quantitative, so the following sections are mostly based on these quantitative results and combine them with qualitative research when possible.

3.2.1.1   International Migration

International migration 'unfolded dramatically with the fall of the Albanian communist regime' (Dahinden 2013, 4). INSTAT data estimates that in 2017, 1.5 million Albanian citizens lived outside of Albanian territory or about one-third of the country's population. The majority of migrant communities are present in two neighbouring countries, Italy (448,407) and Greece (356,848). However, there is a growing trend of Albanians moving to other European Union countries, as well as in North America and Canada (GoA, 2018).

The post-communist phase of international migration in Albania started in 1990, with the so-called 'embassy phenomenon' (Çaro, 2011, 41). On July 2, 1990, more than 6000 Albanian citizens entered fourteen foreign embassies in Tirana, seeking asylum. The West German embassy was the most popular refuge, sought by approximately 3200 asylum-seekers (Tarifa, 1995, 143). The Italian and French embassies represented asylum seeker's second and third choices respectively.

Rumours that the borders had been opened, and that everyone was allowed to leave, spread like wildfire during this time. In July 1990, the Constitution of 1976, which banned the organisation of any opposition parties, as well as all international migration, was still in place, but the idea of getting out had pervaded the entire country. Albanians went to Greece using secret passages in the southern mountains (Vullnetari, 2012).[5] During the last days of December 1990, approximately 16,000 emigrants left the country. On the night of December 31, 1990, more than 5000 people made the trek across the snowbound, mountainous frontier into Greece (Tarifa, 1995, 147). In March 1991, some 25,000 people seized boats in the harbour

---

[5]For more details about Albanian migration to Greece, see Vullnetari (2012).

of Durres and managed to get to the Italian city of Brindisi. In August 1992, a new wave of 17,000 refugees escaped to Bari (Tarifa, 1995, 153).[6]

During the early 1990s, most emigrants were young men (World Bank 2007; Dahinden 2013). Few legal opportunities existed for Albanians to leave the country, and international migration was constructed as a dangerous physical act, requiring strength usually ascribed to masculinity. Albanian women seemed invisible in the international migration movements of the early 1990s, but King and Vullnetari (2012) recommend caution when considering this invisibility. They highlight that women did participate in international migration, including by engaging in dangerous speedboat travel to Italy and taking risky mountain pathways to Greece.

Another critical moment for international migration in Albania came in the wake of the collapse of the pyramidal investment schemes in 1997 (Bezemer, 2001; Korovilas, 1999; Musaraj, 2011). The number of people migrating abroad increased, peaking in 2000 at around 50,000 new migrants per year, and steadily decreasing since then (World Bank 2007, 36). Women's participation in international migration also rose from 20 per cent to 60 per cent of male international migration from 1991 to 2001 (Azzarri & Carletto, 2009, 7). The increasing number of women migrants is due primarily to family unification, as well as student migration (King & Vullnetari, 2012). As in other post-communist countries, Albanian women engage in international migration for various reasons, including to seek economic opportunities and escape from the gendered constraints of their home (Morokvasic, 2004).

According to Morokvasic (2004, 8), women's mobility reflects the newly-acquired post-communist freedom of movement. Still, Morokvasic explains, it might also be the 'result of coercion and human trafficking', offering both new opportunities but also an explosion of precarious jobs and increasing dependence. With regards to the trafficking of women, Albania was considered to be 'one of the centres of the recruitment and transport of women from eastern Europe to other countries, especially western Europe' (Van Hook et al., 2006, 30). Figures on the number of women and girls involved in trafficking, unfortunately, are still not accurate,[7] and in-depth investigations are also lacking.

---

[6] Two well-known movies artistically depict the Albanian boat exodus to Italy. *La nave dolce*, by director Daniele Vicari, is a documentary on the events that unfolded in the early 1990s when thousands of Albanians seized boats in the Durres harbour and went to Italy. The documentary focuses on the story of one boat, the *Vlora*. Through historical documents and interviews, the film digs into the tumultuous situation in Albania and Italy's reaction when faced not only with mass emigration, but an overwhelming number of immigrants at its shores all at once. The second movie, *Lamerica* by director Gianni Amelio focusses on the social and economic developments in Albania in the early 1990s and portrays the poverty and desperation of Albanian migrants to Italy.

[7] I do not go into further details on this issue as it is not the objective of this research. I, however, would like to add that various nongovernmental organisations estimates that as many as 10,000 Albanian women and girls were trafficked by 1997 and 30,000 by 1999 (Van Hook et al., 2006, 30) out of a total population of approximately 3 million (INSTAT, 2002). It is worth mentioning that these figures have been subject to much debate and criticism, especially the methodology followed by the nongovernmental organisations. Unfortunately, the reports on trafficking produced in Albania have often remained at the level of figures and legal frameworks, often falling into the trap of stereotyping trafficked women and girls. For more nuanced and in-depth information and analy-

Since the early 1990s, Albanian women have also emigrated for educational purposes. Italy has been the primary destination country for student migrants, mostly
due to the scholarship programmes offered by the Italian government and the loose
requirements to enter Italian universities. In the early 1990s, one could register at an
Italian university by sending a formal letter of guarantee from an Italian citizen or
institution (most commonly religious institutions) or by depositing around 4000
euros in a local bank in Italy (Këlliçi, 2015). A student could apply for a scholarship
after the first year of studies. In the late 1990s, the only requirement for a scholarship was the applicant's economic situation, and given the poor economic conditions of Albanian families, almost all Albanian students met this condition.

Moreover, virtually all Albanian youth knew Italian, which explains the significant increase in the number of Albanian students in Italy after 1998. However, the
requirements became stricter in 2006 and 2007, and starting in 2008, the number of
scholarships went down significantly (Këlliçi, 2015). While there are no accurate
data on student migration during the early 1990s, around 9000 Albanian students
were studying abroad in 2003–2004 (Gërmenji & Milo, 2011, 347). During the
2007–2008 academic year, the highest number of international students in Italy was
from Albania (Zenelaga & Sotirofski, 2011, 5). There were 11,415 Albanian students in Italian universities, with a gender breakdown of 4659 male students and
6756 female students (Zenelaga & Sotirofski, 2011, 5).

Greece and Italy have been the top destination countries for Albanian international migrants, with an estimated 600,000 and 500,000 Albanian migrants, respectively. Other migrants target Canada, France, Germany, Switzerland, the United
Kingdom and the United States (Barjaba and Barjaba 2015). Social networks and
patterns of chain migration have taken on significant roles in the international
migration process (Vullnetari, 2007). Social network support was present not only
in post-1991 migration but also in earlier migration practices. For example, Albanian
minoritarë,[8] primarily but not exclusively from southern villages, mobilised their
'fossil' networks in Greece to migrate south and obtain residency documents and
employment more quickly than ethnic Albanians (Sintès, 2003, 129). Albanians living in the southern borderland villages revived familial and friendship networks
with Greek citizens to gain support for their migration projects (Sintès, 2010).

Another significant characteristic of the first decade of international migration
for Albanians during the 1990–2001 period, is the circular migration between
Albania and Greece. Albanian migrants were mostly employed on a seasonal or
temporary basis in sectors characterised by informal activity and intense unskilled
labour, such as agriculture, construction, tourism, small-scale family factories and
housekeeping. 'Circular, repeat, multiple, seasonal or frequent migrations became a

---

sis about trafficking in Albania and in other post-communist countries, see Davies (2009), Tarrius
(2011), Morokvasic (2006), Vullnetari (2012) and Ekonomi et al. (2006).

[8] *Minoritarë* refers to members of the Greek ethnic minority in Albania. They benefitted in many
ways compared to Albanian citizens of Albanian ethnicity by, for example, having an easier time
getting visas to enter Greece and obtain residency permits and even Greek citizenship, which
appeared to be quite impossible for those of Albanian ethnicity (Vullnetari, 2007, 2012).

silent feature of migration in the region, particularly around the border regions'
(Gemi et al., 2010, 18). Although these circular movements were illegalised, many
Albanian migrants engaged in them: more than 550,000 unauthorised migrants
worked in Greece by the late 1990s, and most were employed in seasonal work and
returned home in the offseason (Gemi et al., 2010). The participation in circular/
seasonal/pendular practices, though, became problematic after 2000 due to increased
border controls, 'the stricter legalisation procedures' introduced by the Greek government in 1998 and three successive regularisation programmes, implemented in
1998, 2001 and 2005 respectively. These three factors pushed migrants to adopt
strategies for permanent settlement in Greece (Gemi et al., 2010). Unfortunately,
there are no accurate data or information about the circular movements of Albanian
men and women.

Data from the Census of 2011 show that international migration continued during the 2001–2011 decade (INSTAT, 2012). Differences between the numbers of
men and women emigrating have disappeared: 288,000 men and 285,000 women
emigrated between 2001 and 2011 (Bruijn et al., 2014, 17). This development again
indicates a deviation from the male-dominated patterns of international migration in
the early 1990s.

In 2018, the number of people emigrating from Albania was 38,703. These numbers are slightly lower than those of the previous year. However, emigration continues, and in 2018 net migration remained negative by about 15 thousand persons. [9]

3.2.1.2 Internal Migration

Post-1991 internal and international migration in Albania are strongly related and
cannot be analysed in isolation from one another. Over the past decades, individuals
and families have been involved in various movements linking internal and internal
migration (Vullnetari, 2012; De Waal, 2005; King et al., 2008). While crossing
national borders remained challenging, and most emigrants left through illegalised
ways, internal migration was not restricted or controlled anymore as it used to be
during communism. Internal movement started at the same time as international
migration, in the early 1990s. These two migration processes have a robust relationship as often, international migration by one (more) family member(s) was followed
by internal movement by the rest of the family (De Waal, 2005; Vullnetari, 2012;
Çaro, 2011). Another pattern that showcases the connection between internal and
international migration is the process of moving to Tirana to be a step closer to
going abroad. Patterns of chain migration are also found in the process of internal
migration. Çaro (2011) and Vullnetari (2012) emphasise and describe the role that
networks play throughout the internal migration process in Albania.

Internal migration in Albania is not a straightforward rural–to–urban movement,
as it includes urban–to–urban and rural–to–rural mobilities as well. For example,

---

[9] Data consulted on the INSTAT website, www.instat.gov.al, on the 14th of April 2020

approximately 40 per cent of internal migrants moved from rural to rural areas, mostly around Tirana, from 1989 to 2001 (Vullnetari, 2014). Furthermore, internal migration in Albania led to an increase in urban spaces in the main cities, such as Tirana, Durrës, Shkodër, Fier, Vlorë and Korçë, but decreases in other cities, such as Kukës and Dibër. Some cities, such as Saranda and Lezhë, experienced population declines due to international migration but received a substantial population influx from internal migration (INSTAT, 2002, 2012).

An increase in internal movements resulted in the appearance of new urban areas. Post-1991 internal migration, followed by the movement of people toward urban centres, primarily to Tirana and Durrës, led to the settlement of empty land (mostly agricultural lands) and construction of residential buildings meant for housing purposes. These new neighbourhoods were characterised by illegally constructed houses, a lack of infrastructure (e.g., streets, health and childcare centres and schools) and unauthorised access to water and electricity. Housing conditions and infrastructure, however, have improved over the past three decades. The early simple forms of housing called *barake* were replaced by substantial brick houses of one or multiple floors as migrants thought a real brick house would be harder to demolish if the police came to evict them from the home and land they had occupied. This supposition proved to be accurate, and currently, the country is undergoing a thorough but fraught process for the legalisation of these informal settlements. Infrastructure in most areas, especially the peripheries of Tirana, has also been improved since the early 1990s (Çaro, 2011).

The internal population movement also introduced new political and social challenges in both the destination and origin places. As mentioned above, the infrastructure in the places of destination was either inexistent or inadequate, and thus needed to be constructed from scratch or rigorously improved. Furthermore, there was considerable stigmatisation and prejudice towards internal migrants, especially in large urban centres, such as Tirana and Durres. At the same time, internal migration emptied other cities and villages, negatively affecting the development of agriculture, industry, trade and other economic, social and cultural activities. For example, internal movement crippled the country's social assistance scheme (*ndihmë ekonomike*) which was allocated based on a territorial criterion. Many people who left their cities and villages were not registered as residents of their new destination and were thus not entitled to receive social assistance. This example, along with those already mentioned, show some of the policy challenges that Albania would face with regards to education, health care and its social assistance scheme in the early years of the post-1991 era.

In 2011, for the first time in the census history of Albania, the population in urban areas was higher than the people living in villages. In the Census of 2011 (INSTAT, 2012), 53.7 per cent of the population lived in urban areas and 46.3 per cent in rural areas. During the 2001–2011 period, internal migration was characterized by the movement of entire families, as opposed to a partial family movement that was more common in the preceding decade. This growth of the urban population highlights another pattern of internal migration during the 2001–2011 era: internal migrants tended to settle within cities, whereas the majority of movements during the 1990s concentrated in the neighbouring rural areas that later turned to urban peripheries. This change caused a boom in the construction sector and the expansion of new and existing neighbourhoods in the main urban centres. It is also worth nothing another significant characteristic of internal migrants during this period: their relatively young age. More than 50 per cent of migrants who moved from their city or village of origin were 15–34 years old, with most falling in the 20–24 years age group (Galanxhi et al., 2014).

Unlike international migration, internal migration in Albania is female-dominated. It's a trend that mirrors and correlates to a difference described earlier: male family members migrated abroad, while the rest of the family, including women, moved internally. The predominance of women in internal movements has been documented since the pioneering work of Ravenstein (1885), who explicitly stated that women are more involved in internal, short-distance mobilities, whereas men tend to migrate from the country. Data from the first post-1991 Census, conducted in 2001, showed that internal migration from northern regions of Albanian involved all demographic groups, while migrants from the secondary centres[10] tended to be young, educated and female (Galanxhi et al., 2004). During 2001–2011, internal migration by women increased. According to the Census of 2011, women made up 59 per cent of the internal migrants, and the sex ratio of internal migrants was 69 men for 100 women from 2001 to 2011 (Galanxhi et al., 2014, 25). In 2014, the majority of internal female migrants belonged to the age group 20–29 years old. This trend of female-dominated internal migration continues still to date as confirmed by the latest INSTAT data (Arqimandriti et al., 2020). Census data also show gendered differences in the reasons for internal movement: men favour migration for employment, and women for university studies (Galanxhi et al., 2014). The higher numbers of young women engaged in internal migration then may be explained 'by the shares of female students in universities, which are all located in cities' (Vullnetari, 2012, 95). In a study on internal migration in Albania, Çaro (2011, 110) identifies several reasons for internal migration by women: a 'better future for their children', 'better opportunities and a desire for city life' and escape from the 'patriarchal system' in their place of origin and from the 'control of their in-laws'. However, reasons for internal migration (which should not be restricted only to rural–to–urban migration) may vary by civil status, family situation, education and other factors, as explored in the following chapters.

---

[10] Secondary centres are cities in Albania that are less important than Tirana and Durrës, the two main cities in the country (Galanxhi et al., 2004, 63).

3.2.1.3   Return Migration

In 2018, 23,673 migrants returned to Albania[11]. The last Albanian Census of 2011 revealed that 139,827 Albanians returned to the country from 2001 to 2011 (Gemi, 2015). However, the first signs of voluntary returnees—especially from Greece and Italy—can be observed in 1993–1996, after the first wave of migration of the early 1990s. These initial, sporadic movements dissipated due to the collapse of the pyramid schemes and the economic and political crisis that broke out in 1997. More visible rates of return migration emerged after the early 2000s as Albania entered a period of improving economic and political stability, and the main destination countries (Greece and Italy) began to face financial crises (Kopliku, 2016). Indeed, returnees have been mostly men who emigrated to Greece (Galanxhi et al., 2014). Women appear to have been 'reluctant returnees' (Morokvašić, 2015, 368). Gemi (2015, 40) observes that women preferred to stay in Greece despite the problematic conditions they might face under a regime of irregularity. The reasons they give for 'this resistance are linked first to the fact that they continue to work even on different terms and second, the issue of their children's adaptation to the reality of Albania' (Gemi, 2015, 40). Amidst the economic crisis in Greece when many men lost their jobs, migrant women continued to work and adapt to the changing labour market, becoming the sole income providers for their families (Vaiou, 2002).

The main reasons that emigrants decided to return to Albania included the fact that they lost their job in the country of immigration and problems faced by the family they had left behind in Albania (Galanxhi et al., 2014). Other grounds for return included better employment opportunities, investment plans and melancholy and longing for family and country, as identified by Mai and Paladini (2013) and Kopliku (2016). Returning to Albania served as a strategy to handle not only the negative consequences of an economic crisis in the destination country and unemployment, but also de-regularisation of work and residency permits (as observed in some of the cases analysed in this book) (Gemi, 2015).

Figures from the 2011 Census show that approximately 40 per cent of return migrants decided to establish themselves in a location other than their city or village of origin, with Tirana as the most preferred city by returnees (Galanxhi et al., 2014). These data reveal patterns linking return and internal migration. Additionally, after their return to Albania, migrants often decided to engage in circular migration between Italy and Albania to compensate for the difficulties and problems experienced in both countries (Mai & Paladini, 2013). Moreover, after the family's return to Albania, the husband or father often engaged in circular migration to Greece or attempted to migrate to another country (Gemi, 2015). In her research about return migration to the city of Shkodra, Kopliku (2016, 112) highlights that it is often difficult to distinguish the permanent returnee from the transnational migrant as migrants may organise their lives in both the home and the host countries.

---

[11] Data consulted on the INSTAT website, www.instat.gov.al, on the 14th of April 2020

Furthermore, return migrants to Albania may experience difficulties when readjusting, due to a dissimilar work climate and culture in their home country and so consider another migration project (Kopliku, 2016). These patterns reinforce the main thread of this research conceptualising migration as a process with intertwined trajectories (Morokvasic, 1984, 2003; Tarrius, 1993; Kofman 2004; Dahinden, 2009, 2014). The return might not be a permanent move but lead to other migration trajectories (Black & King, 2004).

3.2.2   *Tirana: A 'Magnet' for Internal and Return Migration*

Women in this research come from cities and villages throughout Albania but lived in Tirana at the time of interviews. Tirana is the leading site of this research, so it is necessary to describe the city to better understand the dynamics of migration happening within. Tirana was proclaimed the capital of Albania in 1920 and has since seen a rapid increase in its population (Gëdeshi, 2008) and its importance relative to other cities. Tirana remains the most attractive city in Albania for economic opportunities, education, health care access and cultural activities. During the communist period, Tirana, more than any other city, was the target of internal movement and the most desirable destination for a considerable number of Albanians, especially young people. As a major industrial, politico-administrative, educational and cultural centre, its periphery attracted what Sjöberg (1992) calls diverted migration, the internal movement that was not rural toward urban but intra-rural. Although Tirana was the preferred destination of this intra-rural movement, settling there was quite challenging due to the restrictions of *pashaportizimi* and controlled urbanisation. Thus, people opted for the 'second-best alternative': the rural cooperatives or state agricultural enterprises next to Tirana (Vullnetari, 2014). This unplanned in-migration brought about the growth of the peri-urban settlements of Tirana (Sjöberg, 1992, 14).

After the fall of communism and the end of the restrictions on internal migration, Tirana saw significant population growth. Free movement policies (*lëvizja e lirë*) permitted residents of villages and cities to move to Tirana freely. 'Large-scale internal movements, land grabbing in urban and peri-urban areas followed by squatter settlements' characterised this early period of internal migration to Tirana (Vullnetari, 2014, 51). Only in the 2010s did the Albanian government start procedures to legalise the illegal settlements built in the urban and peri-urban areas mostly by internal migrants.

During 1990–2000, most internal migrants came from the northern and mountainous regions (Galanxhi et al., 2004). During the second decade, migration from other important cities, such as Berat, Fier and Vlora, increased (Galanxhi et al., 2014, 16). Women in this research go through such pattern too. Those from the northern areas migrated to Tirana earlier than those from other southern cities. Considering only the municipality of Tirana, the area saw a population growth of more than 40 per cent from 1989 to 2001 and 20 per cent from 2001 to 2011 (Vullnetari, 2014, 55). Another indicator of the growth of Tirana since 1990 is recorded by Pojani (2010): the urbanised area of Tirana grew from 12 square km in 1990 to 32 square km in 1994 and 56 square km in 2002.

Looking beyond the figures, since 1990, Tirana has been absorbing people from remote, mountainous areas stuck in deep poverty and appalling living conditions (Galanxhi et al., 2004; Çaro, 2011; Xhindi, 2013). Most of the internal migrants from these regions have settled in the peri-urban areas. But others have done so within the municipality of Tirana. Furthermore, most have sought employment and public services within urban Tirana. At the same time, the new 'rich' from other cities have come to Tirana for better business opportunities, education, health services and access to social life (Xhindi, 2013, 86). These trends have made Tirana the city with the most considerable inequalities in living conditions in Albania (INSTAT and World Bank, 2015a, 2015b).

Infrastructure and public services have lagged behind population growth, leaving many gaps in infrastructure, public health and education services and environmental protection (Xhindi, 2013) and transportation (Pojani, 2010). Water and electricity remain scarce and expensive resources in Tirana (Pojani, 2010, 494). As a result of urban growth, increases in small businesses, growing individual wealth, and greater use of electric heaters and air conditioners, electricity demand has risen exponentially. Especially during the winter months, the entire city of Tirana experiences daily power interruptions. Water shortages persist during the summer months. Water and electricity supply interconnect as the post-1991 multi-floor buildings use electric appliances to pump water to the upper floors. Some interviewees highlight these issues, stressing that women, who are responsible for housework, suffer the most from these difficulties.

The continuing internal population movement and the economic crisis in sectors such as construction likely have driven the recent increase in the poverty rate in Tirana. In contrast, poverty in the mountainous area of Albania fell by half between 2008 and 2012, possible due to population shifts from the mountainous regions to other regions. Tirana witnessed a considerable increase in poverty, from 9 per cent in 2008 to 12 per cent in 2012 (INSTAT and World Bank, 2015a, b).

Tirana hosts most public and private education providers, almost all the international organisations and the majority of the NGOs in the country, as well as the majority of Albanian and foreign businesses. The capital city has the highest concentration of economic activity and generates 45 per cent of the Albanian GDP. It also issues more than 70 per cent of all credit to business in the country (Xhindi, 2013).

According to the 2011 Census data, at the time the municipality of Tirana had a population of 418,495 (203,239 men and 215,526 women). Analysing the conditions of women in Tirana remains difficult as such data are lacking. Some existing data disaggregated at the level of the municipality are old and not very relevant. Disaggregated data is also lacking at the mini-municipality level within the city of Tirana. Until June 2015, the city of Tirana was structured into 11 mini-municipalities. The neighbourhoods of Komuna e Parisit (in mini-municipality 5) and Don Bosko (in mini-municipalities 11 and 9) are the two sites of my research where the women interviewed for this book live (see Fig. 3.1[12]).

Don Bosko has been a destination for internal migration, mostly from the northern parts of the country, since the early 1990s. Whereas, Komuna e Parisit was developed later, primarily by internal migrants coming from southern cities. Unfortunately, few statistics have been disaggregated at the level of the mini-municipality, let alone by gender. The only data disaggregated at this level are on poverty, drawn from the ALSMS 2002, which gives a picture of the poverty distribution within the municipality of Tirana. The poverty rate is the highest, at 20–31 per cent, in mini-municipalities 4, 6 and 11, which also have the most massive inflow of migrants (Zezza et al., 2005). In mini-municipalities 6 and 11, which include part of Don Bosko, nearly half the population consists of new residents who arrived between the 1989 and 2001 censuses (Zezza et al., 2005). However, the situation could be different in 2011 as internal migration continued during the second decade post-communism (2001–2011), drawing people from the south who concentrated in mini-municipality 5. Unfortunately, I could not find such data, and thus my

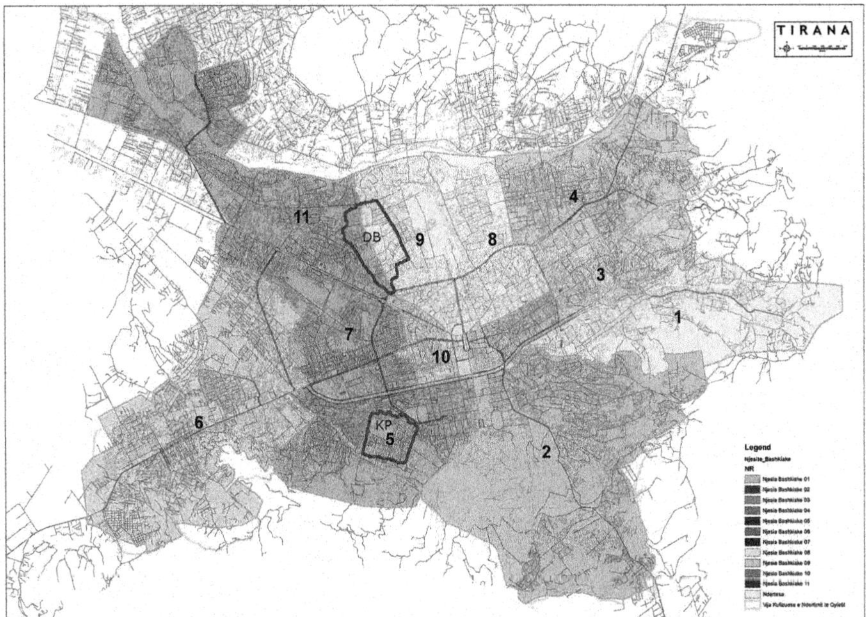

Fig. 3.1 Map of Tirana mini-municipalities and the neighbourhoods of Don Bosko and Komuna e Parisit. (Source: Original map from the Municipality of Tirana (www.tirana.al))

---

[12] These mini-municipalities existed until June 2015, when a new administrative map was adopted for local government. The borders drawn for the neighbourhoods Komuna e Parisit and Don Bosko were adapted for the purpose of this research, as both neighbourhoods have no administrative status but are centred on the streets Komuna e Parisit and Don Bosko and thus referred to by these names. These two neighbourhoods do not have administrative borders, so I have tried to be as approximate as possible in drawing the borders, mostly based on the interviewees' information.

description of my two research sites is limited to the information provided by the participants and to my own observations.

Don Bosko has been populated by internal migration since early 1990. Its newly settled population came mostly from northern regions, according to the key informants and to the 2001 Census data. Initially, few multi-floor buildings existed in the area, and one- or two-floor houses predominated the landscape. Over the years, there was a construction boom characterized by high buildings of all types, leading to an unorganised mixture of low houses and tall buildings that reveals the absence of any deliberate urban planning. The streets still lack in quality, and sidewalks are often inexistent.

In Don Bosko, poor-quality and luxury buildings stand next to each other. During my visits and meetings with the participants, I noticed several low-quality buildings. In some facilities, the construction work had remained unfinished, leaving residents to pay for the rest. Still, the price of these apartments was relatively low compared to apartments in other areas or buildings, and many migrants could not afford more.

While walking around Don Bosko, the heavy car traffic, the lack of sidewalks and the cumbersome large number of shops and coffee bars that line the streets inspire a feeling of chaos. I saw very few playgrounds or green parks (none except at the Don Bosko social centre, which gives the neighbourhood its name). Children played mostly on the sidewalks or courtyards in homes (when they existed). The area has been growing in density, in people, buildings and vehicles. My observations and discussions with people in the neighbourhoods revealed that migrants' origins have changed over the years, shifting from the northern villages to the southern towns of Vlora, Fier, Tepelenë and Gjirokastër.

The situation is somewhat different, and yet in some aspects similar, in the neighbourhood of Komuna e Parisit. Before 1989, Komuna e Parisit was an empty meadow housing only some greenhouses and large swaths of empty fields offering the perfect spot for school-organised excursions and picnics. Today, it is one of the most populated areas in the municipality of Tirana, with buildings piling on top of each other. Komuna e Parisit was developed during the late 1990s, and in particular during 2000s, with population coming mostly from the southern areas. A significant number of women could also be observed in the streets, as was the case in Don Bosko. Women shopped in grocery shops, walked with their children and sat in the coffee bars. Another observation common to both Komuna e Parisit and also Don Bosko, was the significant number of women employed as sellers or workers that managed the majority of shops and services (e.g., dry cleaning and pharmacies).

In both neighbourhoods, I also observed narrow and often-absent streets and sidewalks. In the chaotic urban development and absence of urban planning of Komuna e Parisit, spaces between buildings are small, and green areas and playgrounds are lacking. The only advantage that Komuna e Parisit has over Don Bosko is that Komuna e Parisit is located next to the National Park and Lake of Tirana, which could compensate somewhat for the lack of green spaces and playgrounds. Another marked difference is that Komuna e Parisit is more preferred by students renting shared apartments. Komuna e Parisit is near Bllok, a central area of Tirana highly frequented by young people, and is considered to be safer than other neighbourhoods. Even though apartments in different areas of Tirana might be cheaper, many young people (students and graduates) favour Komuna e Parisit due to its relative safety.

3.3 The Situation of Women in Albania

In this section, I present some main patterns in the conditions of women in Albania during communism and after 1991. It draws mostly from statistical data and provides an overall review that sets the background of the analysis of the experiences of 32 migrant women interviewed for this research. This section starts with a brief overview covering the twentieth century until the year 1991.

3.3.1 Women's Situation Before 1944

It is hard to find detailed, accurate data and information on the situation of women in pre-1944 Albania. I could glean information from popular narratives, such as songs, stories and the literature from that period describing and denouncing the subordinated position of women. Very few women and girls were educated, and female illiteracy was higher than 90 per cent. Illiteracy was more widespread in rural areas and the undeveloped north-east (Gjonca et al., 2008). As in many other countries, women's right to participate in political and social activities was restricted (Musaj & Nicholson, 2011). The health system was fragile, and the infant mortality rate was 148 deaths per 1000 live births (Gjonca et al., 2008, 263). Besides, women's participation in paid employment was low: in 1937, Albania had 345 female teachers, several female gynaecologist doctors and also a few women working in new factories in Korçë, Shkodër, Tirana and other cities (Në Dobi të Gruas Shqiptare 2012). Marriage was almost universal among women, with their average age at marriage younger than 20 years. By 15 years old, 29 per cent of all girls were married, while more than half were married by age 18, and more than four-fifths at 20 years of age (Gruber, 2002). Gruber and Pichler (2002) report that the average age at marriage was 18 years old for women and 28 for men. The wide age gap between spouses is an indicator of their unequal positions within the family, making male domination within the household very real.

During the early 1930s, local newspapers published some articles about feminist ideas and movements in other countries and criticised the position of women in Albania. Furthermore, several organisations promoting women's rights (e.g., education, paid employment outside the home and participation in public and political life) were founded, mostly mainly in urban areas such as Shkodër, Korcë, Vlorë, Tirana and Gjirokastër. In 1928, the Civil Code approved several changes to women's status, at least from a legal perspective. The newly approved civil code marked an official departure from the traditional, customary laws prevalent throughout the county. Instead, it recognised women's 'right to divorce, and equality with the husband regarding the right to inheritance' (Musaj & Nicholson, 2011, 193). Another achievement was the establishment of the minimum age for marriage at 16 years old for girls and at 18 years old for men. This civil code did not include the right to vote as was requested by women's organisations and supported by liberal members of parliament, and women's right to employment remained limited (Musaj & Nicholson, 2011, 193).

3.3.2 'Women's Emancipation Model'—The Communist Period

One of the most substantial policies adopted by the communist regime was the 'emancipation of the woman', to use the government's terminology. This model, applied across communist countries (called the 'women's emancipation model' by Moghadam 1995, 335), included policies supporting women's participation in the productive labour force and the introduction of new laws promoting the equality of men and women. In Albania, the new Constitution of March 14, 1946, declared equal rights between women and men. According to the new law on marriage adopted in 1948, marriage was to be based on the equal rights of both spouses (Keefe et al., 1971, 34). Another major change in this new law concerned the age of marriage which was raised to 18 years for both sexes. The concept of the head of the family, recognised by pre-communist civil law, was scraped. Under the 1948 law, each spouse had the right to choose their occupation, profession and residence and to ask for a divorce (Keefe et al., 1971).[13]

In a 1955 speech at the Fourth Congress of the Women's Union of Albania, Hoxha proclaimed women as 'the proletarian of man' who previously had 'only one right: to bear children and to slave day and night' (Woodcock, 2016). In 1956, in a report on the work of the Albanian Party of Labour, Hoxha criticised the attitudes of Albanian men who continued to consider themselves as heads of the household and who took the credit for all the work done while keeping women's work in the shadows. Regarding women's multiple burdens, Hoxha declared that 'efforts must still be made to extend the range of main products and lower costs. Social catering units, and especially the canteens and restaurants are not up to the task of becoming centres for feeding the family so that they can help to lighten women's household chores so that they can participate in production to a wider extent' (Hoxha, 1974, 536). Such social services aimed at lightening the burden of women's reproductive work emerged throughout the former socialist countries (Gal & Kligman, 2000).

---

[13] The basic divorce law, originally passed in 1948, provided that either spouse may ask for divorce on the grounds of incompatible character, continued misunderstandings, irreconcilable hostility or any other reason that disrupted marital relations to the point where a common marital life had become impossible (Danaj et al., 2005; Keefe et al., 1971).

These social services and structures were first introduced in 1919 in the Soviet Union, to support women's entry in the productive sphere (Sperling, 1996). Hoxha, the leader of the Albania Party of Labour, launched the campaign for the emancipation of women in 1967 with a series of speeches recited again in 1969 (Danermark et al., 1989; Keefe et al., 1971). The new regime made literacy one of its primary objectives, with a particular focus on women and girls. 'Female illiteracy improved from 92 per cent in 1945 to less than 8 per cent in 1989, and by 2002 it was less than 5 per cent…' (Gjonca et al., 2008, 284).

Besides, women's employment was another central policy target of the communist government's 'women's emancipation model' (Moghadam 1995). The full productive engagement of women and girls served several aims: first of all, it was seen as essential to women's emancipation, but also provided a considerable bust to the labour force needed for the reconstruction spearheaded by all socialist countries (Kligman, 1994; Rosenberg, 1991). Most communist countries defined women primarily as workers, a significant change from the pre-war imaginary (Gal & Kligman, 2000). This shift was part of the broader communist commitment to homogenise and equalise the populace so as to eliminate all social distinctions, including gender, and to construct the 'new socialist person' (Gal & Kligman, 2000; Jinga, 2011). The full employment of women and girls was also necessary to bring them into the public sphere, weaken the influence of the old traditions and practices and make it easier to educate them with the new principles of the 'new socialist society'.

Unlike other countries, such as former Yugoslavia, Albania does not have a tradition of feminist movements or feminist organisation, not even during communism. All the activities regarding women resulted from the initiative of the party and the Albanian Women's Union (Fico, 2014). The Albanian Women's Union, founded in 1943, took charge of increasing women's involvement outside the home, especially in public and political life (Jacobs, 1945; Keefe et al., 1971). The parliament of 1974–78 had the highest percentage of women members of parliament in Albania's history, at 35.2 per cent (Keefe et al., 1971).

Albanian women occupied high positions in the communist bureaucracy and served as highly qualified workers in the economy. However, an equal division of roles and responsibilities within the household did not follow. In the case of Romania, for example, studies on women's situation in the early 1970s showed that the unequal division of household labour posed the primary obstacle to women's equal participation in the public sphere (Jinga 2011, 120). Traditional gender roles, that placed women in charge of reproductive work and men productive work, prevailed in the domestic sphere. Sometimes, women's participation in public life (e.g., political and community meetings) demanded many sacrifices, especially in their relationships with their husbands (Çuli, 2012; Keefe et al., 1971). Men did not experience the same pitfalls; they were inherently exempted from unpaid and care work and, in many cases, retained their dominant role within the family. Women had to be as active as men in the public sphere, but responsibility for housework still fell on them. Women's engagement in the productive sphere did not result in the equal participation of men in the reproductive sphere. Policies and propaganda during the communist regime did not include insights about individual liberation or individual rights. They considered women in relation to the man or the state: a mother, a wife, a distinguished worker, etc. Women had to transform their way of life from within, upturn family relations, and re-model patriarchal traits to mirror an ideal socialist family.

Women were praised not only as workers but also as mothers. The cinema, one of the most potent propaganda channels, glorified the image of the woman who worked outside the home and was also a dedicated mother and wife (Puto, 2013). For example, from the 1960s, the Romanian and Bulgarian governments put increasing emphasis on the 'foremost and natural' role of women to give birth to children, due to concerns over declining birth-rates (Brunnbauer, 2000). In the case of Romania, pro-natalist policies became very repressive and abortion was penalised in 1966 (Kligman, 1998; Jinga, 2011). Women thus were burdened with the duty of enlarging the socialist nation and played essential roles in the construction and reproduction of nationalist ideologies (Anthias, Yuval-Davis & Cain, 1993). By dressing and behaving correctly and giving birth to children within legitimate marriages, women both signified and reproduced the symbolic and legal boundaries of the collectivity (Këlliçi & Danaj, 2016).

In Albania, contraception and abortion remained illegal throughout the communist period. Condoms were difficult to procure, no contraceptive pills were imported, education or literature on the reproductive cycle was not provided, and traditional methods of contraception, such as withdrawal (the "pull out method"), were practised (Woodcock, 2016). Kligman (1998) and Jinga (2011) document a similar situation in Romania, where pressures over physical intimacy arose after Ceausescu came to power. The status of abortion and reproductive rights was not uniform across the former socialist countries. For example, in Poland, abortion was legalised during communism and delegalised afterwards, while Russia legalised abortion in 1920, penalised it from 1936 to 1955 and then legalised it again after Stalin's death (Wites, 2004).

Ironically, one of the most notable features of the pre-communist era, the traditional role of women[14] which required that women give birth to children for the sake of the nation, was transferred to the state. In its first decades, the communist regime promoted high fertility and proclaimed mothers of six or more children to be heroic mothers (*nëna heroina*). Interestingly, the fertility rate decline in Albania did not start with the post-1991 transformations that swept the country after the fall of communism, but in 1960, steadily falling from the very high post-war levels. The total fertility rate, which was still close to 7 births per woman in the early 1960s, decreased to 3.0 in 1990 (Danaj et al., 2005; Lerch 2013). This decline happened in the absence of any family planning, unlike in the case of China that has imposed strict family planning policies since the 1970s. The distinctive feature of fertility reduction in Albania, compared to other European countries, was that it decreased for women across all ages and in both rural and urban areas, with only slight differ-

---

[14] 'A female was worthy with reference to the interests of her male protector, her husband, her master, and lord. Her task was to give birth to his children and serve as a symbol and prize for his male honour. This was the traditionalist ideal of a proper woman' (Doja, 2010, 361).

ences. Gjonça, Aasve and Mencarini (2008) attribute this pattern to the increased education of women and girls in rural areas, which was another priority of the communist government, along with higher participation in productive work. Women's double burden provided another reason for unwillingness to have many children, independent of the pro-natalist policies and political discourses of the 1950s and 1960s. The decline of the number of children shows resistance to state policies regarding reproductive rights and as a tactic for coping with the increasing economic difficulties, especially starting in the late 60s. These economic conditions may also explain why the state allowed this decline in the fertility rate to continue without additional interference.

Any analysis of the conditions of Albanian women during communism is complex, and clear-cut, yes/no responses to questions about the liberation (or not) of women under socialism are inadequate.

3.3.3   Post-1991 Period—A Brief Presentation of Women's Situation

The transformation processes in Central and Eastern Europe to date have been subsumed under the frame of a supposed consensus around the neo-liberal market model (Einhorn, 2005). Post-socialist neoliberal programs adopted across the region since 1989 have often resulted in gendered job loss with higher rates of female unemployment and the dismantling of public services of particular help to women (Gal & Kligman, 2000). The transition also bolstered a remobilisation of traditional gender roles (Lelea and Voiculescu, 2017), redefined women's roles in society, and the home was again supposed to be a woman's proper place (Kligman, 1994; 256). The gendered division of labour also sharpened, assigning men to the productive sphere and women to the reproductive one. Brunnbauer (2000) talks about the 'domestication' of women, referring not only to the visible withdrawal of women from the public sphere but also to the early 1990s policies and discourses that discouraged women's participation in productive work and public life. In Albania, too, women withdrew from the labour market and disappeared from politics and the political action and debate (Fico, 2014). 'Male democracies' (a term applied by Sonja Licht, cited in Einhorn, 1993, 148) were created throughout the region, including Albania, and men became the primary beneficiaries of the momentous promises of 1989. Many women, drained by the double burden and influenced by the new ideologies of nationalism and capitalism, at least in the initial period, welcomed the discourse of a return to the domestic sphere and the opportunity to care for their families (Einhorn & Sever, 2003).[15]

---

[15]This paragraph has been previously published as part of the article Danaj, E. (2018) 'I am not a feminist but…': women's activism in post-1991 Albania, Gender, Place & Culture, 25:7, 994–1009,

In this context, in the early 1990s, the 'political action and debate about Albania's past, present and future was completely void of gender analysis' (Fico, 2014, 167). The public debate and the media depicted women either as victims (of political oppression in the past and poverty and sexual exploitation in the present) or as sex objects. Women in Albania and other countries expressed mixed feelings about their place in the productive and reproductive sphere as dictated by the double burden, the restrictions put on the freedom they had experienced during communism and the new economic programmes (for more, see Penn & Massino, 2009).

During 1991–1993, the first women's non-governmental organisations (NGO) in post-socialist Albania were founded. These organisations that dealt with women's issues expanded in the late 1990s and early 2000s. In post-socialist countries, a 'gendering' of the NGO sector seemed to occur, with women more involved in organisations with socio-economic and educational agendas, and men in groups involved in 'high politics' (Kligman, 1996, 72). Nevertheless, this 'gendering' should not undermine the role of NGOs in making visible and raising issues primarily related to the conditions of women and children (e.g., domestic violence, rape, trafficking, informal work and child abuse).

Since 1991, Albania's legal framework has undergone significant improvements through the ratification of a series of international documents, essential amendments and the alignment of national legislation to global conventions, among others. Albania ratified the Convention on the Elimination of all Forms of Discrimination Against Women (CEDAW) in 1993 and its optional protocol in 2003. However, the harmonisation of laws and the implementation of CEDAW in practice took a very long time. Indeed, many necessary changes and improvements still remain to be implemented—especially for the de-facto application of women's rights. While the development of the legal framework has been underway since 1995, the most significant events concerning gender equality, domestic violence, and anti-discrimination date back to 2006 (Kocaqi et al., 2015, 16).[16]

The political participation of women in Albania remained flat until the introduction of gender quotas in the Gender Equality Law and Electoral Code of 2008.

---

[16] The first Law on Domestic Violence was approved in December 2006 in response to a proposal sent to parliament from civil society, supported by the signatures of 20,000 community members. In 2008, the Law on Gender Equality entered into force with a series of measures for the improvement of gender equality, including the establishment of the national gender machinery and women's participation in decision-making in political and public spheres. The Law on Protection against Discrimination in 2010 was followed by the establishment of the Commissioner for the Protection against Discrimination as an independent body that safeguards against discrimination. In a major step, amendments to the Criminal Code in 2012 and 2013 addressed domestic violence and the protection of women and girls from violence and abuse. Albania has drafted two specific strategies on gender equality and domestic violence. First, the National Strategy on Gender Equality and Elimination of Domestic Violence covered the period of 2007–2010. Second, the National Strategy on Gender Equality, Reduction of Gender-Based Violence and Domestic Violence and its action plan covered the period of 2011–2015. The Albanian government has drafted four specific anti-trafficking strategies, including the National Anti-Trafficking Strategy and its national action plan for 2001–2004 and, more recently, the National Strategy on Combating Human Trafficking and its action plan for 2014–2017 (Kocaqi et al., 2015).

These new legal provisions prompted a numerical increase of women serving in parliament, on municipal councils and as mayors. The percentage of women among members of parliament rose to 21 per cent in 2013 and the rate of women among mayors to 14 per cent after the 2015 local elections.[17]

Despite an increase in women's participation in the labour market immediately after the fall of communism, its rate remains low compared to men's. In 2019, 40 per cent of women aged between 15–64 years old are out of the labour market, neither employed (54 per cent) nor unemployed (11,9 per cent) (Arqimandriti et al., 2020). In contrast, 23,1 per cent of men were out of the labour market, 68,5 per cent employed, and 12,7 per cent unemployed. Another significant feature of the labour market in Albania is its gender segregation dimension. Women and men belonging to the 15–64 years old age group work mostly in the agriculture sector. However, the gender gap is significant. In 2018, 42.3% of employed women worked in the agriculture sector compared to 33,5% of employed men.

On the other hand, only 0,5% of employed women work in construction compared to 12.1% of employed men. Being mostly employed in the agriculture sector does not help the economic empowerment of women. They are most engaged as family workers focusing on the family's subsistence (Arqimandriti et al., 2020).

The occupational gender segregation in Albania, both horizontal and vertical is not that different from that of other countries. In gender-based occupational segregation, 'men and women do different kinds of work so that one can speak of two separate labour forces, one male and one female, which are not in competition with each other for the same jobs' (Hakim, 1979, 1). In Albania, the horizontal occupational segregation touches the categories of "public administration, community and social services" that are dominated by women, and "trade and business" dominated by men. It appears that the constructed gender role ascribing women to care and men to breadwinning extend to the labour market structure where women dominate in "care" and social employments (Arqimandriti et al., 2020). Regarding career advancement, women are hurt in vertical occupational segregation as 'men dominate higher-grade higher-paid occupations and women concentrate in lower-grade, lower-paid occupations in the same area of activity' (Hakim, 2006, 284).

In the domestic sphere, women almost exclusively perform unpaid care work. The same source shows that women with young children have less free time and dedicate the most time to unpaid work compared to men and women with older children or no children. Women with no partners and no children spend less time in unpaid work and have the most free time. Employed women have the longest working day (i.e. total work), the least free time and the least time for personal activities. According to the Time Use Survey (INSTAT, 2011), women spend two more hours a day on work of any kind (i.e. paid and unpaid work) than men, seven hours versus five hours, respectively. Men also are more advantaged in free time and personal care compared to women (INSTAT, 2011).

---

[17] Figures drawn from the webpage of the Central Elections Committee (www.cec.org.al)

The data presented above reveal some of the main patterns of women's engagement in paid and unpaid work at the national level. The situation is more complicated than shown here. Still, a post-communist withdrawal of women from the labour market to reproductive care work, resulting in the reconfiguration of the gender roles, can be observed, even among young women. Furthermore, even women with paid employment almost still have sole responsibility for reproductive work and care. The national-level data serve as a frame to better situate and understand the experiences of the women participants in this research.

About education, no significant differences in the numbers of boys and girls appear at the basic education level.[18] However, the enrolment rates are lower in rural areas and among the poor. Problems regarding minority groups' access to education remain. Children with disabilities have a drop-out rate approximately ten times higher than the general drop-out rate, and the school participation rate of Roma girls is significantly lower than that of Roma boys (Wittberger et al., 2012). Visible gender differences, though, emerge at the secondary level, where boys are more numerous especially in rural areas, and the university level, where women outnumber men at an increasing rate (Wittberger et al., 2012).

One explanation for the widening gap among university students is that young men engage more in paid work and international migration (Ekonomi et al., 2006). Another reason is young women's goal to move from their towns or villages of origin (as the cases in this research show). Expanding job opportunities in a labour market where opportunities continue to be scarce is another reason. The high number of female students may be one of the explanations for the fact that internal migration in Albania is female-dominated.

The persistent importance of education for both boys and girls may be one of the lasting legacies of the communist period. The 2011 Census data shows still high rates of education among boys and girls, even across regions and wealth brackets. Moreover, parents' educational attainment seems to have no impact on children's level of education, according to the 2001 Census data (Danaj et al., 2005). Gilyuk (2016) reports a different situation in the case of Russia, finding a correlation between parents' education level and children's linguistic education.

The family is a principal institution in the construction of gender relations and the study of migration, as seen even in cases where women migrate on their own. To complete this national-level contextual panorama, I briefly present some patterns of family formation and family structure in Albania. The marriage rate in Albania remains very stable, at 8.9 in 1990 and 8.1 in 2018, and marriage remains almost universal (Danaj et al., 2005; INSTAT, 2019a, b; Lerch, 2009) Among youth aged 15–29 years old, approximately 0.2 per cent cohabitate (Danaj & Festy, 2006).[19]

---

[18]The educational system in Albania includes non-compulsory preschool education (ages 3–5 years), compulsory primary school (grades 1–6), compulsory lower secondary schools (grades 6–9) and non-compulsory upper secondary school (grades 10–12) (Law Nr 69/2012, On pre-university education in the republic of Albania see http://www.arsimi.gov.al/files/userfiles/arkiva/dok-0029.pdf, in Albanian).

[19]Unfortunately, more recent data on cohabitation are not available.

Nevertheless, slight changes in the age at marriage may be noted, which has risen from 27.3 for men in 1990 to 31.5 in 2018 and from 23.0 for women in 1990 to 26.5 in 2018 (INSTAT, 2019a, b). There are rural-urban differences in the proportion of young married people. According to the 2001 Census data, the percentage of married women in the 16–29 age bracket is higher in rural areas. Also, those with university degrees have lower marriage rates than those with lower education levels. The influence of one's educational level on the marriage rate is more significant at the age of 25–29 years after finishing tertiary studies. In this age group, people with university degrees have the lowest marriage rate (approximately 50 per cent).

The fertility rate in Albania decreased from 3.2 in 1989 to 2.1 in 2001 and 1.37 in 2018 (INSTAT, 2011, 2019a, b). There is also a noticeable decline in fertility rate among young people, as shown in Table 3.1, with an increasing number of childless women in urban and rural areas.

Based on the 2001 Census data,[20] the proportion of childless women at age 25–29 years old is much higher among those with university degrees (more than 50 per cent). Here, again, as with marriage, the influence of education level is evident (Danaj et al., 2005). The decline in the fertility rate, significantly postponing the birth of the first child, marks a change in national family-formation patterns. Besides, less than 1 per cent of births occur outside marriage, indicating that cohabitation rates remain low, similar to the 0.2 per cent rate in 2003 (Danaj et al., 2005). Unfortunately, more recent data are not available.

The decline in the fertility rate is one of the main factors driving the decrease in the average household size from 4.7 members in 1989 to 3.9 in 2011 (INSTAT, 2002, 2012). The other factor may be the decline of the extended family due to migration, both internal and international. According to INSTAT (Bruijn et al., 2014, 19), the number of households 'with more than one family nucleus' decreased from 20 per cent to 10 per cent between 1989 and 2001. Internal movement and international migration triggered a process of nucleation of the family structure in Albania. Nevertheless, this process did not start with post-communist migration, but

Table 3.1 Proportion of young childless women (percentage)

Years	Total	Urban	Rural
20–24 years old			
Albania, 1989	36.9	42.0	34.4
Albania, 2001	64.1	67.5	61.9
Albania, 2011	75.13	79.69	69.34
25–29 years old			
Albania, 1989	12.1	15.6	10.0
Albania, 2001	27.0	31.1	23.9
Albania, 2011	40.57	45.06	34.68

Source: Danaj et al. (2005) and 2011 Census (author's calculation)

---

[20] The fertility decline by education level cannot be calculated from the 2011 Census data, so I base the numbers in this paragraph only on the 2001 Census.

earlier. The first Albanian Census conducted by the Austro-Hungarian occupation forces in WWI (Kaser, 2014) provides a different picture of Albanian household size than the ethnographic studies of the early twentieth century: only 8 per cent of all family households had more than ten members, and the average was five or six members, while nuclear families constituted 39.7 per cent of rural households and 56.2 per cent of urban households (Kaser, 2014, 101–102). After the establishment of the communist government, the 'nuclearisation' of the family structure became part of the regime's 'modernisation measures' (Kaser, 2014, 103). In 1989, the average family size was 4.7, and it has continued to decrease ever since.

It is important to reiterate that the dynamics and nuances within the national-level data presented here are various and complex. Some of these dynamics are explored and analysed in the following chapters that draw from women's voices and experiences.

References

Anthias, F., Yuval-Davis, N., & Cain, H. (1993). *Racialized bounderies: Race, nation, gender, colour and class and the anti-racist struggle*. Routledge.

Arqimandriti, M., Danaj, E., & Garcia, P. R. (2020). *Country gender analysis – Albania*. GFA Consultin Group and European Delegation in Albania.

Azzarri, C., & Carletto, C. (2009, May). Modeling migration dynamics in Albania. *Policy Research Working Paper, 4945*.

Barjaba, K., & Barjaba, J. (2015). *Embracing emigration: The Migration-development nexus in Albania*. Migration Information Source (Migration Policy Institute).

Bezemer, D. J. (2001). Post-socialist financial fragility: The case of Albania. *Cambridge Journal of Economics, 25*, 1–23.

Black, R., & King, R. (2004). Editorial introduction: Migration, return and development in West Africa. *Population, Space and Place, 10*, 75–83.

Bonifazi, C., & Manolo, M. (2004). Past and current trends of Balkan migrations. *Espace populations sociétés, 3*, 519–531.

Bruijn, B. d., Eelens, F., Galanxhi, E., Hoxha, R., Nesturi, M., & Schoorl, J. (2014). *Population and population dynamics in Albania new demographic horizons?* INSTAT.

Brunnbauer, U. (2000). From equality without democracy to democracy without equality? Women and transition in Southeast Europe. *South-East Europe Review, 3*, 151–168.

Çaro, E. (2011). *From the village to the city: The adjustment process of internal migrants in Albania*. Rozenberg Publishers.

Chan, K. W., & Zhang, L. (1999). The Hukou system and rural-urban migration in China. *The China Quarterly, 160*, 818–855.

CIA. (2015). *The World Factbook – Albania*. https://www.cia.gov/library/publications/the-world-factbook/geos/al.html. Accessed 20 Sept 2015.

Çuli, D. (2012). Periudha e Socializmit [Socialist Period]. In E. Gjermeni & M. Dauti (Eds.), *Studime Gjinore [Gender Studies]* (pp. 127–133). MediaPrint.

Dahinden, J. (2009). Migration and mobility: Universality and resulting tensions. *Universality – From Theory to Practice*, 359–376.

Dahinden, J. (2013). Albanian-speaking migration, mid-19th century to present. In I. Ness (Ed.), *Encyclopedia of global human migration*. Wiley Blackwell.

Dahinden, J. (2014). The circulation of people. Understanding the dynamics of transnational formations among Albanian-speaking migrants in Switzerland by bringing in theories of mobility, social inequality and ethnicity. *Working Paper, 6*.

Danaj, E. (2014). Family in Albania as primary solidarity network. In R. Pichler (Ed.), *Legacy and change: Albanian transformation from multidisciplinary perspectives* (pp. 117–134). LIT Verlag.

Danaj, E. (2018). 'I am not a feminist but…': women's activism in post-1991 Albania. *Gender, Place & Culture, 25*(7), 994–1009.

Danaj, E., & Festy, P. (2006). Le passage à l'âge adulte des jeunes Albanais, dans un contexte de brutale transformation socio-politique. *Population et Travail*, 365–375.

Danaj, E., Festy, P., Ekonomi, M., Lika, M., Guxho, A., & Zhllima, E. (2005). *Becoming an adult: Challenges and potentials of youth in Albania*. INSTAT.

Danermark, B., Soydan, H., Pashko, G., & Vejsiu, Y. (1989). Women, marriage and family-traditionalism vs modernity in Albania. *International Journal of Sociology of the Family, 19*(2), 19–41.

Davies, J. (2009). My name is not Natasha. In *How Albanian women in France use trafficking to overcome social exclusion (1998–2001)*. Amsterdam University Press.

De Waal, C. (2005). *Albania today: A portrait of post-communist turbulence*. I.B. Tauris.

De Rapper, G., & Sintès, P. (2006). Composer avec le risque: la frontière sud de l'Albanie entre politique des États et solidarités locales. *Revue d'études comparatives Est-Ouest, 37*(6), 243–271.

Doja, A. (2010). Fertility trends, marriage patterns, and savant typologies in Albanian context. *Journal of Family History, 25*, 346–367.

Einhorn, B. (1993). *Cinderella goes to market: Citizenship, gender and Women's movements in east Central Europe*. Verso.

Einhorn, B. (2005). Citizenship, civil society and gender mainstreaming: Contested priorities in an enlarging Europe. In *Pan European conference on 'Gendering Democracy in an Enlarged Europe'*. Prague.

Einhorn, B., & Sever, C. (2003). Gender and civil Society in Central and Eastern Europe. *International Feminist Journal of Politics, 5*(2), 163–190.

Ekonomi, M., Gjermeni, E., Danaj, E., Lula, E., & Beci, L. (2006). *Creating economic opportunities for women in Albania: A strategy for the prevention of human trafficking*. GADC.

European Commission. (2015). *Albania*. Retrieved September 20 2015, from http://ec.europa.eu/enlargement/countries/detailed-country-information/albania/index_en.htm

Fico, D. (2014). Is there a women's movement in Albania? In R. Pichler (Ed.), *Legacy and change: Albanian transformation from multidisciplinary perspectives* (pp. 165–174). LIT Verlag.

Fischer, B. J. (2010). Albania since 1989: The Hoxhaist legacy. In S. P. Ramet (Ed.), *Central and southeast European politics since 1989* (pp. 421–443). Cambridge University Press.

Gal, S., & Kligman, G. (2000). *The politics of gender after socialism: A comparative- historical essay*. Princeton University Press.

Galanxhi, E., Misja, E., Lameborshi, D., Lerch, M., Wanner, P., & Dahinden, J. (2004). *Migration in Albania*. Tirane.

Galanxhi, E., Nesturi, M., & Hoxha, R. (2014). *Shqipëri, Popullsia dhe Dinamikat e Saj – Horizonte te Reja Demografike? [Albania, population and its dynamics – New demographic horizons?]*. INSTAT.

Gëdeshi, I. (2008). *Introducing Migrant City Tirana, Albania*. Migrant Cities Conference.

Gëdeshi, I., & Jorgoni, E. (2012). *Social impact of emigration and rural-urban migration in central and Eastern Europe: Final country report Albania*. European Commission & GVG.

Gemi, E. (2015). *The incomplete trajectory of Albanian migration in Greece*. Hellenic Foundation for European and Foreign Policy (ELIAMEP).

Gemi, E., Yiannis, A., Michalis, A., & Kyriaki, P. (2010). *Temporary and circular migration: Empirical evidence, current policy practice and future options in Greece*. Neoanalysis Consultants LTD..

Gërmenji, E., & Milo, L. (2011). Migration of the skilled from Albania: Brain drain or brain gain? *Journal of Balkan and Near Eastern Studies, 13*(3), 339–356.

Gilyuk, O. (2016). *Les étudiants russes face à l'internationalisation de l'enseignement supérieur.* Emulations - Revue de sciences sociales.

Gjonca, A., Aasve, A., & Mencarini, L. (2008). Albania: Trends and patterns, proximate determinants and policies of fertility change. *Demographic Research, 19,* 261–292.

GoA. (2018). *The National Strategy on migration governance and action plan 2019–2022.* Government of Albania.

Gruber, S. (2002). *Reproductive patterns in Albania and Serbia.* Leuven: Paper at the Young Scholars' European Historical Demography Conference.

Gruber, S., & Pichler, R. (2002). Household structures in Albania in the early 20th century. *The History of the Family, 7*(3), 351–374. https://doi.org/10.1016/S1081-602X(02)00106-9

Hakim, C. (1979). *Occupational segregation: A comparative study of the degree and pattern of the differentiation between men and women's work in Britain, the United States and other countries.* Department of Employment.

Hakim, C. (2006). Women, careers, and work-life preferences. *British Journal of Guidance & Counselling, 34*(3), 279–294,

Hoxha, E. (1974). Report of the 3rd congress of the Party of Labour of Albania, 25 may 1956. In E. Hoxha (Ed.), *Selected works* (Vol. I, pp. 483–594). 8 Nëntori.

Ikonomi, L. (2009). *E Drejta Migratore: Manual Trajnues [the migratory right: A training manual].* IOM.

IMF. (2019). *Albania.* IMF Country Report No. 19/207, International Monetary Fund.

INSTAT. (2002). *Albania population and housing census 2001.* INSTAT.

INSTAT. (2011). *Albanian time use survey 2010–2011.* INSTAT.

INSTAT. (2012). *Population and housing census 2011.* INSTAT.

INSTAT. (2019a). *Albania in Figures.* INSTAT.

INSTAT. (2019b). *Income and living conditions in Albania: 2017–2018.* INSTAT.

INSTAT and World Bank. (2015a). *Albania: Trends in poverty 2002-2005-2008-2012.* INSTAT.

INSTAT and World Bank. (2015b). *Albania: Trends in poverty 2002-2005-2008-2012.* INSTAT.

Jacobs, J. E. (1945). *Final report of special mission to Tirana.* Department of State Special Mission to Tirana.

Jinga, L.-M. (2011). *Les Femmes dans le Parti Communiste Roumain (1944–1989).* University of Angers.

Kajsiu, B. (2014). *A discourse analysis of corruption: Instituting neoliberalism against corruption in Albania, 1998–2005.* Ashgate.

Kaser, K. (2014). Family and kinship in Albania: Continuities and discontinuities in turbulent times. In R. Pichler (Ed.), *Legacy and change: Albanian transformation from multidisciplinary perspectives* (pp. 97–116). LIT Verlag.

Keefe, E. K., Elpern, S. J., Giloane, W., Jr., Peters, J. M., & White, E. T. (1971). Area handbook for Albania. In *The American University.* The American University, Foreign Area Studies.

Këlliçi, K. (2015, December 5). Albanian student migration in Italy during the 90s. (E. Danaj, Interviewer).

Këlliçi, K., & Danaj, E. (2016). Promoting equality, perpetuating inequality: Gender propaganda in communist Albania. In *In history of communism in Europe (7),* 39–62. Zeta Books.

King, R. (2005). Albania as a laboratory for the study of migration and development. *Journal of Southern Europe and the Balkans, 7*(2), 133–156.

King, R., & Vullnetari, J. (2010). Gender and remittances in Albania: Or, why 'are women better remitters than men?' Is not the right question. In *Trans-Atlantic perspectives on international migration: Cross border impacts, border security, and socio-political responses.* University of Texas San Antonio.

King, R., & Vullnetari, J. (2012). A population on the move: Migration and gender relations in Albania. *Cambridge Journal of Regions, Economy and Society, 5,* 207–220.

King, R., Skeldon, R., & Vullnetari, J. (2008). Internal and international migration: Bridging the theoretical divide. *Working Paper, 52.*

Kligman, G. (1994). The social legacy of communism: Women, children and the feminization of poverty. In J. R. Millar & S. L. Wolchik (Eds.), *The social legacy of communism* (pp. 252–169). Cambridge University Press.

Kligman, G. (1996). Women and the negotiation of identity in post-communist Eastern Europe. In V. Bonnell (Ed.), *Identities in transition: Eastern Europe and Russia after the collapse of communism* (Research Series Nr. 93) (pp. 68–91). University of California.

Kligman, G. (1998). *The politics of duplicity. Controlling reproduction in Ceaușescu's Romania.* California University Press.

Kocaqi, M., Kelly, L., & Lovett, J. (2015). *Mapping violence against women and girls support service- Albania final report.* Council of Europe and UN Women.

Kofman, E. (2004). Gendered global migrations. *International Feminist Journal of Politics, 6*(4), 643–665. https://doi.org/10.1080/1461674042000283408

Kopliku, B. (2016). Return migration in the Shkodra region – what's the next step? In M. Zbinden, J. Dahinden, & A. Efendic (Eds.), *Diversity of migration in south East Europe* (pp. 111–134). Peter Lang.

Korovilas, J. (1999). The Albanian economy in transition: The role of remittances and pyramid investment schemes. *Post-Communist Economies, 11*(3), 399–415.

Lelea, M. A., & Voiculescu, S. (2017). The production of emancipatory feminist spaces in a post-socialist context: Organization of Ladyfest in Romania. *Gender Place & Culture, 24*(6), 794–811. https://doi.org/10.1080/0966369X.2017.1340872

Lerch, M. (2009). The impact of migration on fertility in post-communist Albania. *Southeast European and Black Sea Studies, 9*(4), 519–537.

Lerch, M. (2013). Patriarchy and fertility in Albania. *Demographic Research, 29*, 133–166.

Lévy, F. (2015). *Entre contraintes et interstices, l'évolution des projets migratoires dans l'espace transnational: Une ethnographie des migrants de Chine du Nord à Paris.* EHESS.

Mai, N. (2004). 'Looking for a more modern life…': The role of Italian Television in the Albanian Migration to Italy. *Westminster Papers in Communication and Culture, 1*(1), 3–22.

Mai, N., & Paladini, C. (2013). Flexible circularities: Integration, return, and socio-economic instability within Albanian migration to Italy. In A. Triandafyllidou (Ed.), *Circular migration between Europe and its Neighborhood, choice or necessity?* (pp. 42–67). Oxford University Press.

Moghadam, V. M. (1995). Gender and revolutionary transformation: Iran 1979 and East Central Europe 1989. *Gender and Society, 9*(3), 328–358.

Morokvasic, M. (1984). Introduction. In M. Morokvasic (Ed.), *Current Sociology: Special Edition "Tendances de recherche et approche sociologique des migrations en Europe: perspectives des pays de départ et des pays d'arrivée 1960–1983"* (pp. 17–40). Sage Publications.

Morokvasic, M. (2003). Transnational mobility and gender: A view from post-wall Europe. In M. Morokvasic, U. Erel, & K. Shinozaki, Crossing Borders and shifting boundaries (pp. 101–136). Springer.

Morokvasic, M. (2004). 'Settled in mobility': Engendering Post-Wall migration in Europe. *Feminist Review, 77*, 7–25.

Morokvasic, M. (2006). Une circulation bien particulière: la traite des femmes dans les Balkans. *Migrations Société, 18*(107), 119–143.

Morokvašić, M. (2015). Gendering migration. *Migracijske i etničke teme/Migration and Ethnic Themes, 30*(3), 355–378. https://doi.org/10.11567/met.30.3.4

Musaj, F., & Nicholson, B. (2011). Women activists in Albania following Independence and world war I. In I. Sharp & M. Stibbe (Eds.), *Aftermaths of war - Women's movements and female activists, 1918–1923* (pp. 179–196). Brill.

Musaraj, S. (2011). Tales from Albarado: The materiality of pyramid schemes in Postsocialist Albania. *Cultural Anthropology, 26*(1), 84–110.

Penn, S., & Massino, J. (2009). *Gender politics and everyday life in state socialist eastern and Central Europe.* Palgrave Macmillan.

Pojani, D. (2010). City profile: Tirana. *Cities, 27*(6), 483–495.

Puto, A. (2013). *Gruaja në kinemanë shqiptare të pasluftës* [The woman's image in the Albanian cinema of post-II world war]. http://www.noa.al/artikull/gruaja-ne-kinemane-shqiptare-te-pasluftes/374665.html#sthash.ga4Ow5i0.dpuf

Ramet, S. P., & Wagner, F. P. (2010). Post-socialist models of rule in central and Southeastern Europe. In S. P. Ramet (Ed.), *Central and southeast European politics since 1989* (pp. 9–36). Cambridge University Press.

Ravenstein, E. G. (1885). The Laws of migration. *Journal of the Statistical Society of London, 48*(2), 167–235.

Rosenberg, D. J. (1991). Shock therapy: GDR women in transition from a socialist welfare state to a social market economy. *Signs, 17*(1), 129–151.

Shevchenko, D. (2010, December 15). *Internal passports: 'Without registration, you're a nobody.* Russia Beyond the Headlines.

Sintès, P. (2003). Les albanais en Grèce: le rôle des réseaux préexistants. *Balkanologie, 7*(1), 111–133.

Sintès, P. (2010). Construction des discours d'appartenance en migration: l'exemple des Albanais en Grèce. *Revue ANATOLI, 1*(1), 195–213.

Sjöberg, Ö. (1992). Underurbanisation and the zero urban growth hypothesis: Diverted migration in Albania. *Geografiska Annaler Series B, Human Geography, 74*(1), 3–19.

Sjöberg, Ö. (1994). Rural retention in Albania: Administrative restrictions on urban-bound migration. *East European Quarterly, 28*(2), 205–233.

Sperling, V. (1996). "Democracy without women is not democracy": The struggle over Women's status and identity during Russia's transition. In V. Bonnell (Ed.), *Identities in transition: Eastern Europe and Russia after the collapse of communism* (pp. 45–67). University of California.

Stan, L. (2010). Romania: In the shadow of the past. In S. P. Ramet (Ed.), *Central and southeast European politics since 1989* (pp. 379–400). Cambridge University Press.

Tarrius, A. (1993). Territoires Circulatoires et Espaces Urbaine. *Annales de la Recherche Urbain,* 59–60.

Tarifa, F. (1995). Albania's road from communism: Political and social change, 1990–1993. *Development and Change, 26,* 133–162.

Tarrius, A. (2011). Drogue et travail du sexe: des femmes de retour vers les Balkans. *Multitudes, 1*(44), 115–118.

Uruci, E., & Gëdeshi, I. (2003). Remittances Management in Albania. *Working Papers 05.*

Vaiou, D. (2002). In the interstices of the City: Albanian women in Athens. *Espaces, Populations, Societes, 3,* 373–385.

Van Hook, M. P., Gjermeni, E., & Haxhiymeri, E. (2006). Sexual trafficking of women tragic proportions and attempted solutions in Albania. *International Social Work, 49,* 29–40.

Verdery, K. (1996). *What was socialism, and what comes next.* Princeton University Press.

Vickers, M. (1999). *The Albanians. A modern history.* I.B. Tauris.

Vullnetari, J. (2007). Albanian migration and development: State of the art review. IMISCOE *Working Paper 18.*

Vullnetari, J. (2012). Women and Migration in Albania: A view from the village. *International Migration, 50*(5), 169–188. https://doi.org/10.1111/j.1468-2435.2009.00569.x

Vullnetari, J. (2014). Internal migration in Albania. In R. Pichler (Ed.), *Legacy and change: Albanian transformation from multidisciplinary perspectives* (pp. 47–67). LIT Verlag.

Vullnetari, J., & King, R. (2011). Gendering remittances in Albania: A human and social development perspective. *Gender and Development, 19*(1), 39–51. https://doi.org/10.1080/1355207 4.2011.554020

Wegren, S., & Drury, C. (2001). Patterns of internal migration during the Russian transition. *Journal of Communist Studies and Transition Politics, 17*(4), 15–42.

Wihtol de Wenden, C. (2015). Faut-il ouvrir les frontières? In *Forum 2015. La conference socio-politique de Caritas: Immigration.* Caritas Suisse.

Wites, T. (2004). Abortions in Russia before and after the fall of the Soviet Union. *Miscellanea Geographica, 11*, 217–228.

Wittberger, D., Plaku, A., Jaupllari, V., & Miluka, J. (2012). *The National Report on the status of women and gender equality*. UN Women.

Woodcock, S. (2016). *Life is war: Surviving dictatorship in communist Albania*. Hammer On Press.

World Bank. (1996). *World development report*. Oxford University Press.

Xhindi, N. (2013). *Albania towards a sustainable regional development: The cases of the Tirana, Shkodra and Kukes region*. Universitätsverlag Potsdam.

Zenelaga, B., & Sotirofski, K. (2011). *The `brain gain hypotheses` of transition countries elites and socioeconomic development in their home country (Albanian emigrants in Italy sample)*. Alma Laurea Working Papers.

Zezza, A., Carletto, G., & Davis, B. (2005). *Moving away from poverty a spatial analysis of poverty and migration in Albania*. ESA Working Paper, No, 05–02.

Open Access This chapter is licensed under the terms of the Creative Commons Attribution 4.0 International License (http://creativecommons.org/licenses/by/4.0/), which permits use, sharing, adaptation, distribution and reproduction in any medium or format, as long as you give appropriate credit to the original author(s) and the source, provide a link to the Creative Commons license and indicate if changes were made.

The images or other third party material in this chapter are included in the chapter's Creative Commons license, unless indicated otherwise in a credit line to the material. If material is not included in the chapter's Creative Commons license and your intended use is not permitted by statutory regulation or exceeds the permitted use, you will need to obtain permission directly from the copyright holder.

Chapter 4
Balancing Opportunities and Constraints: The Experiences of Internal Migrant Women in Tirana

This chapter explores the trajectories of those participants who migrated internally to Tirana for reasons other than education. The data draws from interviews conducted with eight women, the majority of whom had already married when Communism collapsed. These women provide distinctive insights as they stand on the verge of and link the late communist years with the post-communist period. The narratives of the following eight women are discussed and analysed at length in this chapter.

Drita, 40 years old, was born in a village near Lezhë, a city in northern Albania. Her husband and his brother migrated to Greece in 1991. Shortly after, in 1992, Drita relocated to Tirana with her parents-in-law and sister-in-law (the wife of her husband's brother). At the time of internal migration to Tirana, Drita had no children. In 2007, her husband returned to Tirana. Drita has completed secondary education. Before moving to Tirana, she worked for a short period in the cooperative, and after that, she withdrew from the labour market for a long stretch of time. In Tirana, at the time of the research, she worked as a domestic care worker for a couple of young professionals. With her husband and son, who was born after Drita moved to Tirana, she shared the third floor of a house in Don Bosko, constructed with the remittances sent by her husband and his brother. Her parents-, sister- and brother-in-law reside on the same premises on the first and second floors, respectively.

Eli is a 39-year-old woman from a village near Fier in central-southern Albania. Her husband migrated to Greece in 1994, and four years later, in 1998, she relocated to Tirana with her daughter, parents-in-law and sisters-in-law (her husband's sister and the wife of her husband's brother and their two children). At the time of the research, in 2012, Eli's husband still lived and worked in Greece. She has completed lower secondary education and has never been employed in either Tirana or her place of origin. In 2012, she and her daughters (one born in Fier and the younger one in Tirana) shared a floor of a house constructed with the remittances sent by her husband and his brothers in Don Bosko. Her parents-in-law lived on the first floor of the house, and her brother-in-law's wife and two children on the second floor. On the third floor were two apartments, one for Eli's family and the other for another

© The Author(s) 2022

E. Danaj, *Women, Migration and Gendered Experiences*, IMISCOE Research Series, https://doi.org/10.1007/978-3-030-92092-0_4

brother-in-law. His apartment was empty most of the time because he lived in Greece and, as of 2012, had no plans to return to Albania. The sister of Eli's husband was married and lived with her husband in another neighbourhood of Tirana.

Manjola, 40 years old, is a native of the city of Vlorë, along the southern coast. Her husband migrated to Greece in 1997 after the collapse of the Albanian pyramid Ponzi schemes. In 2001, she relocated in Tirana with her children and her mother, who cared for the children. A couple of years later, Manjola's husband returned from emigration and joined the family in Tirana. In 2012, they ran a small trading business together. Manjola graduated from university with a degree in economics but had not worked before migrating to Tirana. She lived with her son, daughter and husband in an apartment they owned in Komuna e Parisit.

Arjana, 51 years old, is a native of the city of Fier. She migrated to Tirana with her husband and two children in 2004. A university graduate, she worked as an elementary school teacher in her hometown of Fier. In 2012, she worked as an educator in a private kindergarten in Tirana, and her husband had found work with a private company. In 2012, she lived in Komuna e Parisit with her son and daughter, who were both students at the University of Tirana.

Flutura, 55 years old, is a native of the city Shkodër in northern Albania. In 2002, she migrated to Tirana with her husband and their two daughters. A university graduate, in 2012, she worked in public administration, and her husband as a television journalist in Tirana; one of her daughters worked in Tirana, while the other was a student in Italy. Flutura lived with her husband and one daughter in an owned apartment in Komuna e Parisit.

Silvana, 55 years old, is a native of the town of Lezhë. Her husband migrated to Tirana in 1992, and two years later, in 1994, she joined him with their children. Silvana is a university graduate, and before moving to Tirana, worked in the local administration in Lezhë. In 2012, both she and her husband worked for the central public administration. At the time of the interview, she lived with her husband and one daughter in an owned apartment in Don Bosko. Her other daughter had migrated to France for study purposes. Later, I heard that the other daughter also migrated abroad.

Zhani, 50 years old, from the city of Fier, is a high school graduate. She migrated to Tirana before her husband and two daughters to facilitate their migration. They followed one year later, in 2004. As of 2012, Zhani was self-employed and owned a small shop. Of her two daughters, one was studying at university, while the other was unemployed as of 2012. Zhani lived with her husband and the two daughters in an owned apartment in Komuna e Parisit.

Eleni, 47 years old, is a native of the small town of Tepelenë in southern Albania. Her husband migrated to Greece in 1993, and after his return in 2003, they relocated to Tirana. Eleni has completed secondary education and in 2012 worked as a domestic care worker. Her husband was unemployed due to the crisis in the construction sector. She lived with her two daughters, son and husband in an owned apartment in Don Bosko. One daughter was pursuing university studies in Tirana. The son and the other daughter had already graduated; in 2012, the son was working as a salesperson, but the daughter was jobless. As I heard later, the unemployed daughter had a master's in political sciences and worked in a call centre at the end of 2014.

These short descriptions of the interviewees' partners highlight that what is commonly subsumed under the concept of internal migration includes a variety of different, dynamic mobility configurations. Among these configurations, first, we see that of the husbands who migrate abroad, while the wives—with the children and parents-in-law—move to Tirana. Secondly, entire households move to Tirana at the same time. The third scenario consists of women being the primary migrants to Tirana, while the husbands and children follow. These configurations are explored in-depth in the following chapter.

4.1 Pre-migration: Life in the Cities and Villages of Origin

One of the most common configurations of the early 90s migration in Albania was a twofold one: the husband migrates abroad, and the wife—along with the children and sometimes the in-laws—migrate internally later.

Let us first turn to the husband's decision to migrate abroad and the role the women play in these decision processes. Drita says:

> I was unemployed...Before demokracia[1], we were all employed in the local cooperative. We were penniless, just like everyone else... After that, things became more difficult. I was too young to grasp the situation entirely. I recall my parents-in-law and my husband being anxious because suddenly we found ourselves with no income. I was very young... Then my husband emigrated. Everybody was trying to leave, in fact. What else was there to be done? We had nothing... If I remember correctly, a group of men left first. My husband told me he had no other choice: either emigrate or steal so that we would be able to live. It was tough for me as we were a young couple, but there was nothing I could do. It was the only way. We had no hope. I just told him to be careful and to keep in contact if possible. That was all I was able to say.

Not only did Drita find her husband's departure difficult, but she also expresses a feeling of being powerless, of not being unable to prevent her husband from going abroad. She recalls that at the time, she was very young and could not grasp the complexity of the situation. Drita was living in her husband's household, along with her parents-in-law, brother-in-law and his wife and child. The literature (Ekonomi et al., 2004; Kaser, 2014; King & Vullnetari, 2012) describes such extended patrilo-cal families, of which Drita was part, as following a particular hierarchy, which might partly reflect the dynamics of this migration decision process. In such patrilo-cal households, where wives move after marriage into the house of the husband and the parents-in-law (and sometimes the husband's brother) (Kaser, 2014), hierarchies are organised by age, gender and generation (King & Vullnetari, 2012). In the

---

[1] Some of the women interviewed use the term *demokracia* [democracy] to refer to the post-1991 period in Albania. This usage frequently occurs in everyday communication in Albania, where many people also refer to this period as *tranzicioni*, the transition.

decision-making processes, the oldest man—here, the husband's father (sometimes with his wife)—has the most say within the household (Gjermeni, 2004). The sons have some weight, while wives and daughters are less involved in decision-making processes. This combination of seniority, individual (age) and family factors were decisive in Drita's husband's decision to leave the household and migrate and explains her de facto non-participation in her husband's migration decision.

Eli describes a similar process:

The situation was dire before coming to Tirana. … We [Eli and her husband] were living with my husband's parents. … He [Eli's husband] had already discussed with his father and his brothers…. I didn't know what was going on when suddenly my husband said one day, 'We're going to Greece with a group of young men. They know the route, but you should stay here with my parents'. That was more or less what he told me, and then he left for Greece that very same day in 1994. I recall that I cried all night all night long, feeling lost. We were facing many challenges. We had a little daughter, and it was so difficult for me, and us all, because we were poor. When he left, I felt shattered. His two other brothers left too. I was living with his parents, a younger sister and a sister-in-law…. We were trying to survive there in the village doing our everyday work.

We see that in both cases, migration was—as has been abundantly shown in studies (Stark & Bloom, 1985; Root & De Jong, 1991; Lauby & Stark 1988)—a household decision rather than an individual decision. Again, Eli, similarly to Drita in these patrilocal household configurations, was excluded from the husband's decision-making process to leave for Greece. However, the process is more complicated than this. The interviewees reveal that these decision-making processes cannot be reduced to traditional patriarchal culture, and respectively to the structure of extended families. Instead, it seems that the economic collapse of the immediate post-communist period reinvigorated such power patterns within households. International migration was and is considered to be a solution to improving the challenging financial situations in which these migrants live and can be viewed as a diversifying, risk-minimising household strategy (Stark & Bloom, 1985; Stark & Taylor, 1991).

After the fall of communism, not only men but also women, like Drita, who previously had a paid job, found themselves jobless. At the same time as many state factories and enterprises closed, the social services provided by the state deteriorated. In rural areas, cooperatives shut down, and under Law No. 7501 of July 1991, the land was distributed to the inhabitants of the villages, allowing them to become landowners (Stahl, 2012). Nevertheless, these residents were destitute and did not have the means to work the land and reap its benefits. The situation in the villages was difficult for both men and women as they had no opportunities other than their recently acquired plot of land, as was the case for Drita and Eli. Drita describes the situation in rural areas:

Some time after my husband's emigration, I remembered that we had become owners of a piece of land as the cooperatives had ceased to exist. My parents-in-law and I worked the plot so that we could have something to eat; after that, I worked in the house. My sister-in-law worked more inside [the home] as she had a small child. She had to take care of the baby, too…. it was so tricky because you cannot work the land like that, with no means and by yourself…. I just cannot fathom how we managed to live at that time.

Women's situation in rural areas became more challenging due to the rapid post-communist decline of social services, including child care and health care structures (Danaj et al., 2008; Gjermeni, 2004). Regarding social services in the early nineties, there were no more nurseries or kindergartens, both in rural and urban areas. In 1990, more than 1 in 2 three- to five-year-old children was enrolled in preschool; in 2004, the numbers were less than 1 in 3 (Social Research Center, 2004). Migrating, in any form, was viewed as a solution to the economic and social difficulties of this period. Given this situation, extended households based their decision-making processes on revitalised ideas of gender and seniority.

Women in urban areas faced similar conundrums. Eleni describes her circumstances:

> *When* demokracia *came, we were laid off because my husband was working in the cooperative adjacent to the city (Tepelenë), and it suddenly ceased to exist. The factory where I was working at was closed down as well. I didn't know the reason, but we just learned that there were no more factories. How could we live like this? Yes, you shut down the factory, but where should we go?!! Whom could we ask for explanations? Everybody was like us, laid off. And above all, we had three little children. Only the older child was of school age. The others were younger, so they were staying at home. It was not even a home. It was just a room because we resided in a shared apartment with another family [a couple with two children with no kinship relations to Eleni], and we had one room. The other family was living in the other. Until 1993, we managed to survive and to have food because my husband continued to work in the village. He was able to have some money from time to time. My family [Eleni's mother and brother] back in the village also helped with food, mostly with milk. I was at home with the children.*

Eleni explains that in the early 1990s, she found herself constrained within the house to care for the children, since kindergartens no longer existed, and the factory where she used to work closed down. In other words, the collapse of the communist system—with its feminist perspective on governance—confined women to their role of caregivers and took them out of the labour market.

The mass privatisation that followed in 1992 brought enormous changes to the structure of the labour market. Women withdrew from the labour market in significant numbers (UN Albania, 2004), and men began to adapt to the new market economy through migration and entrepreneurship. In these challenging economic and social conditions, the decision to migrate seemed inevitable for men, even more so once migration became a mass phenomenon and reinforced what Stark and Taylor (1991) call relative deprivation. In this situation, people and households migrate not only to maximise their total incomes but also to improve their position relevant to other reference groups. Such comparisons and the desire to improve one's relative position are significant elements in the decision-making process to migrate.

International migration was seen mostly as men's affair, while women stayed at home caring for the children. The risky and illegal ways emigrants used to leave Albania, as described by Vullnetari (2012), furthered masculinised perceptions of immigration. Men migrated to Greece mostly by crossing the borders through the mountains on foot (Vaiou, 2002; Vullnetari, 2009, 2012). A heroic narrative of migration as dangerous and exhausting, qualities often associated with masculinity, may be seen in Eleni's narration:

Then, in 1993, he [Eleni's husband] took the mountain route to Greece, seven days and seven nights walking in the mountains. They were not aware of anything at that time, where the roads led to, nothing. We had no other choice, except for him to emigrate. Where would we be able to find the money to live?!!! … If he didn't leave for Greece, we would have nothing at all. No other ways were possible to obtain income.

Eleni participated in the decision-making process regarding the potential migration of her husband. However, she recurred to traditional gender representation of the man's role as the breadwinner and the woman's as the care-giver.

International migration by husbands and internal migration by families was not unique to the early 1990s. Another significant migration movement followed the crash of the financial pyramid schemes in 1997, as shown in the research of Korovilas (1999) and Musaraj (2011). Manjola recounts:

It was like the destruction of all hopes. It was like a rupture with what we had hoped and dreamt before 1997. It was like 'boom'. … Everything disappears, and you start from zero. … My husband had worked in the municipality of Vlora. I was not working because our son was two years old, and I was pregnant again. … My parents were in sound financial standing as they were both working and saving all the time, as parents usually do [laughs], so they were helping us. … They lost a lot of money in the pyramid schemes, thankfully, not all of it. Then, after the events in Vlora in 1997, we thought that migrating was the best thing to do. I could not leave at that moment because of the children. That was a period during which people from the south were moving because of the mess. We thought, 'The time has come. Let us try something else other than here…. Agron [Manjola's husband] left in October of 1997.

Like Eleni, Manjola was involved and engaged in the decision-making process regarding her husband's choice to go abroad as they lived in a nuclear family structure. However, again, the outcome of the process—a configuration in which women care for the children and men migrate abroad to become breadwinners—shows how migration is embedded in gender representations. After a period of feminist governance enacted by the communist regime in which most women were engaged in paid work, a remobilisation of 'traditional' division of gender roles occurred in Albania.

Nevertheless, this remobilisation of 'traditional' gender roles is nuanced, as demonstrated by women's experiences while their spouses were abroad. These experiences differed by what sort of economic activity they were involved in, social relations and family structure, among other factors. Although women were responsible for taking care of children, housework and, in many cases, their husband's families, their statements do not reflect the same heroism they ascribe to their husbands' migration. Eleni says:

He [Eleni's husband] was sending money, and I was taking care of the children. The children were very young at that time. I was taking care of everything, dealing with all the issues that arise from having children. I was alone. … My mother and brother lived in a village near Tepelenë. It was impossible to visit with them often—the same with my husband's parents and brother. I could only rely on the neighbours, the majority of whom were also people from the villages around Tepelenë. They were poor people like us. Sometimes they helped out with children, sometimes with food. We helped each other as much as possible.

This quotation shows that Eleni took care of everything related to the household and had to overcome any difficulty by herself while her husband was away. Men could migrate because women took charge of caring for the family and housework. Social relations, in this case, neighbour networks, were generous support.

We go back to Eleni:

I sometimes did handcraft. I worked at home and then sold the work in Gjirokastër [the city adjacent to Tepelenë, a more central hub]. My neighbour from a village in Gjirokastër helped me sell some of the handcrafts. Little things, very little money, but better than nothing.

In the case of Eleni, neighbour networks allowed her to generate some additional income in a time of acute economic constraints for herself and her children. Her story also shows how Eleni tried to adjust to the new economic opportunities by mobilising her skills of handcrafting, an activity that women in Albania usually do for free as a "female" hobby. This change illustrates how women's skills gained new value in the market environment and provided new income opportunities, as found by Gal and Kligman (2000) in the case of the multiple entrepreneurial initiatives undertaken by women in the post-socialist space.

In addition to neighbour networks, women's parents often took on new roles while husbands went abroad, as the case of Manjola illustrates:

It would not have been wise for me to stay at home alone with my son while pregnant. I thought it was better to go to my parents; they had enough space for me. At first, I thought of staying only for a few months following the birth of my daughter. But I changed my plans along the way [laughs] … as it was very comfortable for me to stay there. My parents were helping me all the time.

Sometimes, women also mobilised these networks to find additional ways to earn money. For instance, Manjola stated in her interview that she found an opportunity to rent their apartment (her and her husband's). She decided to live with her parents for longer than planned so that through the renting of her apartment, she could have some income in addition to her husband's earnings. As both cases illustrate, women not only had to deal with all the difficulties that taking care of their children and households presented, but they also make efforts to improve their financial situation, even though their husbands abroad were in charge of earning money for their families.

4.2 Moving to Tirana

The interviews show that social networks played a highly significant role and provided a wide range of social support in these women's move to Tirana. The time when women migrated to Tirana was an essential factor in this regard. Internal migration in the early 1990s was characterised by a lack of knowledge about the place of destination, fewer social networks in the destination and consequently more insecurity about what would happen in this new location. For instance, Drita, who migrated to Tirana in 1992, talks about how the villagers and cousins of hers who had already relocated to Tirana, shared the information she needed about the land where to construct a house and other practical advice:

> *… Some cousins of my mother-in-law told her what was most necessary to take with us and to sell the rest of the things (clothes and furniture) because the money would be quite useful in Tirana… I had no idea where we were going to live and how it would be there.*

The other interviewees left later in the nineties and early 2000s and could rely on a broader network of social relations and information. In the case of Eli, her husband and brothers-in-law had moved to Tirana to settle their families' accommodations and other matters, and the rest of the family followed them later:

> *They [Eli's husband and brothers-in-law] came back for a few months to arrange things with the house, and so on. They were staying in Tirana and first built a tiny house so that we would not have to live under the open sky. After some time, they came back to Fier, and we moved all together to Tirana. A few days later, they left again for Greece as they had to work, and we also needed money to live and to add some rooms to the house.*

Another striking result from the interviews, which corresponds to the results drawn in the previous section, is that women living in nuclear families were far more knowledgeable about the city. They had gathered information from family and social networks or gone there themselves to evaluate the situation. Manjola is an illustrative case:

> *I thought of buying two small apartments, one to live in and another on the first floor to use as a small shop, as we needed income. … My parents were caring for my children as I was going to Tirana to deal with the search for apartments and all the procedures to follow, and a cousin of mine drove me back and forth as I wanted to go in the morning and return to Vlora on the same day.*

Manjola organised the entire process of the family's move to Tirana, handling not only logistical matters but also preparing a strategy to settle down fully. She relied on her mother, who took care of her children, and on her cousin, who drove her. This assistance again illustrates how deeply migration decisions were embedded in broader family networks. However, to find a job in Tirana, Manjola needed social networks that she lacked at this time. Thus, she found another way to overcome this obstacle: by turning to self-employment. She used her available financial resources, given her lack of social networks in the destination place. With the money she had saved from renting her apartment in Vlora and from the remittances sent by her husband, she bought two small apartments, one to live in and one to turn into a shop, which she still ran with her husband at the time of the interview in late 2011.

Other women prepared for migration to Tirana by asking for the direct and indirect support of their kin and friends. These persons—friends, cousins and parents—were crucial for access to living spaces, apartments, houses and even investment opportunities. As Flutura states:

> *He [Flutura's husband] found an apartment through the friends and acquaintances he had in Tirana. It was not as big as the apartment we had in Shkodër, but here [in Tirana], it was more expensive, and we could not afford a better one.*

Zhani speaks of similar issues:

I had some cousins in Tirana who had found a space for rent on the first floor of a building. They asked if we wanted to join and share the rent and space as I had a shop in Fier, and they knew that we were planning on going to Tirana. I could have my shop now in Tirana and continue the same activity.

In addition, Zhani speaks of how her cousins in Tirana hosted her until she could find an apartment for herself and her family. In this case, kinship networks served to appease and share the risks of economic investments and the internal migration process. Silvana recounts a similar situation, showing the role that family and relatives played in accessing living spaces in Tirana:

The search for a house to live in turned out to be problematic as apartments in Tirana were very expensive compared to Lezha. Even if we had sold our apartment in Lezha, the money would not have sufficed. But my family [Silvana's parents] was willing to host us for an undetermined period until we could find an apartment.

Discussing internal migration to the municipality of Kamza, Çaro (2011, 184) highlights that migrants relied on their resources throughout the process and received little support from municipalities or other state structures. Gjermeni (2004) and De Waal (2005) describe similar situations. Moving to Tirana was organised through the mobilisation of social networks to obtain housing and employment, as frequently highlighted in this chapter and the following ones. Furthermore, the population growth on the peripheries of Tirana (that were mainly empty spaces before 1990) and the overpopulation of Tirana did not lead to the appropriate development of road infrastructure, schools, health care centres or laws. For instance, for a long time, migrants to Tirana or its peripheries could not register in the Offices of Civil Registry, so they could not enrol their children in school or benefit from the services of the labour offices (Social Research Centre, 2004).

4.3   Balancing Opportunities and Constraints: The Experiences of Internal Migrant Women in Tirana

Analysing the experiences of internal migrant women allows us to explore the opportunities and the constraints these women faced in Tirana. These included the challenges of beginning the settling process and the strategies and the resources the interviewees mobilised to meet their new social reality in Tirana. When settling in a new place, there are challenges that arise from having to adapt to a new and unfamiliar environment, the nostalgia one feels for their city or village of origin, not to mention the need to adjust to new everyday life practices, as well as structural challenges. In the early period of their settlement in Tirana, the living conditions were often not as good as expected, and for some, this engendered a significant sense that they had been deceived. As Drita explains:

The initial time in Tirana was very challenging. Our first house was terrible. I could have never imagined living in such a place. Why had we moved here to live under these condi-

tions? However, after a few months, things started to change as we had begun construction on a new house. My husband and his brother had contracted some workers here in the area to build our home. They were migrants like us, but they were working here, not abroad.

At the beginning of their stay in Tirana, many internal migrants had to contend every day with the lack of infrastructure that accompanied life in newly populated areas. Eleni describes one such situation:

I was climbing eight floors every day, even twice a day, carrying water and food. … The building had a place for an elevator, but the owner never built it. The builder said he was going to solve this, and then he asked us for money. But we were all newcomers in this building, and if we had money, we would have found another building, not this one. … In the beginning, the electricity was unsteady as there were no regular electricity lines but wires that were connected messily by the inhabitants themselves. … I had to wash clothes by hand, but we didn't even have water.

The disillusionment many women experienced at the beginning of settling is also explored in Gjermeni's (2004) research on internal migration to the area of Bathore, next to Tirana. A lack of adequate infrastructure, electricity and water and the presence of many muddy pathways were most problematic for women in charge of reproductive work. A similar situation of women overburdened by a lack of facilities, such as water and electricity, is also reported by Danaj et al. (2008), who held focus group discussions with women in Tirana and other urban areas of Albania. Despite inadequate infrastructure and facilities, some areas did improve, such as the newly created municipality of Kamza, a former periphery of Tirana populated by migrants (Çaro, 2011). Nevertheless, the continuous internal migration to Tirana has spurred ongoing construction in Don Bosko and Komuna e Parisit, hindering the improvement of the infrastructure in these areas.

4.3.1 Accessing the Labour Market in Tirana: The Double Face of Informality

Involvement in economic activity was a significant concern for some interviewees as life in Tirana imposed on them new financial constraints. This subsection scrutinises the experiences of the interviewees who attempted to find jobs in Tirana, noting the main challenges they faced and the ways they overcame them. The interviewees make important points about accessing the labour market, especially navigating its informal nature in Albania. Labour market informality became tangible in two main ways. First, most Albanians found their jobs through informal connections (e.g., kinship, friends and acquaintances), as mentioned by the interviewees. Second, available jobs often lacked regular contracts and social insurance. Let us stop and analyse in depth these two points.

First, social networks, consisting mostly of relatives and friends, played a significant role in job finding. All the interviews show this pattern, although the types of connections mobilised and the types of the job found differed. Silvana's story is illustrative of this pattern:

> *I moved to Tirana after having found a job. It was a job in the public sector, not very well paid, but somehow more secure than the jobs in the private sector. It was made possible through my relatives in Tirana who themselves had found suitable employment in public administration and had many essential acquaintances.*

Unlike Silvana, who found a job in Tirana that was similar to what she had been doing in her city of origin, Arjana could not find a place as a teacher. However, through her friends' network, she managed to secure employment as a kindergarten educator.

> *I had been a teacher in Fier, and I knew that it would be hard to find a job as a teacher again. … After some months, I found a career as an educator in a private kindergarten through some friends of ours who had moved to Tirana earlier than us. It's not a teaching position, but to be honest, it pays better than being a teacher; thus, I don't care.*

It is worth noting that what Arjana emphasised about her new job in Tirana was its salary. It shows that she placed more importance on the income than the type of position she could get, whether it was the same as the job she had held pre-migration. Money holds more significant value in times of economic insecurity such as those experienced in post-1991 capitalist Albanian society.

Some women had been unemployed before migrating or had withdrawn from the labour market to care for their children and home and/or because their previous employment structures (e.g., factories and cooperatives) had shut down. Most women, such as Eleni, Drita, Eli and Manjola, had long relied mostly on the income sent by their husbands for their livelihood. Their spouses' return from abroad and the mounting financial costs of living in Tirana, meant families needed more revenue which, in turn, made it necessary for the women to enter the labour market. (Re) entering the labour market in Tirana was difficult for these women as long-time unemployment decreases women's human capital and makes them less competitive in the labour market (Kligman, 1996; Miluka, 2009). To increase their employment opportunities, the internal migrant women resorted to their available resources and adapted to the demands of the labour market in Tirana. These resources included skill they had learned without necessarily expecting to make money out of them, such as Eleni's handcrafting and tailoring:

> *I had been without a regular job since 1993 when my husband left for Greece. When we moved to Tirana, I stayed at home for three months, and then I found a job in a small tailoring business. I have this gift for tailoring...*

The interviewees fit in with the broader context of the Albanian labour market where jobs, for both migrants and non-migrants, are found primarily through kinships and other connections, not through institutional channels (Danaj, 2014). However, we may assume that non-migrants possessed more connections than later arrivals to Tirana and thus held an advantage in finding better jobs.

Second, the interviews show that most of the jobs available for internal migrants existed in the informal sector of the labour market. In this context, it is hard to ascertain what constituted a better job; for some, it was the security of a regular contract and paid insurance, and for others, it was a good salary. For instance, Arjana and Eleni state that a fair wage compensated for the lack of social insurance and formal contracts, despite the possible consequences for their health and their future pension once they retired.

> *Arjana: Social insurance contributions are paid only by some employees at work. We [the others] are not declared [to the social insurance institutions], … but the salary is excellent.*

> *Eleni: Now I have a good salary, but I have no insurances.*

In other cases, the absence of social insurances was accompanied by low salaries. Consequently, these jobs were precarious, putting women in vulnerable, unstable financial situations. As Eleni says about her first jobs after migrating to Tirana:

> *Ah, in the beginning, they told us that we would have a good salary with social insurance and contracts and everything. Then, nothing of that sort happened. I changed several tailoring shops. The pay was meagre, without contracts, without insurance, nothing. Only some people were insured, most of them were family members of the owner, while the others were not. … Then, I stayed one and a half year at home with no job at all until I found a career as a babysitter.*

In 2012, Eleni, as well as Drita, worked as domestic care workers. In their interviews, they mention that they found these jobs through their networks of friends and acquaintances who were also internal migrants working as domestic care workers. More details about this emerging informal sector of the labour market in Tirana follow in the next section.

4.3.2 Domestic Care Workers and Complex Care Chains in Tirana

Within the growing city of Tirana, a new sector has emerged: that of domestic care workers, who take care of cooking, cleaning, caring and the full range of activities that domestic work and care may involve. The experiences of domestic care workers illustrate the informality of the labour market highlighted in the previous section: accessing the informal labour market through informal channels. Domestic care work was often underpaid, undertaken with no contract or social insurance coverage to speak of. Furthermore, those who took on these positions often found them through informal channels, i.e., through friends and family, or other internal migrants. These cases also provide insight into the complexity of chare chains and their intersection with migration. This section first discusses some elements of domestic care workers' jobs and then the complex care chains connecting these domestic care workers and other migrant women.

The emerging sector of domestic care work in Tirana employs mostly internal migrant women, as illustrated by Eleni:

I found a job as a babysitter, where I am still working. … This is the second family where I have worked. … Another domestic worker, an e ardhur [internal migrant] too, helped me to find this second family, so I wouldn't stay jobless after my first child grew up.

Most domestic workers have no contracts but only verbal arrangements setting the work schedule, holidays and other rules of the job. Eleni states that she worked informally, with no contract and no social insurance but had a good relationship with her employer:

I have had a good understanding with both families where I have worked. I am like this. I want to have good relations with people. They are highly educated people, very gentle, so if they need me to stay some extra hours, I remain, and if I need to take a day or some hours off, they allow me.

She also adds that she had a good salary, and her employers gave her three weeks of paid summer holidays. Moreover, at the time of the interview, Eleni says that her current employers were using their connections to help her daughter find a job. The connections of Eleni's employer thus became a resource for her daughter, too. Bonizzoni (2016) analyses the mobilisation of informal employers as a resource to solve various issues in the case of migrant domestic workers in Italy. Such collaboration with informal employers arises in the case of international migrants employed as domestic workers in Greece (Chap. 5). So far, there are no official or unofficial data on the sector of domestic workers in Albania, leaving this area almost entirely unexplored.

Consequently, the working conditions, salary and participation in the social insurance scheme for domestic workers are almost unknown (Ekonomi & Arqimandriti, 2012). Nevertheless, the interviews show that many women are involved in such work and help each other by sharing practical information, such as average salaries in the sector and families needing domestic workers or babysitters. Possibly, internal migrants adopt a form of solidarity in the face of the constraints of the labour market in Tirana.

As mentioned, and according to the interviews, it is mostly 'të ardhura' (internal migrant), women who perform these jobs. These internal migrants working as domestic workers are involved in various care chains (Hochschild, 2000), which brings us to the second part of this section: the complex care chains to which these internal migrant women belong. The first care chain configuration consists of internal migrant workers who take on the caregiver role for other women in Tirana engaged in the paid, productive workforce.

Drita: I work two hours per day. I work as a cleaning lady for a young couple here in Don Bosko. He is a lawyer, and she works at XX [a mobile corporation]. I clean, and sometimes I go grocery shopping for them.

Eleni: Where I work now, we are three women, one in charge of the cooking, me as a babysitter, and another woman who does the cleaning and all. We are all from different cities; one of them is from the south, the other from the north, and the employers are from the town of Fier. I don't know what they do exactly, but they are quite wealthy, they both run their business, and as long as they give me a good salary, I am thrilled.

Eleni reveals a second element of the care chains: the female employers may be migrants themselves. Thus, internal migrant women work for other internal migrant women. These care chains account for the relationship of inequality between women, as Parreñas (2001) emphasises in the case of the international migration of domestic workers. Some women, in our case migrants and natives of Tirana, can enter productive work as they are able to hire other women—mostly less wealthy internal migrants—to take care of their household work and members. Furthermore, the internal migrants employed as domestic workers transfer their caregiver role to other family female members, as in the case of Drita, whose mother-in-law took care of her son when she started to work as a domestic worker.

And here is the third link of the care chain: intra-familial solidarity. The interviews with the women discussed in this chapter show that they sought support mostly from female relatives to perform their caregiving duties and allow them to enter productive work. For instance, Zhani migrated alone to Tirana as her daughters could do the housework. This was also the case for Drita, as mentioned, and Manjola, who says:

> I was working all day at the shop to put things in order and have a successful business. … My mom stayed with us during our first months in Tirana as someone had to take care of the children. There were no kindergartens in the neighbourhood at that time.

This quote again emphasises the significance of intra-familial solidarity—the support that mothers, mothers-in-law and daughters offer by taking over reproductive care work so that Manjola, Drita and Zhani could find employment or be self-employed and bring money home.

These women's cases reflect a set of complex care chains (further expanded in Chap. 5), but they are not only about migrant women's various experiences with their role as caregivers. What they also show, is that the post-1991 political and social upheaval did not result in new gender arrangements that replaced traditional gender roles: men do not take on the caregiver role; rather, women transfer these roles onto other female relatives or employees.

4.3.3 Relations in Extended Families: Shifting Toward a Nuclear Family Life

Research on internal migration (Çaro, 2011; Gjermeni, 2004) shows that internal migration in Albania is often followed by a shift from life in an extended family to the creation of a nuclear family. The interviews illustrated this pattern too. Internal migration was indeed accompanied by the nuclearisation of the family structure, which had far-reaching consequences for gender issues.

This nuclearisation affected different domains. First, the nuclear families within an extended family often still lived in a shared building (in the form of owned houses) but organised their physical space within the home into separate apartments. Drita and Eli, the two interviewees who lived in extended families before migrating to Tirana, describe this physical separation:

Drita: Within a year [of migrating to Tirana', the house was finished, and now we each [nuclear] family has our part of the house. This is what I wanted [laughs].

In this excerpt from Drita, *nuclear family* refers to a number of nuclear families: that of her parents-in-law; herself, her son and her husband (even if initially he was still in Greece); and her brother-in-law's family. In their new house in Tirana, each family lived in a separate apartment on each of the three floors. Drita adds that while in the village, she often dreamt of living alone with her husband and cooking what she wanted, watching some television or sleeping a little more in the morning. She states that she could not do these things while she was living with her in-laws as there was much work to do and only a small television in the dining room primarily 'reserved for the father-in-law'.

That brings us to a second point concerning this nuclearisation process. The physical separation of living spaces in Tirana affected a number of other aspects of life among nuclear families. Eli describes how the household economy was split, giving her more responsibility and power:

[In the big house,] I live with my children, my parents-in-law and the family of my brother-in-law. I live with my kids on the third floor, and the parents-in-law live on the first floor as they are old and cannot go up the stairs. … We live off the money my husband sends. … In the beginning, when we came here, it was my father-in-law that was managing the money. But over time, and especially after having built the three floors of the house and separated the floors into apartments [each for a nuclear family], we are managing money separately. … I feel relieved as I don't have to ask them [Eli's parents-in-law] for money…

This situation changed Eli's relations with her parents-in-law, and she felt more comfortable now that she did not need to ask them for money. Beyond not having to discuss money with her parents-in-law or other members of the extended family (e.g., sisters-in-law), Eli also shares that in living in an apartment with her children only, she could now cook whatever they wanted.

We eat quite often together with the parents-in-law, especially during lunch, but in the evening, we stay at our apartment, and I can eat and cook what my kids and I want. I like this. I can cook other things that the others [members of the extended family] don't like.

This example further illustrates that life in Tirana was organised differently than life in villages, focusing on the nuclear family rather than the extended family.

However—and that is the third aspect of the nuclearisation process raised in the interviews—these transformations that gave the women more power were negotiated and did not arise automatically. Eli describes her situation:

He [the husband] is the man; he has to know everything about what we do or if something has happened, how girls are doing in school and if they have had any problems. When he returns, it will be more comfortable. I will be relieved as I won't have to carry the responsibility for everything. If something happens, I won't have to give explanations to others; I will be responsible only to him. My daughter fell very ill once, and I wanted to take her to the hospital. The hospital is nearby, and I was terrified as I didn't know what to do to cure her. So, I told my parents-in-law that we had to bring her to the hospital, but my mother-in-

law kept saying that it was nothing, my daughter would be well soon, and we didn't need to spend a lot of money on the doctors. I didn't want to argue with them, so I called my husband and discussed it with him. He also agreed with me that we had to take her to the hospital, and he talked to his father, and we took a taxi and went to the hospital.

In this case, we see that Eli did not want to challenge openly the position of her parents-in-law but used another tactic to accomplish her goal. In this family, husbands were the ones who made serious decisions, and Eli mobilised this in her favour even though she was operating in an unfavourable context. Eli's experience shows how women display agency in the practices of everyday life (De Certeau, 1984) as Eli challenged the authority of her parents-in-law by instrumentalising the role of the husband. The following sections present similar situations when women used various tactics to negotiate gender roles.

As Gjermeni (2004) and Çaro (2011) report, this shift to nuclear families represents a change for women, giving them a 'sense of liberation', in the words of Çaro (2011, 113). The interviewees emphasised this very experience. Having separate apartments led to positive changes for Drita and Eli in their everyday lives.

4.3.4 *Negotiating Gender Roles and Relations Within the Nuclear Family*

Internal migration to Tirana has frequently triggered transformations in the gender roles between spouses. The economic situation in Tirana is a significant factor contributing to this redefinition of spouses' gender roles. Finding a job in Tirana is difficult for men and women and, as shown, primarily requires mobilising social networks. Additionally, the economic crises experienced by Albania since the late 2000s have hit specific sectors of the labour market harder than others, especially construction. These crises have limited the employment opportunities available to male migrants returning from Greece, who mostly work in this sector. This crisis had direct consequences for Drita and Eleni, whose husbands returned from Greece after working in the construction sector for many years. Once in Tirana, they continued to do the same work, as the construction sector was doing very well at first. However, the growing crisis in this sector changed things. Drita talk about how her husband:

came back [from Greece] five years ago, and he has been, working in construction. Now it is complicated to find jobs in construction, and he has to move a lot in the south or in the coastal areas where construction is continuing.

Eleni tells a similar story, and at the time of the interview, her husband had been unemployed for the past three years.

Now we live off my job. … We are living off my salary as a babysitter.

This new gendered family configuration with men unemployed or holding unstable jobs as in the case of Drita and women as breadwinners does not abruptly transform the spouses' share of productive and reproductive work. Eleni illustrates this:

He [Eleni's husband] had been working for so many years, and now he is sick. I cannot ask him to help me with the housework. He is depressed because of not having work. I can't add to this depression.

Eleni continues to perform both the breadwinner and the caregiver role. Other cases beyond Albania present the same configuration. For instance, Camille Schmoll (2006) reports that Tunisian circular migrant women work as traders and are their family's breadwinners through circular migration to Italy. Yet, they also continue to be in charge of the reproductive sphere. Despite 'the inverted roles in the productive sphere, migration does not generate significant ruptures in the family order' (Schmoll, 2006, 9).

However, Schmoll (2006) adds, women, do gain respect and legitimisation for their productive work. Eleni's experience illustrates a similar dynamic, although in her case, the respect that she receives comes mostly from her children:

Now that my husband is not working, it's me who brings the primary income in the house. … And the children often say, 'Fortunately, we have you because otherwise, we would have starved to death'. But I tell them it is because of your father that we are here, because he worked hard in Greece, and now he is sick. I don't want him to be hurt because of this situation.

However, this added respect for women's role as breadwinners, coupled with other financial constraints, lead to a crisis of masculinity, as Eleni's words indicate. In a study on poverty in Hungarian households, Fodor (2006, 15) finds that 'one of the major gender differences in the experience of poverty is that men often find themselves in a gender role crisis when they are too poor to function as successful breadwinners. Women, on the other hand, tend to feel their roles as caretakers intensified and thus avoid a conflict with (newly) hegemonic ideals of femininity'. Fodor (2006, 14) adds that women help their husbands by alleviating this role crisis and the 'gender shame' derived from it. Accordingly, Eleni recounts of how she protected her husband in front of their children who questioned his role as breadwinner.

Another final point worth analysing is how Eleni, conscious of the transformation of the gendered configurations within her family, attempted to preserve and not destabilise them. She chose to cope with the weakening of her husband's breadwinner role by not upsetting relations within the family. Such behaviours, as Kabeer (1999, 448) writes, 'reflect a certain degree of caution on the part of women—a strategic virtue in situations where they may have as much to lose from the disruption of social relationships, as they have to gain'. At the same time, women are conscious that gender relations within the family have changed.

4.4   Conclusion—Discussing the Findings

The women interviewed in this chapter are internal migrants in Albania. At their age, they have lived through both late communism and the succeeding post-communist period. They provide a vantage point for exploring the fissions in gender regimes unleashed by the collapse of communism and the new gender regimes that emerged during and following the aftermath. In this section, I highlight four main findings and compare and contrast them with the current research on gender and migration to find where they overlap and undermine each other and where my results depart in fundamental ways from recent contributions on the intersection of migration and gender.

First, the interviews show that migrating in any form is seen as a solution to the economic and social difficulties experienced at any given moment, particularly by the rural population, which accords with Çaro's (2011) findings on internal Albanian migration more specifically. However, the migratory response to difficult economic and social conditions is gendered: international migration is mostly considered to be a male affair, and internal migration is reserved for women. While the husband migrates abroad, the wife, children and other family members migrate internally. In this context, interviews show that families pick Tirana as their destination for multiple reasons: it offers the best economic, social and educational opportunities for internal migration, and it is the most feasible option for a family migration project, balancing the needs of all family members and offering support from already-established social networks in Tirana (as elaborated in the second main finding).

The interviews also show that migration is a household-wide decision, not an individual one, confirming the findings of extensive international research (Root & De Jong, 1991; Lauby & Stark 1988). However, these researches neglect to consider that household decisions regarding migration are gendered. Interestingly, both the migration decision-making process and the preparation for the move to Tirana assign different positions to women living in extended and nuclear families. Women in nuclear families have greater negotiation power in migration decisions and often lead the preparation for the move to Tirana. Whereas, the women in extended families lack this negotiating power.

Second, the internal migrant women interviewed in this chapter talk about how they rely heavily on the social network systems built during communism and how they expand and renegotiate those networks anew after communism. The interviewees give accounts of chain migration; people migrate to other cities where they have kinship or friendship networks, a feature of internal migration in Albania highlighted also by other studies (Çaro, 2011; Vullnetari, 2014). Internal migrant women have no choice but to rely on their kin and social relations in the absence of internal migration policies to facilitate free movement in the labour market, infrastructure and various services and in the context of a weak welfare state. While family and kinship networks appear to have the central role during the entire internal migration process by married women, these women create new social relations upon their arrival in Tirana. One such case is that of domestic care workers who create social networks with similar women to exchange information about job vacancies, average salaries and other matters. These new social networks evidence women's agency in adapting to their new social realities in the place of destination. This adaptation is illustrated by the informal professional network of internal migrants working as domestic workers. Such 'solidarity' networks of mutual support among migrant women are also prominent among Ukrainian female migrants working as domestic workers in Italy (Vianello, 2009). Schmoll (2006) also stresses how Tunisian migrant women use different types of solidarities throughout their migration process to Italy.

I now turn to my third main finding in this chapter on married internal migrant women: the transformation of the family structure and the new negotiations of gender relations. It is interesting to note that in many cases, internal migration parallels a nucleation process, in which extended families that used to live together in their place of origin, separate and live in nuclear families in individual apartments in the same building following their internal migration. The decline in extended families is not a recent, post-communist phenomenon in Albania. Contrary to the common belief, the number of nuclear families was already significant before the communist period and grew more after 1944, under the communist government's modernising policies (Kaser, 2014). Internal and international migration further contribute to this nucleation process, as shown by the few cases in this chapter. The nucleation of extended families seems to affect gender relations within the family, although it does not necessarily lead to a reorganising of gender hierarchies. The husband remains the head of the household, with the most decision-making power in the home. Nevertheless, the interviews show that women view nucleation as a positive change in their everyday lives. The physical separation in housing is followed by a reorganisation of economic responsibilities, giving women more power and driving new negotiations of gender relations within the extended household.

Gender relations within the nuclear household are also renegotiated. As shown, the nuclear family sometimes faces a crisis of masculinity. For instance, women discuss their husbands' d state after being laid off. Even while unemployed and out of the sphere of paid, productive work, men do not perform domestic work. Furthermore, when women become the primary breadwinners in the family, they still go to great pains to maintain the façade of the man being the head of the household in front of the children. New negotiations of gender relations within the family take place amid this destabilisation of gender roles. Paradoxically and despite evidence to the contrary, the women interviewed work to maintain and not disturb gender hierarchies neatly. No significant ruptures in the existing gender arrangements within households appear. This brings us to the matter of care chains in which some women pass on their caregiver role to other women.

Thus, in my fourth point, I discuss the issue of care work. The cases here confirm findings on the complex post-1991 dynamics of care in Albania for both children and ageing parents through intra-familial support and paid, employed care providers. Vullnetari and King (2016) explain that paid childcare providers in Tirana have increased in number, where domestic care workers may be Albanian internal female migrants as well as Filipina immigrants. The interviews in this chapter illustrate the entanglement of these complex care chains with migration. First, as in some of the cases discussed in this chapter, women's internal migration becomes possible as their care-giving duties are transferred to their parents or shifted around, passed on from mothers to daughters. The intra-familial care chain, or family solidarity, frees women to migrate. Second, women living in Tirana who enter the labour market employ internal migrants to take care of their children, ageing parents and domestic tasks.

Interestingly, the women who employ internal migrants as domestic care workers include both non-migrants and other internal migrants. In Chaps. 5 and 8, I develop further the dynamics of care for children and ageing parents and the intersections between internal and international migrant care workers. Third, as Hochschild (2000) investigates, the number of links in any care chain may vary. Internal migrant women transfer their mothering and caregiver roles to other female family members so they themselves can be employed by other women as domestic care workers. These cases illustrate the entanglement of multiple care chains with internal migration in the particular space of Tirana.

The 'marketisation of care' (Hochschild, 2000, 133) seems to have influenced the emergence of the informal sector of domestic workers in Tirana. The invisibility and informality of this new sector, which employs mostly internal migrants, does not help at all domestic care workers. They are stuck in a precarious job situation, lacking regular contracts and excluded from the social security scheme. This is a developing yet under-researched sector that demands future in-depth investigation.

References

Bonizzoni, P. (2016). The shifting boundaries of (un)documentedness: A gendered understanding of migrants' employment-based legalization pathways in Italy. *Ethnic and Racial Studies, 40*(10), 1643–1660.

Çaro, E. (2011). *From the village to the city: The adjustment process of internal migrants in Albania.* Rozenberg Publishers.

Danaj, E. (2014). Family in Albania as primary solidarity network. In R. Pichler (Ed.), *Legacy and change: Albanian transformation from multidisciplinary perspectives* (pp. 117–134). LIT Verlag.

Danaj, E., Plaku, A., Ekonomi, M., & Cavo, Z. (2008). *Unpaid care work - the invisible burden of women.* ASC and UNIFEM.

De Certeau, M. (1984). *The practice of everyday life.* University of California Press.

De Waal, C. (2005). *Albania today: A portrait of post-communist turbulence.* I.B. Tauris.

Ekonomi, M., & Arqimandriti, M. (2012). *Mapping Women's economic situation in Tirana, Vlora, Shkodra and Elbasan.* GADC.

Ekonomi, M., Danaj, E., Dakli, E., Gjermeni, E., Budowski, M., & Schweizer, M. (2004). *Gender perspectives in Albania.* INSTAT.

Fodor, E. (2006). A different type of gender gap: How women and men experience poverty. *East European Politics & Societies, 20*(1), 14–39. https://doi.org/10.1177/0888325405284248

Gal, S., & Kligman, G. (2000). *The politics of gender after socialism: A comparative - historical essay.* Princeton University Press.

Gjermeni, E. (2004). *Ardhja në Tiranë: Migrimi femëror në Shqipëri [Coming to Tirana: Female migration in Albania]*. Doctoral Dissertation (Unpublished).

Hochschild, A. R. (2000). Global care chains and emotional surplus value. In W. Hutton & A. Giddens (Eds.), *On the edge: Living with global capitalism* (pp. 130–146). Jonathan Cape.

Kabeer, N. (1999). Resources, agency, achievements: Reflections on the measurement of Women's Empowerement. *Development and Change, 30*, 435–464.

Kaser, K. (2014). Family and kinship in Albania: Continuities and discontinuities in turbulent times. In R. Pichler (Ed.), *Legacy and change: Albanian transformation from multidisciplinary perspectives* (pp. 97–116). LIT Verlag.

King, R., & Vullnetari, J. (2012). A population on the move: Migration and gender relations in Albania. *Cambridge Journal of Regions, Economy and Society, 5*, 207–220.

Kligman, G. (1996). Women and the negotiation of identity in post-communist Eastern Europe. In V. Bonnell (Ed.), *Identities in transition: Eastern Europe and Russia after the collapse of communism* (pp. 68–91). University of California.

Korovilas, J. (1999). The Albanian economy in transition: The role of remittances and pyramid investment schemes. *Post-Communist Economies, 11*(3), 399–415.

Lauby, J., & Stark, O. (1988). Individual Migration as a family strategy: Young women in the Philippines. *Population Studies, 42*(3), 473–486. https://doi.org/10.1080/0032472031000143596

Miluka, J. (2009). *Education, migration, and labour Markets in Albania: A gender perspective*. ProQuest LLC.

Musaraj, S. (2011). Tales from Albarado: The materiality of pyramid schemes in Postsocialist Albania. *Cultural Anthropology, 26*(1), 84–110.

Parreñas, R. S. (2001). *Servants of globalization: Women, migration and domestic work*. Stanford University Press.

Root, B. D., & De Jong, G. F. (1991). Family migration in a developing country. *Population Studies, 45*(2), 221–233.

Schmoll, C. (2006). *Moving "on their own"? Mobility strategies and social networks of migrant women from Maghreb in Italy*. IIIS Discussion Paper 154.

Social Research Center. (2004). *Early childhood care and development*. INSTAT and UNICEF.

Stahl, J. (2012). *Rent from the land. A political ecology of Postsocialist rural transformation*. Anthem Press.

Stark, O., & Bloom, D. E. (1985). The new economics of labour migration (NELM). *American Economic Review, 75*, 173–178.

Stark, O., & Taylor, J. E. (1991). Migration incentives, migration types: The role of relative deprivation. *The Economic Journal, 101*(408), 1163–1178.

UN Albania. (2004). *Albania common country assessment*. UN Albania.

Vaiou, D. (2002). In the interstices of the City: Albanian women in Athens. *Espaces, Populations, Societes, 3*, 373–385.

Vianello, F. A. (2009). *Migrando Sole; Legami transnazionali tra Ucraina e Italia*. FrancoAngeli.

Vullnetari, J. (2009). Women and migration in Albania: A view from the village. *International Migration, 50*(5), 169–188.

Vullnetari, J. (2012). *Albania on the move: Links between internal and international migration*. Amsterdam University Press.

Vullnetari, J. (2014). Internal migration in Albania. In R. Pichler (Ed.), *Legacy and change: Albanian transformation from multidisciplinary perspectives* (pp. 47–67). LIT Verlag.

Vullnetari, J., & King, R. (2016). 'Washing men's feet': Gender care and migration in Albania during and after communism. *Gender Place & Culture, 23*(2), 198–215. https://doi.org/10.1080/0966369X.2015.1013447

Open Access This chapter is licensed under the terms of the Creative Commons Attribution 4.0 International License (http://creativecommons.org/licenses/by/4.0/), which permits use, sharing, adaptation, distribution and reproduction in any medium or format, as long as you give appropriate credit to the original author(s) and the source, provide a link to the Creative Commons license and indicate if changes were made.

The images or other third party material in this chapter are included in the chapter's Creative Commons license, unless indicated otherwise in a credit line to the material. If material is not included in the chapter's Creative Commons license and your intended use is not permitted by statutory regulation or exceeds the permitted use, you will need to obtain permission directly from the copyright holder.

Chapter 5
Returned, Yet Still Not Back: The 'Status Paradox' of International Female Migrants Returning to Albania

This chapter focuses on the group of women who migrated internationally. To distinguish them from the women who migrated abroad for education (Chap. 7) but to avoid limiting this group to only women who migrated for work purposes, I refer to them as *international migrant women*. Common to this whole group is that after their international migration experience, they returned to Tirana instead of their hometowns. The majority of the women in this group are married, while two are single, and two are divorced. The women who form the core of this chapter are the following:

Marta is a 34-year-old woman from the city of Fier. Marta had finished high school in 1996, but she had been unable to find paid employment since graduating. So in 1998, she migrated to Switzerland with a fake passport to join her husband, who had migrated there earlier through illegalised ways, and together they requested asylum. During her stay in Switzerland, Marta was exclusively in charge of housework, as well as caring for her husband and her daughter. In 2006, Marta returned to Tirana with her child after failing to obtain asylum in Switzerland. She divorced from her husband a few years later. Her ex-husband still lived in Europe as an illegalised migrant, though he had left Switzerland. In 2012, Marta was self-employed and lived with her daughter in a rented apartment in Don Bosko.

Migena is a 40-year-old woman from the city of Pogradec. She lost her job in the early 1990s and migrated to Greece with her fiancée in 1994. She migrated on a regular, short-term visa but could not obtain a long-term residence permit and stayed there in an illegalised way. In Greece, Migena worked mostly as a babysitter and domestic worker, while her husband was in construction. After failing to regularise her long-term residence in Greece, she returned to Tirana in 2002. In 2012, at the time of the interview, she lived with her husband and her child in an owned

Parts of this chapter have been published in the article (Danaj, 2019). The material "Albanian women's experience of migration to Greece & Italy: a gender analysis, in Gender & Development, Vol 27/1" is adapted by the publisher with the permission of Oxfam, Oxfam House, John Smith Drive, Cowley, Oxford OX4 2JY UK www.oxfam.org.uk. Oxfam does not necessarily endorse any text or activities that accompany the materials, nor has it approved the adapted text.

© The Author(s) 2022

E. Danaj, *Women, Migration and Gendered Experiences*, IMISCOE Research Series, https://doi.org/10.1007/978-3-030-92092-0_5

apartment in Don Bosko and worked for a private bank in Tirana. Migena has a master's in economics.

Elona is 39 years old, comes from Lezhë and first migrated to Greece in 1994. Upon graduating from high school in 1991, Elona started work in the flour mill factory in Lezhë. She left Albania on an illegally purchased visa to follow her boyfriend to Greece. During her stay in Greece, Elona first worked as a domestic and care worker in a village, while her partner worked as an agriculture worker. Later, she was employed in a bakery shop. In 2004, Elona and her husband returned to Tirana, where they ran a bakery together. She lived with her husband and children in an owned apartment in Komuna e Parisit.

Juli is 38 years old and from a village near the town of Tepelenë. In 1993, she had already graduated from high school and was jobless. That year, she migrated to Greece with her husband, his brothers and their wives, crossing the border through hidden pathways in the mountains. In Greece, Juli worked as a domestic and care worker, a cleaning lady for various businesses and later as a hairdresser. While in Greece, she divorced from her husband, who remained there. She returned from Greece after 13 years and lived with her child in Tirana, in an owned apartment in Komuna e Parisit, where she ran a hairdressing shop. Juli had obtained Greek citizenship.

Denisa is 45 years old and from the city of Gjirokastër. In Gjirokastër, Denisa worked in local government but lost her job in the mid-1990s. In 1996, she migrated to Greece on her own, while her family (husband and child) stayed in Gjirokastër. Denisa migrated in a legalised way based on her Greek ethnicity. She engaged in a pendular movement between Greece and Albania, working as a domestic worker in a tourist village 6 or 7 months a year and returning to Gjirokastër for the rest of the year. In 2007, Denisa, her husband, child and parents-in-law moved to Tirana. In 2009, she emigrated again. This time she went to the United Kingdom with her child, while her husband and his parents stayed in Tirana. She returned to Tirana in 2012, while her child remained in the UK. She and her child have obtained Greek citizenship. She has a university degree, and in 2012, she worked in Tirana as a domestic worker and lived with her husband and parents-in-law in an owned apartment in Komuna e Parisit.

Arlinda is 46 years old and from Kukës. She earned a professional high school diploma and worked as a nurse in the regional hospital in Kukës. With her family, husband and two children, she migrated first to Tirana in 1999, where she was unable to find a stable job, and then to Greece in 2002. A Greek employer vouched for them, making their migration possible. In Greece, she worked as a domestic worker and cleaning lady. In 2007, she returned to Tirana with her husband, while her children remained in Greece to study. In 2012, she had retired from the labour market and lived with her husband in an owned apartment in Don Bosko, while her children lived abroad.

Mimoza is 44 years old and from Saranda, the southernmost city in Albania. She left for Greece in 1993 with her husband, who belonged to the Greek minority population in the country. In 1993, Mimoza had graduated from university and worked as an accountant in a factory in her native town. She and her husband migrated with regular visas. In Greece, she worked as a cleaning lady at several places, as well as a domestic worker. Mimoza, her husband and her child returned to Tirana in 2004. In 2012, she ran a dry-cleaning business with her husband. Mimoza, her husband and her two children obtained Greek citizenship through her husband's Greek ethnicity. Their family lived in an owned apartment in Komuna e Parisit.

Irida is 36 years old and from a village near the city of Shkodër. In the early 1990s, she migrated with her parents and brothers to the city of Shkoder. In 2000, Irida migrated to Italy on a regular work visa after graduating from the University of Shkodër and not finding a job. In Italy, she first worked as a domestic worker, then as a hairdresser and undertook professional training in body care and hairdressing. She returned to Albania in 2007. In 2012, she was single and lived alone in Tirana in a small, owned apartment in Komuna e Parisit, where she ran a beauty centre. Irida had a long-term Italian residency permit.

Rovena is 42 years old and from Fier. She migrated to Greece in 1993, after graduating from the professional nursing high school of Vlora and working as a nurse in Fier. Rovena migrated alone with an illegally purchased short term visa, while her parents stayed in Fier. In Greece, she worked first as a domestic care worker and later as a nurse. She returned to Tirana 14 years later. In 2012, Rovena worked as a nurse in a hospital in Tirana, was single and lived alone in an owned apartment in Don Bosko. At the time of this research, Rovena had a Greek long-term residency permit.

5.1 Leaving Albania

5.1.1 Multiple Motivations to Migrate Abroad

These women's migration projects were triggered by diverse, entangled factors. First, challenging economic situations and loss of employment appear to be significant motivations for migrating abroad. Family and kinship relations were essential drivers in the decision-making process to migrate, as highlighted by Julie Vullnetari (2012). Decision-making involved negotiation with household members, rather than being individual choice. Family is the institution where the interplay of gendered power relations is most substantial. The interviews showed that these women held different positions in this interplay. Some women have the same say as their husbands or parents in the decision to migrate. Others bypassed their parents when they posed an obstacle. Some used the support of their family to be able to migrate and achieve their objectives. Others were relegated to a marginalised role in the interplay of the gendered power relations behind the decision-making process.

Focussing further on the specific reasons these women decided to migrate abroad, the interviews discussed here show that diverse and entangled factors trigger these women's migration projects. Irida, aged 36, had first migrated with her family from a rural area to a city when she was 16 years old:

> *The economic situation of my family was awful. We had moved from the villages to the city of Shkodër, but we were in even a worse position as my parents were unemployed, and we lived on only the salary of my brother.*

In Irida's story, the first internal move did not translate into a bettering of the family's financial situation, which in turn prompted an international movement. This time, Irida migrated on her own to Italy, at the age of 24. International migration is often the next step when internal migration does not accomplish the expected outcomes. A second research participant, Rovena, recounted a similar story: she had left on her own for Greece early in the 1990s, when she was aged 23, because of her family's difficult economic situation. But unlike Irida, when Rovena decided to immigrate to Greece, she made no mention of her plans to her parents.

> *I told them nothing about my plans … I told them a few days before that I was leaving. I was 23 at that time. My poor mother, she was terrified by this idea. She was expecting me to marry and settle down, and now I was telling her that I was going away alone. I told them only once I had prepared everything, as otherwise, it could have been harder … Me, that young, a young woman migrating alone, how terrifying that would have been for my parents if they knew beforehand. Them not knowing about my plans was more comfortable for them and me.*

Rovena's account showed how her migration on her own to Greece transgresses the pre- vailing gender expectations regarding marriage and settling down. So they would not impede her plans to migrate, Rovena sidestepped her parents and prepared to relocate with the support of her cousins who had already settled in Greece. Irida, in contrast, said she had taken the decision together with her parents and brother, in a consensual way due to their shared financial hardship.

Irida and Rovena stand out as young, single women who migrated internationally intending to help their families who faced financial hardship. Cases like this do not usually figure in the common imaginary of Albanian migration, but they do exist. Economic migration and the need to earn a living for a family is associated with masculinity, but these roles are not exclusive to men; single women, too, migrate to support their parents financially, as shown by these interviews. In the challenging economic and social conditions of post-1991 Albania, the decision to relocate seems to have been inevitable for many women, as well as men.

Loss of employment also provides the primary motivation for Denisa, who has Greek ancestry and whose parents had already moved to Greece in the early 1990s. She says that after she lost her job, and her husband downgraded in a less paid position, the family's economic conditions deteriorated. Denisa migrated on her own to find work in Greece, while her husband, daughter and parents-in-law stayed in their native city of Gjirokastër. Similarly, Migena was pushed to migrate to Greece and work as a babysitter after losing her job after the fall of the communist regime:

> *I was unemployed. … I had worked at an elementary school, but some of the positions were eliminated. I was young and a new hire, so I was also among the firsts to be dismissed. … In Pogradec, there were no opportunities in sight.*

Nevertheless, even though the acute economic crisis was often what motivated these women to migrate, it was by no means the exclusive reason to do so. There were a multitude of other reasons that pushed women to migrate. Mimoza left for Greece in 1993, at the age of 25, as a young married woman. Her husband was a *minoritar* – a member of a Greek ethnic minority in Albania. They benefited from this as they were able to get visas to enter Greece quickly and obtain residency permits and even Greek citizenship, which was quite impossible for those of Albanian ethnicity (Vullnetari, 2012). Mimoza pointed out that the couple were not in bad economic shape at the time. She says:

> *I was working in a factory as an accountant. It was a good job, an excellent job indeed for the time. However, at the beginning of the 1990s, things changed, and what was previously considered a fantastic job, it wasn't anymore. … Many of the people we knew, friends, relatives, they had already migrated or were planning to leave for Greece. I think it was more this environment that pushed us to go, rather than proper financial reasons.*

According to Mimoza, more than 'proper financial reasons', it was the environment of widespread migration around them that pushed her to leave with her husband. As many Albanians migrated to Greece post-1991 and international migration became a mass phenomenon, this reinforced the sense of relative deprivation. In relative deprivation, individuals and households migrate not only and necessarily to maximise their total income but also to improve their position in comparison to other reference groups (Stark & Taylor, 1991). Mimoza's case reveals the influence of what is called the 'culture of migration' (Massey et al., 1993, 452) that emerges within sending areas. In essence, migration drives further migration because people's values and cultural views shift as it becomes commonplace, increasing the probability of future migration.

Another reason for migration is to use it as a strategy to escape constraining gender expectations in women's home towns. Elona reported:

> *I didn't want my family to know about my boyfriend as a lot of troubles would come of it. I didn't know if they would agree, so we preferred to keep it a secret. If they knew they could separate us or force me to marry someone else or not … I didn't know what could happen if they knew … When he told me that he was thinking of leaving for Greece, I immediately felt that I should go with him. So we could solve our situations with our families. If we left together, they wouldn't be able to oppose us anymore but would have to accept our relationship.*

Migration thus becomes a means of salvation not only from economic hardship but also from gender constraints, particularly the fear of arranged marriage. John Davies (2009) and Adriana Baban (2003) both highlight the persistence of arranged marriage in contemporary Albania, and John Davies (2009) reports young women leaving the country through the practice of elopement due to fear of arranged marriages by their families and the social control of their kin. Arranged marriage continues to be present in Albania, especially in rural areas, where gender norms and expectations for young women and girls are more prevalent and have a higher restraining power.

For other women, like Juli, their decision to migrate was also tied to the geographical imaginaries related to migration, as highlighted in the previous chapter. Julie speaks about the motivations that pushed her to migrate:

> *The idea that I had about 'abroad' was lovely. ... The young female dancers on TV, the clothes that other emigrants were sending back to the village ... I am not sure I was thinking about ... making money. It was more about some beautiful dresses and hair models [laughs] and this kind of things that I had in mind before leaving for Greece.*

Juli's story illustrates how the migratory project is shaped by imaginaries, fuelled both by earlier migration (e.g., the clothes sent to Greece by earlier migrants) and by television. The glittering imaginary of abroad seen on tv, influences the migration processes of young Albanians, as explained in the previous chapter and by Mai (2004) in her research on the role of television in Albanian migration. Television depicts an imaginary of 'alternative lifestyles' (Mai, 2004, 18), 'beautiful clothes and hair models' that, for Juli, contrast with her life in her hometown.

Finally, I present the case of Marta, a case which centres on family unification: she migrated to join her husband, who had previously migrated abroad. Women's migration for family reunification purposes is a well-known aspect of late 1990s Albanian migration (King & Vullnetari, 2012). Marta says that she had no specific reason or desire to migrate, but her husband insisted that she join him:

> *My husband was telling me on the phone that we needed to be together as couples do and also that he needed me there as migrant couples in Switzerland received better treatment.*

Moreover, she adds that her father told her that by migrating, she could help her parents who were in a difficult financial situation. Marta found herself in a situation where both her parents were pushing her to relocate so that she could support them and her husband was pressing her to migrate so that he could improve his own living conditions.

To conclude, the cases analysed in this section fit into the framework of those studies that approach migration as a process that cannot be explained by a single motivation (Vianello, 2009; Kihato, 2009; Riaño & Baghdadi, 2007). These cases demonstrate, instead, that the migration process is triggered by various entangled reasons and factors related to both the sending and the receiving countries.

5.1.2   Crossing Country Borders – The Role of Social Networks

Before going into the details of the role of social networks and the different migratory regimes undertaken by these women, I need to talk about the factors that push these women to migrate abroad and not to Tirana, like the women in Chap. 4 did. Expanding on the roots of this migratory choice gives us further insights that can deepen our analysis of the role of social networks and migratory regimes themselves. The interviews reveal two primary reasons that drive the decisions to migrate internationally instead of internally. First, Greece and Italy appear to offer better financial opportunities and living conditions than Tirana. These are quite significant reasons for those women migrating for economic reasons, as their statements indicate:

> *Denisa: In Greece, I could work and earn money, which was impossible in Albania.*

Rovena: I had no [economic] opportunities in Albania, for sure.

Irida: I just wanted to go to another country and work there to help my family and myself.

International migration to Greece and Italy was and is considered to be a solution for improving complicated economic situations and can be considered to be a diversifying and risk-minimising strategy for households.

However, not everyone has the same opportunities to migrate internationally, which brings us to the second main reason that determines the type of migration these women undertook: the feasibility of the migration project. Almost all women in this group state that they chose an international destination where they had family or friendship or acquaintance networks that were already settled in these places. Similarly to internal migration (Chap. 4), international migration appears to be achievable due largely to pre-existing connections. Various types of social networks—friends and acquaintances, family and parents—are mobilised to enable the move to Greece, Italy and Switzerland by taking care of logistical details for crossing the border, accommodations and employment, for instance. In Albanian migration, social networks stand as critical factors determining the decision to migrate and the choice of destination (Vullnetari, 2007).

In the following, I go into more detail about the role of these social networks in leaving Albania and entering other countries. I elaborate on the legalised and illegalised ways used by these women to cross national borders. Boyd and Grieco (2003) and Wihtol de Wenden (2015) say that the decision to undertake a migratory project is not the same as being allowed to exit or to enter a particular country. Nation-states enact policies and affected the gendered international migration process through constraining the crossing of borders. This also arises in the context of Albanian migration. As mentioned in Chap. 3, since 1993, Albanian citizens have not been legally impeded by their own government from freely leaving the country. Still, to enter another country, they have to comply with its generally strict migration policies and visa regime. When confronted with the impossibility of entering some countries with regular documents, many Albanian migrants made the choice to enter through illegalised ways, especially to two neighbouring countries, Italy and Greece.[1] Migrating through illegalised ways (e.g., mountainous paths to Greece and speedboats to Italy) has further shaped perceptions of Albanian migration as a male affair, with men seen as more likely to take on these risks.

The women in this chapter had mixed experiences of crossing borders and entering other countries. Social networks play roles in all the interviewees' narratives, so let us first consider the cases of those women who migrated through legalised ways. Irida immigrated to Italy on a regular work visa after her close kin succeeded in finding her a job with a standard contract and an employer available to sign

---

[1] As explained by Vullnetari (2012), Italy and Greece should not only be considered from a geographical perspective - Macedonia is another neighbouring country, for example, but sees less migration from Albanians. Italy and Greece, besides being neighbour countries, they are, above all, members of the European Union and thus more developed economically compared to the other neighbouring countries of Albania.

documents for her. Denisa and Mimoza migrated to Greece on legal documents due to the *minoritar* status of their mother and husband, respectively. *Minoritars* have advantages over Albanian citizens of Albanian ethnicity in getting entry visas to Greece and obtaining residency permits and even Greek citizenship (these are quite impossible for those of Albanian ethnicity) (Vullnetari, 2007, 2012). Again, kin networks lend significant support. Denisa took on the project of working in Greece after her parents' migration as she could find a job through their acquaintances. Mimoza says that her husband's relatives waited for them at the Albanian-Greek border checkpoint and took them to Athens, where they provided accommodations for several months. Also, Arlinda and Migena migrated to Greece on regular visas made possible by their kinship and networks of acquaintances. For Migena, her father's acquaintances enabled her to get a short-term visa and find a job as a babysitter in Cavalla:

> *My father had established some networks with Greek business people who were coming to Korçë and Pogradec, and he found me this opportunity in the city of Cavalla in Greece. They also helped him with my visa.*

Similarly, Arlinda recounts that her husband's relatives who migrated earlier to Greece facilitated their move to the same country, helping them secure the documents necessary for a visa and getting jobs for Arlinda and her husband. Parents, relatives and acquaintances networks are mobilised in the cases of the interviewed women migrating through legalised ways.

Other women have migrated through various illegalised ways, according to their interviews. Juli speaks about her migration to Greece:

> *We left together, my husband and I and his brothers with their wives. … We went illegally through some border villages near Gjirokastër. … What I remember is that we could not carry much with us as we had to walk and climb a lot. … We took with us some* byrek *and a little milk and water; that is what I remember. A villager from the near villages who was often doing this thing for money took us near the Greek border. I have no idea where it was exactly. If you told me now to go and find the place, I could not. I think I was very much shocked by what was happening. The only thing I remember is that we had to walk and hide in some woods for a couple of days until we met the guy who would pick us up on the Greek side.*

Juli states that people from their village who had already migrated to Greece helped them contact local smugglers who knew how to navigate the illegalised mountain paths. These smugglers from nearby villages in Gjirokastër also collaborated with residents of the Greek border villages. Juli adds that during her family's first months in Greece, their co-villagers who had already settled in the country hosted them.

Fake documents and illegally purchased visas are among the other ways these migrant women used to leave Albania. Elona, Rovena and Marta left with illegally obtained visas or counterfeit passports. As Elona says in her interview, she migrated 2 years after her boyfriend left via the mountain border. With the money he sent, she arranged for a Greek visa through a visa dealer in Tirana. Elona had to handle all the paper and preparation in Albania by herself as her family did not know about her plans:

The hardest part was to go to Tirana for the visa because I had to go in secret, without tell-
ing my family.

Likewise, Rovena says that she had to deal with the passport and visa issues herself. She had no passport at the time, so she had to apply for a new one, which was not accessible due to bureaucracy. To pay the bribes for the passport and to buy a Greek visa through a dealer in Tirana, she borrowed money from her cousins in Greece. Marta says that she migrated with a fake passport arranged by friends of her husband. She flew to Switzerland through Italy and was *'frightened to hell'* as she had never left her hometown, and now she was travelling with a fake passport, and *'anything could happen'* if the border police caught her. In addition to the support of partners, husbands and relatives, the networks mobilised to migrate through illegalised ways included co-villagers who had previously migrated and networks of visa dealers and migrant smugglers.

Juli, Elona, Rovena and Marta show that young women also migrate through unsafe, illegalised channels. Although these women might be fewer than men, the image of the Albanian man who migrates through risky, clandestine ways does not provide a complete picture of Albanian migration. Women, too, have undertaken risky migration projects. In the context of Eastern European migration, Andrijasevic (2003, 256) explains that the persistent absence of women from visual depictions of border-crossing emerges in a discursive scenario that figures migrant women not as protagonists but as characters endowed with little or no agency. In sum, Albanian women who cross borders through risky, illegalised ways remain under-researched and under-documented but certainly exist.

5.2   Life Abroad

In this section, I analyse some particular elements of the economic experiences of the interviewed women while they were abroad. Their experiences abroad are far more expansive than I can present in this section. Due to space constraints and the need to focus on their post-return experiences, here I concentrate particularly on their economic activity that builds a unique, yet still familiar story of these women's bargaining power and capacity to adapt to new social realities. The section also highlights some migration trajectories mostly invisible in the broader picture of Albanian women's migration, such as pendular migration.

5.2.1   *Filling the Care Gap in Greece and Italy*

Greece and Italy seemed to be the most accessible countries for finding a job for Albanian migrants, at least until the mid-2000s when the first signs of the global economic crisis emerged. While these two countries' proximity to Albania accounts for a significant portion of their attractiveness to Albanian migrants, equally important is the structure of each country's labour market and welfare systems that allowed Albanian migrants, men and women, to find jobs. In particular, Southern European countries were attractive to migrants due to their extended informal sector (Vaiou, 2002; Vianello, 2009; Lyberaki, 2008), employing men mostly in the construction industry and women in the domestic industry. Accordingly, most women discussed in this chapter work in the domestic sector, and this subsection focuses on domestic care workers.

Three main points regarding these migrant women's economic activities in the destination countries emerge from the interviews. First, Albanian female migrants appear to fill a care gap in Italy and Greece, often allowing Italian and Greek women to engage in productive work. For instance, Elona's first job in a Greek village consisted of performing housework and babysitting. She says that her employers were a Greek couple who owned the property where she and her boyfriend worked. After Elona's arrival, the wife, who previously dealt primarily with the household, started to work with the husband, in the production and sales of olive oil and jam. The arrival of Elona enables her Greek female employer to shift from housework and care duties to business-related tasks. Rovena also says that she cared for an old couple, allowing their daughter to return to her productive employment as a full-time lawyer in a law firm. After the mother's illness, and prior to Rovena's arrival, her Greek employer had shifted to part-time work while caring for her parents, but Rovena's position allowed her to resume her full-time job. Migela describes a similar situation:

> *I was working as a babysitter for a young couple in Cavalla. I was also teaching some English to the two little children I was caring for. ... They were quite a wealthy couple; they were both dentists and had their own dental cabinet. The wife had stayed at home for some time as the children were little and only one year apart. ... They were looking for a young, educated woman to care for the children regularly. She [the female employer] returned to her job, and they both were at work all day long.*

These cases illustrate and confirm the results of other research showing that most women migrants in Greece have filled the care gap left by women entering the domain of productive work. In the context of 'rudimentary' (Lyberaki, 2008, 18) or 'insufficient and inadequate' (Vianello, 2009, 187) welfare states in Greece and Italy, the productive work of Greek and Italian women created a vacuum of domestic and care work that needed to be covered. Migrant women then served as the *'deae ex machina'* ('just-in-time goddesses' Lyberaki (2008, 12) performing domestic and care work and facilitating Greek women's entry into the productive sector.

A second common point is the interviewees' engagement in informal jobs and bargaining within their informal economic activities. Almost all report working informally. Sometimes, they combined informal and formal employment to comply with the procedures for their legalised stay in Greece, as Arlinda highlights:

> *I was doing two jobs, one with a regular contract and the other informally so that I could get some extra cash that we were just putting aside.*

The interviewees explained how they bargained with their informal employers for their work status with the intention of increasing their financial resources:

> *Mimoza: Both jobs [Mimoza was doing] were unreported as it was better for the employers and me. They were paying me directly in cash.*

Similar setups arise in the accounts of other interviewees, such as Rovena, Denisa, Elona and Migena, who state that they were paid in cash for their informal work. Rovena reports that working informally suited both her and her employers best, as they did not have to pay taxes. She knew that if she were a declared employee, then her salary would be lower, hence this mutual arrangement. As Vaiou (2002) elaborates, the informal sector of southern European countries attracted migrants, and the state allowed the informal sector to fill the care gap. Working in the black created arrangements that allowed migrant women to save more money, but such an arrangement became necessary as many of these women were illegalised migrants Lyberaki (2008, 16). In this context, female domestic care workers emerge as active subjects in a continuous process of bargaining.

However, informal domestic care work also entails many disadvantages, starting with the fact that it is not regulated by national labour codes. Women involved in this sector are deprived of any labour right and access to the social security scheme (Michel, 2011) and may be subjected to low pay and long working hours. Furthermore, the lack of regular contracts and payment of social insurance contributions keeps them from applying for residency cards. For instance, Migena explains how the process of getting a residency card was complicated for her. She had mostly worked informally and did not have the social security stamps necessary to apply for a residency card. As explained by Hatziprokopiou (2006), these stamps prove that employers have registered the employee and paid contributions to the employee's social insurance. Consequently, only applicants who were formally employed could obtain residency permits, and the women, who mostly worked in the black, were disadvantaged in this regard (Hatziprokopiou, 2006). For example, in 1998, in the first regularisation programme conducted by the Greek government, Albanian migrant women made up only 17 per cent of the Albanian migrants who applied (Vullnetari, 2012, 71).

Moreover, Migena, Juli and Elona report that often they had to work extra hours and sometimes had no days off during the week. Nevertheless, they also mention that they needed this extra work to save money and gain their employers' much-needed support to find other jobs or 'even a respectable and not expensive paediatrician' as Elona says. Employers also helped migrants manage administrative issues and the difficult application procedures for obtaining residency permits. For instance, Rovena reports:

> *It was necessary to have a good relationship with her [Rovena's employer]. She and her husband knew a lot of people, and I needed their help if I wanted to apply for my residency card. ... I didn't need holidays back then but rather a good relationship with my employers.... After her [Rovena's employer] parents passed away, she and her husband helped me find another job, as a nurse, with a regular contract and paid insurance. ... If it weren't for them, I could never have gotten a residency permit. ... I still keep regular contact with her [Rovena's employer] and her daughter.*

Rovena's case illustrates the bargaining between working informally (with no labour rights and social security) and the advantages of the employers' support in a wide range of issues. Female migrants and their employers have a negotiating relationship. Bonizzoni (2016) has analysed similar accounts of combining informal with formal jobs as a means to make money and obtain legalised residency permits among migrant women in Italy.

The third main point concerns the low-skilled jobs these women take on, such as positions as domestic care workers, cleaners in offices and factory workers. These jobs are beneath the educational level of most women interviewed. Among the interviewees, the lowest school degree obtained by the women was a high school diploma, while four women had university diplomas. Nevertheless, these jobs appear sufficient to grow their financial capital. The figure of the skilled migrant working in low-skilled jobs that is beneath their educational or professional qualifications appears in much of the literature on migration (Morokvasic and de Tinguy, 1993; Gërmenji & Gëdeshi, 2008; Kofman et al., 2000). Parreñas (2001) refers to this situation as contradictory class mobility, as women undertake less socially valued but better paid jobs for a reduced social status and improved financial situation.

Similarly, Vaiou (2002) reports that migrant women in Greece worked in positions that were below their skill level and education but were better paid than jobs in Albania. This contradictory situation of Albanian migrants may also be described by what Nieswand (2011, 3) calls the 'status paradox of migration': migrants' qualifications are undervalued in their destination countries, and they accept lower, informal positions, resulting in a loss of social status in the receiving country. At the same time, amid growing global economic inequalities, the higher financial capital in the receiving state gives migrants higher status in their native countries as they send remittances or when they return. Similarly, the women at the focus of this research bargain with their qualifications by doing informal, low-skilled jobs and bargain with their informal employers to increase their financial capital. Their experiences fit within the frame of the status paradox of migration, as is further observed upon their return to Tirana.

5.2.2 *Engaging in Pendular Migration Practices*

As already shown in this research and other studies (Vullnetari 2012; Olsson 2014) Albanian women are much more present in the migration process than represented the imaginary of post-1991 Albanian migration. As seen in this study, Albanian migrant women not only migrate internally and internationally but also engaged in multiple migration trajectories, combining internal and international migration, and even circular migration practices, as illustrated in the case of Denisa. In fact, Denisa embraces pendular migration, travelling back and forth and spending several months a year in her country of origin as defined by Fokkema, Cela and Witter (2016, 142). Though this is one particular case, I think it is important to go more in-depth into her experience and highlight some moments of her migration process.

Denisa reports that she worked with several families, Greek and foreigners, in a coastal area, where many people owned summer houses. With her primary objective being to save money, she says that she was fortunate as she could live for free at her parents' home. She worked only from March to October, and during the winter, she stayed with her husband, child and parents-in-law in Gjirokastër:

> *That was an excellent solution as I could work [in Greece]. On the other side [in Albania], I was spending about half of the year with my family, so that they would not forget me [laughs]. ... I could take care of my daughter... and I was quite serene as the money was not lacking, and I knew I had a job, quite a fruitful career indeed.*

Pendular migration is appropriate for Denisa as it allows her to be the primary breadwinner in her family but also continue, as much as possible, to perform her role of mother and caregiver. Denisa's accords with research on pendular migration by women who move without settling in the destination country. Pendular migration with a neighbouring country is related to constructed gender roles positioning women as caregivers (Morokvasic, 2003; Dahinden, 2010) and allows them to combine productive work and caring for the family (Dahinden, 2010; Morokvasic, 2003) and to be a 'transnational mother' (Hondagneu-Sotelo & Avila, 1997, 549). This position of transnational motherhood is possible as Denisa's parents-in-law have stepped into her caregiver role by taking care of her child while she is away. In most cases, this transference of the caregiver role enables migration by mothers, as highlighted in the findings of Hondagneu-Sotelo and Avila (1997) and Olwig (1999). The case of Denisa, a breadwinner in Greece and caregiver in Albania, exemplifies the notion of transnational double presence (Morokvasic, 2008; Vianello, 2013) when women have a presence in two different realities, the public and the private sphere, paid labour and the family, the destination and the sending country. Through pendular migration, Denisa thus can combine the breadwinner and the maternal role.

Denisa can move between Albanian and Greece as she has obtained a residency permit based on her mother's Greek ethnicity. With a Greek residency permit and later a Greek passport, Denisa can quickly move between the two countries and construct a transnational double presence. Doing so would be very difficult if she were staying illegally or if she were in the process of legalising her stay in Greece. This would entail a very complicated process of re-entering Greece, as shown by Olsson's (2014) work with migrant women in Greece. Women without a legalised presence in Greece cannot go back and forth between Greece and Albania due to the physical difficulties and high costs of the illegalised border crossing (Olsson, 2014). The case of Denisa is particular as most of her migration project follows a pendular trajectory. Nevertheless, other circular trajectories may be observed among returnee women upon their return to Albania, as shown in the next section.

5.3   Return from Abroad and Life in Tirana

In this final sub-chapter, I elaborate on the participants' reasons for returning to Albania and settling in Tirana rather than their hometowns. The interviewed women returned before the economic crisis of the late 2000s in Greece and Italy. Thus, unlike other recent research on return migration in Albania, the financial crisis in the destination country does not appear among the reasons for return.

These international migrant's relocation back to Albania was not a straightforward case of return migration. Rather, it was also entailed a move to a new settlement – Tirana, the capital of the country – which makes it challenging to define their movement as a simple return. In the interviews, it became clear that the women's double move is a complex process precipitated by various reasons which pushed these women to return from international migration and move to Tirana rather than their native cities or villages. The variety of significant reasons that drove the women to leave their destination countries and return to Albania included: the desire to invest in their native land; the need to care for family members; and the impossibility of staying legally in the destination country. They preferred Tirana over their other hometowns as it offered better opportunities for entrepreneurship, employment, and their children's education.

5.3.1   Returning from Abroad

Let us first observe the reasons behind the decision of these migrants to leave Greece, Italy and Switzerland and return to Albania. First, based on the interviews, some women returned to Tirana to invest in their own business. As Elona says:

> We [Elona and her husband] were planning our return. … We wanted to start our business … We thought that probably it was time to return and begin this adventure of ours.

Returning to invest in Tirana was also the reason that motivated Mimoza's return. She says that she returned to Albania with her family (husband and children) as she and her husband had saved some money and wanted to invest in Albania. They now run a dry-cleaning shop. Juli also says that she returned to invest in her own business as a hairdresser, knowing that she could have more opportunities in Albania than Greece. Plus, Juli needed support to care for her child. Juli says that after divorcing from her husband, she lived in Greece with her child and had difficulty working and caring for the child at the same time, as she had no other support. In Albania, she could more easily devise a solution to her child care and housework problem: she could hire a domestic worker. Juli's return project is thus supported by the opportunity she had in Albania to transfer her caregiver role to a domestic worker who required a lower salary than a domestic worker in Greece would require. The migration trajectories presented here are linked to women's constructed roles as caregivers. Irida, reasons for returning are double-edged too: she wanted to invest in her own business and also care for her parents. Irida adds that she needed to build a successful business to continue to help her parents in Shkodër financially and at the same time, be closer to them.

That brings us to the women's second main reason for returning from abroad: caring for family members. In addition to Irida, Rovena and Denisa also mention this reason as one of their motivations in their interviews. Gender affects the return project as caring for relatives (in this case, parents), is considered women's responsibility. Following Sri Tharan (2010), being close to an ageing parent is often a main motivation driving migrant women to return to their native countries. Rovena clearly states that her main reason for returning to Albania was to take care for her parents because they were quite old. Sine Tirana is close to Fier, where her parents lived, she visit them almost every weekend to check on her parents' needs. Similarly, Denisa reports that after an additional migration trajectory to England, she has returned to Albania to take care of her parents-in-law:

> And I came back last August. ... My parents-in-law are quite old now. They have more health issues. It is now a time when they need more care and attention. They need me here now.

In the case of Denisa, having Greek citizenship serves as significant capital, facilitating her various migration trajectories.

Here, we come to the third motivation for returning to Albania: obtaining (or failing to obtain) legal residency permits or passport. Similar results are noted in other research on Albanian return migration (e.g. Mai & Paladini, 2013; Gemi, 2015; Kopliku, 2016). Marta recounts that she returned to Albania with her child because of the impossibility of obtaining legal residency in Switzerland:

> My husband moved to another European country illegally. We could not obtain the residency permits, so we had to leave Switzerland.

Arlinda says that it was difficult and expensive to continue the process for the regularisation of the documents for all the family members, so Arlinda and her husband decided to return. At the same time, their children remained in Greece with student documents. Similarly, Migena and her husband returned to Tirana because she could not succeed in regularising her residency permit. She had worked informally, as mentioned in Sect. 6.2.2, and was unable to get a Greek residency card. She adds:

> The situation in Albania [in 2002] was not as bad as during the 1990s, which made our return not that painful. ... In Tirana, we could do a master's to complete our education and find a good job, an office job. ... There seemed to be many opportunities as a lot of Greek banks and companies were already established in Tirana. ... We thought it could be easy for us to find a job in these companies as we knew Greek and English very well.

In 2012, Migena worked for a Greek-owned bank. Her statement illustrates the complexity of the motivations to return and the difficulty in determining clearly, in some cases, whether the return is voluntary. On the one hand, these women have to face the constraining conditions of being an illegalised domestic worker migrant in Greece. While, on the other hand, there is the attraction of working in a better, more prestigious job in Albania.

In contrast, migrants with long-term residency permits and passports often return to Albania to open businesses, find jobs in their professions or stay close to their families. These migrants are somewhat secure in their standing as they can quickly leave Albania again if the need arises. Rovena presents a typical case. She returned to Albania after obtaining a ten-year residency permit in Greece that allows her to move again to Greece if she wanted. Similar, Juli decided to return after securing legal documents in Greece so that, as she says, 'in case of disappointment in Albania', she could return to Greece or leave for another country. Irida and Mimoza narrate familiar stories: they have returned with 'the reassurance', as they say, of moving again if their return does not work. Possessing so-called 'regular papers' is considered to be a 'safety valve' for many Albanians (Mai and Paladini 2013, 50). Becoming a citizen of the European Union (or a Schengen area) country is regarded as the most valuable status as then migrants can return to Albania, but also leave it quickly if they wish.

5.3.2 Return by Moving to a New Destination, Tirana

These women's return entails a double move, as it also includes their relocation to a new city, Tirana, instead of their hometowns. The conceptualisation of return migration as part of a broader migration process, as a movement to another place in which the migrant has to re-adjust, becomes concrete (and literal) for most women discussed in this chapter. They return to their country and a new destination. Here, I focus on their reasons for choosing to go to Tirana rather than returning to their hometowns. In the interviews, the women indicate that they moved to Tirana due to the significant opportunities the city offers compared to their hometowns, particularly with regards to investment, employment and children's education. Let us examine their reasons for moving to Tirana in more detail.

First, they consider Tirana to offer more opportunities for setting up businesses. For instance, Juli says she knew that a low demand made it not worthwhile to open a business in her native Tepelenë, whereas Tirana was a growing, developing city:

> *My cousins [in Tepelene and Tirana] had told me not to attempt to open my parukeri [beauty salon] in Tepelenë as it would soon fail. People are leaving Tepelenë, and you see, Tirana is growing every day, and there are so many women and girls here who go to beauty salons.*

For Juli, moving to Tirana was not a matter of luck, but a deliberate, informed decision based on her social relations in Albania. That fits with Cassarino's (2004) and Ley and Kobayashi's (2009) emphasis on preparedness as a significant pattern of return migration; return is thus anticipated, and transnational connections contribute to the preparation phase, as mentioned by Juli. Irida too shares that she knew that she could build a more successful business in Tirana *'because people in Tirana are in a better financial situation so they can spend more money on beauty care'*. Mimoza also says that they decided to come to Tirana as *'it is only in Tirana that you can invest well, as there are more opportunities.'* She also adds that Tirana has the best schools. Second, Migena and Rovena say that they decided to move to Tirana to find good jobs that better match their education and skills. As a growing city with numerous private, state, and international institutions, Tirana appears to offer more employment opportunities than the women's towns of origin, Pogradec and Fier, respectively.

Rovena highlights the third reason for moving to Tirana: she also returned to Tirana as she wanted to continue to live independently. After so many years spent apart from her family and relatives, it would be challenging to have them 'all-around', she says. Boccagni and Decimo (2013) explain that migrants' increased personal autonomy or the individualisation of migrants may create social tensions between them and their families and communities in their hometowns. Similarly, Irida moved to Tirana not only for the business opportunities but also for the ability to live on her own and be near her parents at the same time. In this context, Tirana emerges as a 'middle way' between living abroad and in one's hometown. This locus allows one to be closer to one's parents while preserving some of the autonomy constructed through international migration.

Marta's case is a bit different. She moved to Tirana instead of her native Fier as her parents-in-law had moved to Tirana while she was abroad. Following a patrilocal family structure in which wives move into the house of the husband and the parents-in-law (Kaser, 2014), Marta returned to Tirana to live with her in-laws.

5.3.3   *Manifesting the Entrepreneurial Spirit*

Economic reasons and investing in Albania are among the main reasons for returning from abroad for some of the women in this chapter. In this section, I expand more on their entrepreneurship experience as this experience involves specific gender patterns. Most women interviewed here exhibited a clear entrepreneurial spirit, much more visible upon their return to Tirana, challenging the dominant post-communist configuration of gender relations: entrepreneurship for men and domesticity for women (Heyns, 1995). The cases examined in this section challenge these cultural, gendered expectations and highlight the tactics and strategies mobilised by these returnees to succeed in their entrepreneurship efforts. Interviewed women in this section mobilise three types of resources upon their return to Tirana: social networks, know-how (e.g., their new skills, work experience, and language), and financial resources.

Elona, Juli, Mimoza and Irida saw investing in their own businesses as their main reason for returning to Tirana. Elona says that when she and her husband returned from Greece, they knew that they wanted to open a bakery as she had worked in a bakery for many years and knew *'how to do things'*. Investing their savings and know-how gained while abroad seems to be a common strategy for some returning migrants, both couples and women alone.

Mimoza's story is similar to Elona's. Using their savings and the know-how they had acquired in Greece, Mimoza and her husband had planned to open something '*of their own*' in Tirana. They decided to open a dry-cleaning shop. Juli and Irida returned from abroad, one divorced and the other single, with the wish to establish hairdressing and beauty centres. They had both explored the possibilities of opening businesses through preliminary contacts with their relatives and friends living in Albania. They, too, made use of their savings and professional knowledge they had acquired abroad. It appears that they actively participated in the process of migration by gaining professional expertise with the aim of opening up better opportunities for their lives and work. As found by other researchers (Kopliku, 2016), family businesses are common investments for returning migrants. Service businesses dominate among return migrants' entrepreneurship initiatives as they offer good self-employment opportunities, are more affordable financially and are less risky (Kopliku, 2016).

Let us turn now to their concrete entrepreneurship experiences, particularly the process of registering a business, doing paperwork and following bureaucratic procedures. Juli and Irida report significant bureaucratic difficulties while trying to start their respective businesses.

> *Irida: You cannot imagine the time I spent going from one office to another to obtain documents and for other procedures. … It was impossible to sign the rental contract as the owners said that they could not trust me, where my money was coming from. … Sometimes similar doubts were being raised even in state offices. Sometimes my brother came with me. It was easier to have him with me as they did not consider me to be an unaccompanied young woman anymore.*

Irida using the tactic of bringing her brother along to overcome the discrimination and constraints imposed on her as a woman.

Juli, for her part, says that she '*had screamed louder than a man*' with the team building her beauty centre as they were not taking her seriously and delaying the works. She adds that what she '*hated*' most was the oft-asked question: '*Why does not your husband come to deal with this*'? She heard it while she was handling the needed documents to get a licence to open her business and to register in various tax offices.

> *I got so angry sometimes; it's unbelievable. … I was at the tax office for some registration, all this stuff, you know. And I was just dragged from one desk to another, unbelievable. … I was talking angrily mostly to myself, you know, as I didn't know whom to shout to. And one of the ladies working there came close to me and said to me, with a low voice, you know, 'Why doesn't your husband come to deal with this? … It's easier for a man to deal with "office issues". … My God, at that moment, I just went crazy, and I thought, 'No more smiling and politeness. I'm just gone yell at everyone here. Otherwise, it's in vain'.*

Juli also says she often faced mistrust when she claimed that it was her project and her own money:

> *I needed some documents at the Labour Office, and I was explaining all my story and everything… The employees at the office there started to ask me 'Oh, that's so good your husband is giving you the money to open the* parukeri'*. And I said, 'No, it is my own money. I am divorced'. You cannot imagine the look in their eyes, and the smiling, you know what that smile that meant 'Yeah, yeah, as if we believe you'. The worst of thing is that you feel angry and humiliated at the same time, as I had been breaking my back working so many years to*

save this money, and now instead of some support [for investing], I face a wall because I don't have a husband. … I'm offering people a job, but this is not important; the important thing is that I don't have a husband. … Oh, I just get angry now that I'm talking to you. … Do you hear my voice? [Laughs] I've practiced to make it sound like this, raucous, smoking has helped me a little [laughs]. … I need such a voice so that I can sound like a man [laughs loudly].

Unlike Irida, who brings her brother along while dealing with the procedures to open her business, Juli uses the tactic of adopting a masculine behaviour, or yelling with a raucous voice, as she says. Gender influences the process of establishing a business, putting women in an unfavourable situation compared to men not only in informal relations but also in state institutions, whose laws and strategies presumably promote gender equality. Statistics (INSTAT, 2016) show that women made up 31.3% of entrepreneurs in 2015. However, the majority of these enterprises are small enterprises (1–4 employees). That means that despite the growth indicators of women entrepreneurs, their businesses may face the risk of stagnation or even failure in a short or medium term.

Moreover, almost half (43 per cent) of the female-owned or -administrated enterprises are concentrated in Tirana. Albania had no state policy or programme promoting female entrepreneurship until the Action Plan for Women Entrepreneurs 2014–2020 was drafted in 2014. In an analysis of women's entrepreneurship in Albania, Beqo and Gehrels (2014) recount the difficulties women entrepreneurs face in Albania. Discrimination against women occurs during the process of opening a business, navigating the bureaucracy and handling financial issues. Women have more difficulty getting bank loans than men as they own less property. In this context, Juli and Irida say they used their savings from abroad to open their businesses in Tirana. Although investing in their own companies was not initially a part of their migration plan, the investment opportunities in Tirana were among their reasons for returning. Their savings in Greece and Italy took an added value in Albania, where labour and start-up costs are cheaper, and they could envision opening a business.

Mimoza and Elona did not report any gender-related difficulty during the initial phases of establishing businesses as they largely passed this task to their husbands. As Elona illustrates:

Altin went to the notary offices and the license office and everything. I went there only to sign. Why lose all that time when nobody would listen to me but him anyway? I had so many other things to do with the preparation of the venue and so on.

Mimoza and Elona overcome gender constraints merely by avoiding them, which is a tactic adopted by them in an unfavourable context. They anticipate, as Elona states, that *'nobody would listen'* to them, so they shift the task to the male figure. Like Irida, who uses her brother, Mimoza and Elona appoint their husbands to handle the unfavourable gendered environment of undertaking business procedures. Similarly, Beqo and Gehrels (2014) report that in the absence of fair treatment for women, women entrepreneurs often find a male figure to help them move forward the process of opening a business.

I end this section with the case of Marta, which is somewhat different from that of the other women. She returns not with the aim of investing in her own business but as she was unable to regularise her stay in Switzerland. Marta was a housewife throughout her stay abroad, but she learned tailoring from the daughter of her Albanian neighbours while in Switzerland. Almost a year after her return to Tirana, she started a small, informal tailoring business:

> *That [tailoring business] was significant to me. First of all, as I could finally have my work and have some income but also as I got to know other women and interact with them. I was tired of staying at home all the time, doing housework and watching TV.*

She adds that her husband's family was not very happy with this decision and action on her part, as according to them, she needed to care for the child, and the family did not need money. Marta's husband helped her financially at the beginning after she explained to him that the space for the tailoring business was in the same building where they lived. It was also a private space, not visible to the public, where she could also bring their daughter and care for her.

Marta engaged in twofold negotiations. To open this business, she had to assure her husband and his family that she would continue to care for their daughter and that the space where she worked was private. This twofold negotiation reassured her husband and his family that the traditional gender roles, Marta as the domestic caregiver and her husband as a breadwinner, would continue. The negotiation process for Marta as she attempted to open her small business took place in the family sphere. Her shop was an informal one, and she did not attempt to register it or seek a permit. It was more an extension of her domestic space and a way for her to earn some income and establish connections with other women. As in Eleni's case in Chap. 4, we see here how women's skills take on a new value in the post-socialist market environment and how women mobilise these skills to increase their income (Gal and Kligman 2000) and their connections, as in the case of Marta.

At the time of the interview, Marta had shifted from the informal status to that of registered self-employed worker. She continued to work as a tailor and lived alone with her daughter after divorcing from her husband, who was then living abroad. She recounts that her parents and the connections she had made through tailoring helped her overcome the challenges of the divorce and formalise her business.

5.3.4 Tirana as a Space of Entangled Care Chains

Here, the focus goes to the negotiations and tactics these women undertake in their role as caregivers. Most interviewees stress this particular element, so it is worthy of further development. As mentioned above, the possibility of transferring the caregiver role to another woman gave Juli one reason for returning to Albania. Other interviewees also shed light on the complex care chains among migrant women. Let us look at the care chain configurations brought out by the women discussed in this chapter.

In a first care chain configuration, the returned international migrant woman hires an internal migrant woman as a caregiver. Juli says:

> *Now that I have my beauty salon, I spend most of the day working there. This is what I have to do if I want this to continue. … My family lives in Tepelenë, and here in Tirana I'm alone with my son, so I hired a woman who is also from Tepelenë. She is a lovely person, and she cooks and cleans. She practically does everything in the house until I return from work.*

Juli's case involves a complex care chain in which internal migrants work as domestic workers for return migrants who are engaged in productive work. This also indicates a status paradox of migration: in Greece, Juli worked as a domestic worker, and now as a returnee, she employs an internal migrant to take on her care work. Mimoza also claims to have hired two internal migrants to work primarily in the house but also in the shop if she needs support. These two internal migrants are from poor, rural families, and Mimoza tries to help them as much as possible, as she was aided when first came to Greece. Migrant women who once required work and support in a new place are now in a position to give work and support to other migrant women.

A second configuration is illustrated by Denisa, who previously worked as a domestic care worker in Greece as well. Returned from international migration, Denisa still finds employment as a domestic worker for a wealthy family that migrated to Tirana from southern Albania. We see here a configuration that is the opposite of the one above but that again intertwines internal and international migration trajectories. Denisa says:

> *I have a very relaxed work schedule. I need to go to work only during the mornings, do all the housework, pay the bills, electricity and water, shop for the groceries or anything else they ask me for, cook, leave everything ready for the family when they return from their jobs. … It is very appropriate for me as I have the rest of the day for me and my family [husband and parents-in-law].*

Denisa's case not only illustrates a particular care chain: a return international migrant working as a domestic worker for an internal migrant; her case also demonstrates the family solidarity configuration of care as she takes care of her parents-in-law.

The third and final type of care chain on display here is the intra-familial care chain. We saw earlier that when Denisa migrated to Greece, her parents-in-law took on her caregiver role. Next, Denisa returned from abroad principally to care for her parents-in-law, who were getting old and needed closer care and support. Likewise, Migena says that both her parents, who lived only a few minutes away, helped her, transporting her child to school and doing cooking and shopping. As Vullnetari and King (2016) highlight, there is an intersection of mutual care within the family: grandparents take care of the grandchildren but later will rely on the care of their children. These cases show how complex the care chains configurations are and how the place migrant women occupy in these configurations may vary by the migration phase.

5.3.5 *Circular, Return and Remigration Projects: What's Next?*

From the interviews, I draw three main points concerning the returnees' future migratory plans. Some express no wish to migrate again, while others articulate a strong desire to do so. Yet others, primarily those possessing residency permits from other countries, do not exclude the possibility of migrating again and engage in circular migration with their destination countries.

Arlinda and Migena say they do not plan to emigrate again. Arlinda reports that she has already settled well in Tirana, and her children visit her and her husband often, so she has no particular reasons to think about migrating again. It appears that Arlinda's primary motivations for migration—her financial situation and her children's education—have been satisfied, and no other reason pushes her to reconsider the option of migration. Likewise, Migena reports that she worked in Greece for a long time and did not want to do 'those kinds of a job' again.

Caring for one's parents is another reason that prevents plans for long-term international migration. Denisa, for example, says that her daughter lives in the UK, so *'the biggest issue is solved'*. She adds that she lives in Tirana with her husband and parents-in-law, who *'need more care now than before'*. Similarly, Rovena states she cannot leave Albania as long as her parents are alive as she could not bear to leave them alone at this age. However, she adds that later, she could quickly return to Greece. Caring for family members again emerges as a significant gendered factor informing the migration project. Additionally, Rovena says that she visits Greece regularly with a long-term residency permit. Possessing the long-term residency permit allows her to both care for her parents and maintain her networks and contacts in Greece.

Here, we come to the second topic in this section: returnees who engage in circular migration trajectories and transnational experiences. This activity is made possible by the fact that they possess regular residency documents in their host countries. For example, Irida says she maintains her relations in Italy and goes there a couple of times a year to keep up with new fashion trends and hairstyles and products. She adds that she does not want to cut all her ties with Italy and needs to renew her residency permit as *'one day it is possible that I return to Italy for good'*. Like Rovena, circular migration allows Irida to combine caring for and being closer to her parents while running her own business and maintaining her transnational ties with Italy. According to Mai and Paladini (2013), documented returnees—migrants with Italian citizenship or a permanent/long-term residency permit—return to Albania as they feel that they have completed their migratory experience but still maintain structural links with Italy. In this case, Irida's circular migration is enabled by her Italian legal documents and driven by her need to advance in her new profession.

Furthermore, the cases of Irida and Rovena confirm Black and King's (2004, 80) claim that return migrants 'continue to value the professional contacts and other social networks they have made abroad after their return, and indeed in many cases continue to travel overseas'. In research on return migration to the city of Shkodra, Kopliku (2016, 112) contends that distinguishing the permanent returnee from the transnational migrant can be difficult as often migrants organise their lives between their home and host countries. Having regular papers from another country serves as capital. It allows return migrants to make more flexible plans, knowing that, unlike other Albanian citizens, they can leave Albania at any time. None of the women who possess these documents expresses any concrete wish to migrate again but leave the possibility open.

A third point arises in connection to Marta, who is the only returnee to express a wish to emigrate again openly. Marta says that she would like to migrate due to her daughter and the pressure she feels as a divorced mother:

> *My work is going well, and I have many clients, but I am not happy here. My parents are in Fier, and here [in Tirana] I am alone with my daughter. It's not easy for a woman alone with her child, especially when you are divorced. … I always have this feeling that people know that I am divorced. Someplace else could be better. We would be on our own, and in western countries, they support you when you are a divorced woman with a child. … I don't want my daughter to be raised here. I'm trying to gather some information where I could migrate so that I don't have to migrate illegally or with fake documents as I did before. Now I have my daughter, and I have to think about her first. I've heard that the American lottery seems to be a good idea. … I would like to leave together with my daughter so that she could go to better schools … and not go through my experiences.*

Interestingly, Marta's professional and economic situation is not the primary motivation pushing her to migrate again. Instead, it is the gendered prejudices and the social weight that she feels as a divorced mother, in addition to her desire to raise her daughter in a place other than Tirana, that drives her to consider migrating again. Paradoxically, Tirana—that is often imagined as modern and free city—exhibits many gendered prejudices towards a divorced mother, along with young women living on their own. Monika Kocaqi (2013), a researcher on violence against women, emphasises that divorced women in Albania are stigmatised more than men, primarily as marriage remains a highly socially accepted value. Similar accounts about divorced women are reported concerning Chinese (Lévy, 2015) and Turkish female emigrants (Erel, 2009). These analyses show how, in addition to economic reasons, escaping from prejudices and discriminatory contexts is another motivation for divorced women to migrate.

Additionally, Marta's interview reveals how the migratory project for her daughter and her is based on the contrast she draws between 'equal western countries' and Tirana. Against Tirana, Marta projects a less prejudicial and more supportive 'abroad'. Her case again illustrates how the 'imaginaries of equality' influence and shape women's migration-related projects and actions, as highlighted by Riano (2015) in the case of Latin American women's migration to Europe.

5.4   Conclusions—Discussing the Findings

This chapter analyses the experiences of female migrants who returned to Tirana after migrating to the neighbouring countries of Italy and Greece for other reasons other than education. In what follows, I start with the overall findings and then emphasise three particular findings.

Overall, the narratives of the women engaged in a double trajectory migration, returning from abroad by moving to a new destination such as Tirana, shed light on their multiple, overlapping reasons and motives for migration. In contrast to the dominant portrayal of Albanian international migration—men migrate to help their families economically, and women only join later through family reunification—the narratives in this chapter show that single and married women migrate on their own to support their families financially. When relocating internationally, women not only transgress the borders of accepted gender roles. Moreover, faced with the impossibility of entering other countries legally, they also cross the boundaries through illegalised ways, contradicting the dominant figure of Albanian migration that attributes risk and physical strength to masculinity.

In the interviews, we observe that the women's double move is a complex process precipitated by various reasons which pushed these women to return from international migration and move to Tirana rather than their native cities or villages. The participants' multiple principal reasons for leaving their destination countries and returning to Albania are the desire to invest in their native country, the need to care for family members and the impossibility of staying in a legalised way in the destination country. These women choose to move to Tirana over their other hometowns as it offers better opportunities for entrepreneurship initiatives, employment and their children's education. It also serves as an intermediate space that allows the women to be closer to their parents while preserving the autonomous life to which they became accustomed while abroad. Some of the cases analysed also show that their return is not permanent but may be part of circular migration trajectories and transnational relations with the destination country. These trends accord with the findings from other research on migration (Cassarino, 2004; Black & King, 2004; Dahinden, 2010; Ley & Kobayashi, 2009), particularly on Albanian migration (Mai & Paladini, 2013; Kopliku, 2016).

I now turn to the three particular inputs of this chapter. First, these women display bargaining power about their economic activity abroad and the status paradox of migration. Their bargaining power first emerges in their complex relations with their employers abroad that involve both dependency and support. Dependence arises from the absence of regular formal contracts and the need for regular work contracts for those wishing to legalise their status. Albanian migrant women depend on their employers for their salary, working hours and holidays. At the same time, (in)formal employers assist the migrants in overcoming administrative issues and creating new social networks. Sometimes, employers are mobilised as a resource in the process of residency permit legalisation, as also examined by Bonizzoni (2016) in the case of Italian immigration.

Moreover, informality is not a one-direction relation benefiting only the employers but also gives certain advantages to migrant women, who prefer to increase their income by not declaring it formally. They acquire negotiating and bargaining skills in their relationships with their international employers. All these bargaining processes account for the agency exhibited by women in their migration trajectories.

Second, the financial and knowledge resources these women earn while abroad indicates what Nieswand (2011) calls the status paradox of migration. During migration, female migrants often experience a devaluation of their social status, accepting jobs in low-income segments of the labour market, including the informal sector. Nevertheless, the acceptance of these positions involves a bargaining process. Upon returning to Tirana, these women's economic and social status increases again due to their financial capital and knowledge, which they often invest in enterprises, self-employment and employment. Confirming the status paradox of migration, they regain and even exceed the status they once left behind.

A further point in this change of status through migration can also be illustrated by the complex care chain configurations in which some interviewed women occupy various positions. The interviews show that these women take on care jobs in Greece and Italy to fill the care gap and allow other women to engage in productive work, putting themselves in an international care chain. After returning to Albania, some of these same women are still in care chain nets but now in the position of employer, not employee. To fill the care gap in Albania and engage in productive work, entrepreneurial initiatives in some cases, these same women hire internal migrants as domestic and care workers. We see here Tirana's embeddedness in entrenched global care chains. We also see how the women's regained status in Albania is based primarily on their increased financial capital. Care chain configurations frequently appear in this analysis, with women often situated in various positions within them at various points in their lives and migration trajectories.

In this chapter, we see that the state is a significant actor in women's migration process. Boyd and Grieco (2003) argue that the decision to undertake a migratory project is not the same as being allowed to exit or to enter a particular country. These constraints affect men and women differently, as frequently highlighted in this chapter. The policies of nation-states are the main actors in the gendered international migration process, limiting the pathways of border crossing. Likewise, internal labour and welfare policies influence the types of jobs male and female migrants may access, as shown in the case of migrants engaged in informal care work—a sector dominated by women.

However, there is more to consider about the role of the state, and I now turn to the core of this second input: the masculine state that returnees face upon their return to Albania. Whereas their experience abroad is characterised mostly by informal negotiations with employers, and only a few interactions with the state bureaucracy, the challenges they face back in Albania differ. Advancing a feminist theory of the late modernist state, Wendy Brown (1995) examines how gender marks state power. The masculine state described by Brown (1995) is diffuse, encountered and experienced by subjects on different scales. In deepening involvement with the government, women exchange dependency on individual men for regulation by contemporary institutions and processes of male domination (Brown, 1995, 173). Protection codes are significant technologies in which the state extends its masculine powers. For the returned female entrepreneurs discussed in this chapter, bureaucratic institutions are sites where the state becomes tangible. As shown, when encountering state institutions, women require protection by and from men. They employ tactics such as being accompanied by a male relative and embodying masculine behaviours. Paradoxically, they instrumentalise the same power whose dominance they attempt to challenge.

Third, and finally, most women interviewed exhibit a clear entrepreneurial spirit, much more visible upon their return to Tirana, challenging the dominant post-communist configuration of gender relations: entrepreneurship for men and domesticity for women (Heyns, 1995). In the post-communist space, women employees are associated with the public sector, which is perceived as more secure and relaxed, offering a fixed job schedule more appropriate for a caregiver—meaning a woman. Thus, entrepreneurship is mostly related to masculinity and the culturally defined masculine values, such as risk, competition, independence and aggression (Gal & Kligman, 2000; Meshcherkina, 2000). Entrepreneurship is a matter of cultural expectations. In this case, after the fall of communism, women are expected to withdraw to the domestic sphere or stay in the public sector, and men to undertake entrepreneurship initiatives in the new, capitalist private sector.

However, women show their capacities and entrepreneurial spirit in mobilising their skills and resources to achieve their initiatives, even when small scale (Gal & Kligman, 2000). In the same line, the analysis here shows that women continuously negotiate the spaces between public and private gender constraints to achieve their entrepreneurship initiatives. Not only do they handle structural and state masculinity, as mentioned, but they also challenge their relationships within the household, with their husbands and parents, by deciding to embark on entrepreneurial initiatives. The interviews also show that these women strategically activate their know-how and financial resources earned during migration to accomplish their entrepreneurial objectives.

References

Andrijasevic, R. (2003). The difference borders make: (Il)legality, migration and trafficking in Italy among eastern European women in prostitution. In S. Ahmed, A.-M. F. Claudia Castañeda, & M. Sheller (Eds.), *Uprootings/regroundings: questions of home and migration* (pp. 251–272). Berg.

Baban, A. (2003). *Domestic violence against women in Albania*. UNICEF.

Beqo, I., & Gehrels, S. A. (2014). Women entrepreneurship in developing countries: A European example. *Research in Hospitality Management, 4*(1 & 2), 97–104.

Black, R., & King, R. (2004). Editorial introduction: Migration, return and development in West Africa. *Population, Space and Place, 10*, 75–83.

Boccagni, P., & Decimo, F. (2013). Mapping social remittances. *Migration Letters, 10*(1), 1–10. https://doi.org/10.33182/ml.v10i1.106

Bonizzoni, P. (2016). The shifting boundaries of (un)documentedness: A gendered understanding of migrants' employment-based legalization pathways in Italy. *Ethnic and Racial Studies, 40*(10), 1643–1660.

Boyd, M., & Grieco, E. (2003). *Women and migration: Incorporating gender into international migration theory.* Migration Policy Centre.

Brown, W. (1995). *States of injury: Power and freedom in late modernity.* Princeton University Press.

Cassarino, J.-P. (2004). *Theorising return migration: A revisited conceptual approach to return migrants* (EUI Working Paper(2004/02)).

Dahinden, J. (2010). Cabaret dancers: "Settle down in order to stay mobile?" Bridging theoretical orientations within transnational migration studies. *Social Policies, 17*(3), 323–348.

Danaj, E. (2019). Albanian women's experiences of migration to Greece and Italy: A gender analysis. *Gender and Development, 27*(1), 139–156.

Davies, J. (2009). My name is not Natasha. In *How Albanian women in France use trafficking to overcome social exclusion (1998–2001).* Amsterdam University Press.

Erel, U. (2009). *Migrant women transforming citizenship: Life-stories from Britain and Germany.* Ashgate.

Fokkema, T., Cela, E., & Witter, Y. (2016). Pendular Migration of the older first generations in Europe: Misconceptions and nuances. In I. V. Horn & C. Schweppe (Eds.), *Transnational aging: Current insights and future challenges* (pp. 141–162). Routledge.

Gal, S., & Kligman, G. (2000). *The politics of gender after socialism: A comparative – Historical essay.* Princeton.

Gemi, E. (2015). *The incomplete trajectory of Albanian Migration in Greece.* Hellenic Foundation for European andForeign Policy (ELIAMEP).

Gërmenji, E. & Gëdeshi, I. (2008). Highly skilled migration from Albania: An assessment of current trends and the waysAhead. Brighton: Development Research Centre on Migration, Globalisation and Poverty, 34 pp.

Hatziprokopiou, P. (2006). Globalisation, migration and socio-economic change in contemporary Greece. In *Processes of social incorporation of Albanian and Bulgarian immigrants in Thessaloniki.* Amsterdam University Press.

Heyns, B. (1995). Review of Cinderella goes to market: Citizenship, gender, and Women's movements in East Central Europe by Barbara Einhorn. *American Journal of Sociology, 100*(5), 1343–1345.

Hondagneu-Sotelo, P., & Avila, E. (1997). "I'm here, but I'm there": The meanings of Latina transnational motherhood. *Gender and Society*, 548–571.

INSTAT. (2016). *Women and men in Albania.* INSTAT.

Kaser, K. (2014). Family and kinship in Albania: Continuities and discontinuities in turbulent times. In R. Pichler (Ed.), *Legacy and change: Albanian transformation from multidisciplinary perspectives* (pp. 97–116). LIT Verlag.

Kihato, C. W. (2009). *Migration.* University of South Africa.

King, R., & Vullnetari, J. (2012). A population on the move: Migration and gender relations in Albania. *Cambridge Journal of Regions, Economy and Society, 5*, 207–220.

Kocaqi, M. (2013, December 5). *Sexual harassment and other types of violence against women in Tirana* (E. Danaj, Interviewer).

Kofman, E., Phizacklea, A., Raghuram, P., & Sales, R. (2000). *Gender and international migration in Europe: Employment, welfare and politics.* Routledge.

Kopliku, B. (2016). Return migration in the Shkodra region – what's the next step? In M. Zbinden, J. Dahinden, & A. Efendic (Eds.), *Diversity of migration in South East Europe* (pp. 111–134). Peter Lang.

Lévy, F. (2015). *Entre contraintes et interstices, l'évolution des projets migratoires dans l'espace transnational: Une ethnographie des migrants de Chine du Nord à Paris.* EHESS.

Ley, D., & Kobayashi, A. (2009). Back to Hong Kong: Return migration or transnational sojourn? In D. Conway & R. B. Potter (Eds.), *Return migration of the next generations: 21st century transnational mobility* (pp. 119–138). Ashgate.

Lyberaki, A. (2008). 'Deae ex Machina': Migrant women, care work and women's employment in Greece. In *GreeSE Paper No 20*. Observatory.

Mai, N. (2004). 'Looking for a more modern life…': The role of Italian Television in the Albanian Migration to Italy. *Westminster Papers in Communication and Culture, 1*(1), 3–22.

Mai, N., & Paladini, C. (2013). Flexible circularities: Integration, return, and socio- economic instability within Albanian migration to Italy. In A. Triandafyllidou (Ed.), *Circular migration between Europe and its neighborhood, choice or necessity?* (pp. 42–67). Oxford University Press.

Massey, D. S., Arango, J., Hugo, G., Kouaouci, A., Pellegrino, A., & Taylor, J. E. (1993). Theories of international migration: A review and appraisal. *Population and Development Review, 19*(3), 431–466.

Meshcherkina, E. (2000). New Russian men: Masculinity regained. In S. Ashwin (Ed.), *Gender, state and Society in Soviet and Post-Soviet Russia* (pp. 105–117). Routledge.

Michel, S. (2011). Introduction. In *Women, migration and the work of care: The United States in comparative perspective* (Woodrow Wilson International Center for Scholars). USS: Occasional Paper Series, 1–5.

Morokvasic, M. (2003). Transnational mobility and gender: A view from post-wall Europe. In M. Morokvasic, U. Erel, & K. Shinozaki (Eds.), *Crossing borders and shifting boundaries* (pp. 101–136). Springer.

Morokvasic, M. (2008). *Crossing borders and shifting boundaries of belonging in Post-Wall Europe. A gender lens.* migrationonline.cz.

Morokvasic, M., & de Tinguy, A. (1993). Between east and west: A new migratory space. In M. Morokvasic & H. Rudolf (Eds.), *Bridging states and markets: International Migration in the early 1990s* (pp. 245–264). Sigma.

Nieswand, B. (2011). *Theorising transnational migration: The status paradox of migration.* Routledge.

Olsson, F. (2014). *Between dreams of papers and a house: Everyday life of Albanian undocumented migrant women in Greece.* University of Lund.

Olwig, K. F. (1999). Narratives of the children left behind: Home and identity in globalised Caribbean families. *Journal of Ethnic and Migration Studies, 25*(2), 267–284.

Parreñas, R. S. (2001). *Servants of globalization: Women, migration and domestic work.* Stanford University Press.

Riaño, Y. (2015). Latin American women who migrate for love: Imagining European men as ideal partners. In E. Begonya & J. Roca (Eds.), *Rethinking romantic love. Discussions, imaginaries and practices* (pp. 45–60). Cambridge Scholars Publishing.

Riaño, Y., & Baghdadi, N. (2007). "Je pensais que je pourrais avoir une relation plus égalitaire avec un Européen". Le rôle du genre et de l'imaginaire géographique dans la migration des femmes. *Nouvelles Questions Féministes, 26*(1), 38–53.

Sri Tharan, C. T. (2010). *Gender, migration, and social change: The return of Filipino women migrant workers.* University of Sussex.

Stark, O., & Taylor, J. E. (1991). Migration incentives, migration types: The role of relative deprivation. *The Economic Journal, 101*(408), 1163–1178.

Vaiou, D. (2002). In the interstices of the City: Albanian women in Athens. *Espaces, Populations, Societes, 3*, 373–385.

Vianello, F. A. (2009). *Migrando Sole; Legami transnazionali tra Ucraina e Italia.* Milano.

Vianello, F. A. (2013). A transnational double presence: Circular migrations between Ukraine and Italy. In A. Triandafyllidou (Ed.), *Circular migration between Europe and its neighbourhood. Choice or necessity?* (pp. 187–211). Oxford University Press.

Vullnetari, J. (2007). *Albanian migration and development: State of the art review* (MISCOE Working Paper 18).

Vullnetari, J. (2012). *Albania on the move: Links between internal and international migration.* Amsterdam University Press.

Vullnetari, J., & King, R. (2016). 'Washing men's feet': Gender care and migration in Albania during and aftercommunism. *Gender Place & Culture, 23*(2), 198–215. https://doi.org/10.108 0/0966369X.2015.1013447

Wihtol de Wenden, C. (2015). Faut-il ouvrir les frontières? In *Forum 2015. La conference socio-politique de Caritas: Immigration.* Caritas Suisse.

Open Access This chapter is licensed under the terms of the Creative Commons Attribution 4.0 International License (http://creativecommons.org/licenses/by/4.0/), which permits use, sharing, adaptation, distribution and reproduction in any medium or format, as long as you give appropriate credit to the original author(s) and the source, provide a link to the Creative Commons license and indicate if changes were made.

The images or other third party material in this chapter are included in the chapter's Creative Commons license, unless indicated otherwise in a credit line to the material. If material is not included in the chapter's Creative Commons license and your intended use is not permitted by statutory regulation or exceeds the permitted use, you will need to obtain permission directly from the copyright holder.

Chapter 6
Education as a Platform for Migration – Young Women Migrating to the 'Big City' on Their Own

This chapter analyses the experiences of young women from various villages and cities across Albania who migrated to Tirana to study. Here, 'on their own' refers to single[1] women who moved to and lived in Tirana by themselves while their parents and siblings stayed in their city or village of origin. Upon their graduation, which had happened within at least three years at the time of the research in 2012, they did not return to their native communities. Below, I introduce briefly the eight young women who migrated to Tirana to study.

Eriola is a 28-year-old native of Pogradec, a town in eastern Albania. She migrated to Tirana in 2002 to study political science and has completed a bachelor's and a master's degree. In 2012, she worked for a private television station in Tirana and lived in a rented apartment with two other young, internal migrant women in Komuna e Parisit. At the time of the research, Eriola's parents resided in Pogradec. She is an only child.

Kiara is a 27-year-old native of the city of Fier, in southern coastal Albania. She migrated to Tirana in 2003. Kiara holds a bachelor's and master's degree in psychology and another bachelor's degree in economics. In 2012, she worked for an NGO providing psychological counselling and research. Kiara rented a small studio apartment in Komuna e Parisit. While at university, she lived in public university housing, and after completing her studies and finding a job, she rented a small studio apartment by herself. Kiara's parents resided in Fier, with her younger brother, who has been ill since childhood and cannot walk.

Olisa is a 28-year-old native of Fier. She migrated to Tirana in 2002 and obtained a bachelor's in political sciences and a master's in gender studies. At the time of the

---

Parts of this chapter have been originally published as Danaj, E. (2019) Young, educated, and female: narratives of post-1991 internal Albanian migration, in Bonifacio G. (ed) Global Youth Migration and Gendered Modalities", Bristol: Policy Press, 235–255. Republished with permissions of Policy Press (an imprint of Bristol University Press, UK).

---

[1] In this research, single women means women who were not married, not cohabiting and not in a stable relationship during the time of the fieldwork.

© The Author(s) 2022

E. Danaj, *Women, Migration and Gendered Experiences*, IMISCOE Research Series, https://doi.org/10.1007/978-3-030-92092-0_6

interview, she worked in a call centre in Tirana and lived in a small, rented studio apartment in Don Bosko. In 2012, Olisa's parents and older brother, with his wife and young child, lived in Fier. Olisa's brother had migrated to Greece for work and returned a few years before 2012.

Iris is an only child and a 27-year-old native of Librazhd, a small town in the central-eastern part of the country. She migrated to Tirana in 2004, where she completed a bachelor's and a master's degree in law. As of 2012, she worked as a journalist in a private television station, where she first began work as a secretary. Iris lived in Don Bosko, sharing a rented apartment with a young internal migrant woman from Pogradec. At the time of the research, Iris's father resided in Librazhd, and her mother had passed away soon after Iris 'finished her bachelor studies in law.

Erida is a 30-year-old native of Lezhë, a town in northern coastal Albania. Erida migrated to Tirana in 2000, and she completed a bachelor in social work and master's in political sciences. After working on a temporary contract as a social worker in an institution for orphan children, she worked in a call centre. She lived in a small, rented studio apartment in Don Bosko in 2012. At the time of the research, Erida's parents resided in Lezhë. She had two sisters, 13 and 11 years older than her, who were married and lived in Shkoder and Lezhë. Both had graduated just at the beginning of the 90s.

Alba is 28 years old and an only child from Rrëshen, a small town in northern Albania. In 2002, Alba migrated to Tirana and completed a bachelor's and master's degree in political science. In 2012, she worked as a consultant for a think-tank in Tirana and lived in a small, rented studio in Don Bosko. Alba recounts that before coming to Don Bosko, she rented an apartment with two other young internal migrants, in another area of city.

Erjona is 26 years old and from a village in the district of Gjirokastër, in southern Albania. Erjona migrated to Tirana in 2005 and obtained a bachelor's and a master's in law. As of 2012, she worked as an assistant in a law firm and lived in a small studio apartment in Komuna e Parisit. At the time of the research, Erjona's parents and younger sister still lived in their village in Gjirokastër, running a small agritourism initiative. Her younger sister was very passionate about the family's agritourism business and wanted to be involved in running it on a daily basis.

Marjola is 26 years old and an only child from Fier. She migrated to Tirana in 2004 and earned a bachelor's and a master's in information technology (IT). In 2012, she worked as an IT specialist in a project office and lived in a small, rented studio apartment in Komuna e Parisit. At the time of her interview, Marjola's parents resided in Fier but were thinking about moving to Vlorë and starting a business in the tourism sector, according to Marjola.

6.1 The Pre-migration Phase—Rationalising Migration

While education provided the main motivation behind the reason women migrated, as this chapter shows, it was by far not the only cause. I examine these young women's decisions to migrate, taking into account their broader social relations to their family and relatives.

6.1.1 Education as a Platform for Migration

This section explores the reasons and motivations informing these young women's move to Tirana. First, the belief that a university degree would provide better job opportunities emerged as a significant motivator in all the interviews. People see bachelor and master degrees as an advantageous qualification in securing better white-collar jobs. University studies were becoming an increasingly attractive means to obtain economic security, especially for women who were disadvantaged in the labour market compared to men (INSTAT, 2012). As Erida states:

You know, they say that a university diploma for a young woman is an open window to a job. I am not sure if this is true, but without a university diploma, it is certain that it is more difficult to find a job. ... And I wanted to have a good job, but just to be precise—not in Lezhë. That is why I wanted to go to university in Tirana.

Still, the benefit of obtaining a university diploma was not limited to its indispensability in finding a good job; for some women, it was also an important marker of self-achievement, as highlighted in Iris's story:

I cannot imagine myself without a university diploma. What could I do without a degree? No job, nothing. I would be a failure. ... That is why I decided, together with my family, to attend the University of Tirana and later, maybe somewhere abroad.

"Education in Tirana" or "education abroad" seem to be the code words used by these women to express their desire for higher education. Indeed, succeeding in their career by having a university degree is a proper motivation to move to Tirana.

Second, migration in and of itself is also a sound and solid motivation. Some of the young women interviewed come from cities where there are no universities, making the decision to move elsewhere obvious. However, for them, the desire for higher education is combined with the desire to move to Tirana more specifically, which is the biggest city in Albania. Kiara, for example, says she wanted to have a university degree, but at the same time, she "always" wanted to leave her small city and go to Tirana. Marjola describes a similar situation:

He [my father] was saying that it might be better to go to the University in Vlora,[2] as it was close to Fier, and he had relatives and friends in Vlora, who could help me if I was in need. But I didn't want to go to Vlora because it resembled Fier a little. In Tirana, it was

---

[2] Vlora is a coastal city next to Fier, and physically closer to Tirana. It has its own public university.

different. … I told my mother that it was not worth going to Vlora at all. Vlora was like Fier, with no opportunities at all, and I would have all the relatives and friends of my father looking over me worse than in Fier. And also, the purpose of these studies was to find an excellent job in Tirana, not just to go from one city to another.

Marjola's story shows the intersection of the desire to migrate in order to improve one's chances to getting a better job, with the desire to live in a big city farther away from home.

Marjola's words bring to the forefront the third motivation that behind many young women's desire to migrate to Tirana: escaping the social control exercised by relatives and kinship over women specifically in their attempt to enforce gender norms in the native home. As a reason, it often takes centre stage in the narratives of these women. Social control here refers to attempts by one or more individuals to manipulate and direct the behaviour of another person or persons (Gibbs, 1981). In their narratives, the women often lamented this social pressure they experienced in their native homes. For instance, multiple women talk about how people in their hometown would frequently comment about what they saw as the women's inappropriate clothing or behaviour. As Kiara states:

They would gossip if they saw me with a boy, even a classmate and if possible, they would immediately tell this to my parents.'

Similarly, Iris says:

What was there to do in Librazhd? It's such a small city where nothing ever happens. My life in Librazhd was confined to school and home. …it was so suffocating. Even if I had the permission to do something else, I could not, because you have nothing to choose from in Librazhd. The only entertainment was to go to Pogradec in summer with your parents. Thus, the only thing I was doing was watching TV, all the telenovelas, and getting good grades in school so I could come to Tirana.

Iris's answer identifies a fourth reason women migrate, one that is related to the need to escape, but this time not simply from the social control exercised by family members, but from the lack of activities and the boredom associated with their native towns and villages where, the women say, nothing ever happens. Since the political upheaval 1991, the underdeveloped cultural and artistic infrastructure for young people in Albania has attracted very little attention by the appropriate institutions. Only a few cities have movie theatres, and they are non-existent in most of the country. A handful of public or private libraries exist outside Tirana. The coastal towns that cater to tourists boast few cultural activities during or outside of summer.

Television is the leading form of entertainment for women and girls, while men spend their leisure time drinking coffee in the numerous city bars and various sports and games parlours (Danaj et al., 2008). Since television is women's primary source of information, their desires are shaped by the imaginaries displayed there. On numerous Albanian television stations, Tirana has an air of brightness. It is the epitome of modernity, boasting well-dressed, fashionable young women and men, high-rise buildings, nightlife, cinemas and festivals. Tirana contrasts sharply with the small cities and villages where these young women live and where, according to the interviewees, TV was the main cultural activity. Tirana contrasts with the 'suffocating' community and kinship pressure they felt and the lack of activities in their hometowns. It, therefore, can be assumed that, as in international migration (Kim, 2012; Mai, 2004), the media play an essential role in offering a bright image of Tirana as a destination that was very different from their hometowns, as these women express. Discussing the international migration of Albanian youth to Italy, Mai (2004) stresses that television provides information about potential destinations, in particular about 'alternative', more 'modern' 'lifestyles' that are 'independent from parents' (Mai, 2004, 14, 18). Focusing on female international student migration, Kim (2012) reveals how the media drive these migratory projects by generating imaginaries of alternative Western lifestyles and work.

6.1.2   Parents' Role in the Decision to Migrate to Tirana

When it comes to the decision to move to Tirana, the parents' and the women's desires converged. The interviews show that there were no substantial disagreements between the parties on this point. Indeed, for some women, it wasn't only their wishes but also their parents' desires that drove them to leave, as the women's parents imagine they will have more opportunities in Tirana than their cities or villages of origin. Olisa talks about her experience:

My parents, especially my father, wanted me to go away to the city, to have other opportunities in life. He is still pushing me to find a way to go abroad, for a master's or something, and not to come back. That is why I am continuing to apply to find a master programme abroad, even though I have already obtained an MA degree, and now I have a job.

Eriola also states that she decided to pursue her university studies Tirana with the total agreement with her parents. Kiara concurs:

It was a mutual desire, my parents' and mine. … My parents have always encouraged me, even before coming to Tirana, to take classes in foreign language or take other courses. It was my parents' drive, combined, for sure, with my desire. I could not imagine myself without academic development.

There is a lot of value placed on education in Albania, an attitude forged since the early years of the communist regime through campaigns supporting education for all, especially girls and women, and through the construction of schools throughout the country. Even after the fall of the communist regime, the value of education persisted as a means to achieve social mobility. Parents' desire for their children to obtain better educational and job opportunities triggers their children's migration, both sons and daughters (Ekonomi et al., 2004). In the same line, the interviews reveal that parents see their daughters' education in Tirana as an opportunity for further professional development, as well as for independence.

Parents are not only willing to let their daughters go to Tirana to study at the university to have better and "other opportunities in life," as Olisa noted. They supported them financially as well as protecting them from adverse reactions in places of origin. Parental support is much needed because, as Kalaja (2014) observes, it is unusual for young women to migrate on their own to Tirana. Parents play a significant role when faced with gossip about their daughters' migrating on their own. The interviews show that, paradoxically, it is not within the family that social control materializes; instead, the close nuclear family plays the role of a shield against kinship/community reactions and gossip. According to Drotbohm (2010), gossip is not "just talk" but a powerful tool for exercising social control. Kiara's experience supports this point of view:

> My family has never impeded my education and advancement. The relatives yes, but not my family… But I did not feel the pressure of my relatives because my parents protected me. They told me that they had many issues with the broader kin regarding my education, the various classes I was taking before coming to Tirana, or my plans to advance in my career rather than planning to have a family and a kind mother-in-law. My mother told me later how my relatives were gossiping or criticizing my parents for the freedom I had.

Parents use various strategies and tactics when faced with gossip about their daughters' moving and living alone. Eriola describes how her mother handled it:

> I remember my mother told the neighbours that we have some relatives in Tirana, and I was going to stay with them. It was a lie because we had no relatives, and I stayed in the dormitory. But she was concerned with what the neighbours would say, and so she just invented this story to be left in peace by their gossip.

Eriola's mother's tactic was to invent a set of so that the reactions of their kin and neighbours would not affect negatively Eriola's migration to Tirana. At the same time, her mother took great care to destabilise neither relations nor gender expectations within the community.

These situations defy the stereotypical, clear-cut distinction between modern children and traditional parents. In this regard, Moujoud's (2011) analysis of the discourse surrounding migration and age shows that parents, mostly mothers, are often portrayed as 'guardians of tradition' opposed to young migrant women. Although Moujoud (2011) conducted her research in another context than mine, her analysis helps uncover this often-stereotypical opposition of tradition versus modernity. My interviewees' parents were their daughters' primary protectors against traditional social practices. In these cases, we can hardly portray the role of parents as 'traditional' or 'backward.' Similar narratives also emerge from Turkish migration. Erel (2009) shows that parents often valued and encouraged the education of young Turkish women.

6.1.3   Transiting to Tirana, with Parents' Support

Despite the ever-growing number of students, Tirana suffers from a lack of dormitories or residencies for students. The private universities rarely offer residencies, and the main dormitory is within the City of Students, which is associated with the State University of Tirana. Thus, the accommodation is quite an important moment for the process of moving to Tirana. Many of those who study at the State University aim to find a place at the City of Students' dormitory because it is the cheapest and the most affordable option. Those who attend private universities mostly live in shared, rented houses in some specific neighbourhoods of Tirana such as Komuna e Parisit or Don Bosko. The process of sharing a rented apartment is also discussed and negotiated with parents so that they can be sure that their daughters are living in a safe place, with 'good persons' coming from 'good families' as Erjona says. The conditions in the public dormitory are subpar, lacking electricity or heating, etc. Nevertheless, due to the very modest financial standing of their families, the dormitory is a very convenient place for many of them. Kiara and Eriola illustrate this:

Kiara: During my University studies, money was in short supply because of some family issues. So, the alternative was to go to the dormitory because it was less expensive. I was lucky to have some excellent roommates who became good friends. But that period was very difficult, the life in the dormitory was very difficult: Miserable conditions, a tiny room, no space for personal hygiene, no privacy at all. The conditions were not conducive of studying there.

Eriola narrates a similar situation:

The worst thing in the dormitory was the lack of electricity and water. It was hard to read and study with the power turned on and off. We could not even have a proper shower without water and electricity. But as long as I was not working, my parents could not provide more money, so I had to endure the few years until I finished school.

Parents are considerably more worried if their daughters live in rental apartments, compared to those living in the dormitory, as Erjona says. She says that her mother was very anxious until they met with her roommate, who was also from her native city. Olisa describes a similar situation:

Olisa: My parents were often coming to Tirana: To bring food, to check if I was eating well, if the apartment was tidy, if my two roommates were excellent and we were not having problems with each other, and this kind of stuff. My mother was visiting more often. They were worried because we were three girls living alone, and they were worried. But, in the neighbourhood, the majority of people around were students sharing apartments so, it was not only us.

The anxiety that surrounds the girls who live in shared apartments could be explained by the fact that the dormitory is considered a public infrastructure, with hundreds of other young women and men, with rules to follow, with guards at the doors, etc. Thus, there might be imagined a degree of institutional control and security compared to privately rented apartments. In reality, the interviews report that there were no such rules or safety.

Iris says:

with a little money, you could provide access to anyone wishing to enter the dormitory. I mean a man could come in our female-only dormitory, so it's not that we had that much of a security. If I had the financial means I would not have stayed there; I'd have rented an apartment.

In this group, there seems to be no clear correlation between social and wealth standing of parents, the choice of the university (whether public or private) and accommodation choice. During the time period in which these women studied, the number of private universities was still low. Hence, no exhaustive conclusion can be made about such correlation. Not all students in private universities are coming from wealthy families; there are many young women and men who come from modest economic backgrounds (e.g., parents that have worked as teachers and received a low to average salary have saved for a long time to pay their daughters' studies as shown here). Nevertheless, it might also be said that children of the wealthiest families in general study in private universities in Albania, or in universities abroad. It's worth recalling here the findings of Danaj, Festy, et al. (2005) about no visible correlation between parents' and children' education, but the existence of inequalities based on region and wealth conditions. These inequalities have been amplified with the increase of the State University tuition fees that fueled a series of strong protest during December 2018[3].

6.2   Life in Tirana

The first section highlighted one significant finding, among others: education is seen not only as a means for a better career but also a substantial value mobilised by these young women to migrate to Tirana in a more socially acceptable way. Education is also a platform mobilised by the women to escape from the social control exercised by their community and kinship in their hometowns.

This second one expands on the paradox embodying these women's situation in Tirana: in the city, they experience less social control by family and community, but at the same time, they face highly gendered and sexualised prejudices and constraints that arise from the same mechanisms as those they escaped and that put them in new forms of precarity and dependency.

6.2.1   Anonymity as Freedom

Anonymity is a way to get away from social control. *'The fewer people know you, the freer you are'*, as the ability of others to impose specific gender norms and roles onto these women is likely or at least, less harmful. Tirana is a large, growing city with new communities being created as people come from all corners of the country. In this setting, people barely know each other, and this provides an anonymity that young migrant women appreciate. Anonymous, they feel less pressured and controlled, as illustrated by Erida's story:

> *When I came to Tirana, I remember that I started to dress differently. This was not the case in the beginning, but after some months, I began to look at other girls here and the 'clothing*

---

[3] https://balkaninsight.com/2019/01/10/albania-s-student-protesters-hail-victory-over-fear-01-09-2019/

stores. It was suddenly possible to wear a miniskirt or stretch jeans, which I could not wear in Lezhë. I added blond highlights to my hair as it was the fashion at that time to dye your hair like that. … At first, I could not go to Lezhë dressed as I did in Tirana, and when I went back home, I got back into my old clothes [laughs]. Now it is different as it looks like things are changing a little in Lezhë too, and people don't give you weird looks because of your clothes.

In the same vein, Erjona adds:

I hate to cook. Yes, now I know a little how to cook, small things, but in general, I hate it. When I was in Gjirokastër, my mother tried all the time to teach me how to cook, how to prepare desserts, how to prepare dough to make byrek, *and all these traditional meals, which I like to eat but not to cook. But it was like an obligation to know these things, and I had had enough. I wanted to read instead, and I remember that I was always angry when I had to learn how to cook. … Here, I don't cook. I can buy* byrek *if I want to, but in general, it's toasts and salads.*

Young women who migrated to Tirana began to engage in new social activities, with things like going out to bars and nightclubs being particularly noteworthy, given how radically different these experiences were from life in the interviewees' city or village of origin. For example, Marjola says that in Tirana, she goes out to have coffee by herself. She did not do that commonly in her city of origin as people would look at her and judge her; but in Tirana, where she knows few people, she does not care if they will look at her or not. These young migrant women appreciate this dimension of life in Tirana and prefer the liberating anonymity and indifference (Simmel [1903] 2002) of the big city compared to their places of origin, where people know each other. Migrants to the big city find that the physical distance separates them from the 'prying eyes of the community' (Kihato, 2009, 86). Alba adds:

Fortunately, in Tirana, you don't know a lot of people, and like this, you are less controlled, and you can live without this damn fear about she saw me doing this, he saw me doing that.

Similarly, Kiara says that in Tirana, one can get lost in a crowd, which provides the crux of the freedom Tirana offers compared to her hometown.

The streets in Albania, as Musaraj (2009) aptly notes, carry ambivalent connotations. The interviewees often present walking the streets of Tirana without knowing people as much-appreciated anonymity and freedom. In contrast, the streets of their hometowns represent the place where social control is exerted at full force. For instance, the coffee shop in their hometowns is a 'forbidden' space for these young women, especially those coming from towns and villages. Appropriating such a 'forbidden' space in Tirana appears to give the young women a greater sense of freedom than in their places of origin.

6.2.2 The Other Side of the Paradox: New Gendered and Sexualised Prejudices and Constraints

A paradox manifests quickly after these young women arrive in Tirana. As these cases show, even in Tirana, they face gendered and sexualised prejudices as women living on their own, far from their families, is perceived as transgressing the borders of accepted femininity. Moving from the provinces and living alone in Tirana makes them vulnerable to prejudice and discrimination from non-migrants and other migrants alike. From the perspective of those living in Tirana, almost all other cities of the country are considered the provinces. Thus, when young migrant women arrive in Tirana, their behaviour is often perceived as that of people 'liberated from chains', to use a local expression whose negative connotations implies a certain lack of restraint in women's behaviour and choices. This view complements the many prejudices against young female students moving on their own to Tirana, or *'konviktoret'* ('dormitory girls') as they are often called. Iris illustrates this point:

> As dormitory residents, we were all seen as whores. It is mostly older men and other people who think so. You must know this expression 'dormitory girls'. It means that these girls have all the worst qualities of the world, they are all whores, and they just want to get money from married men. We were and still are considered women who ruin marriages and families. That is not true, but even if it was, what about these good men who were betraying their wives with younger women and also paying them? But, as we all know, men are always good people, and we are the whores.

Kiara says that these prejudicial views against them are hold only by non-migrants, but also by other internal migrants, primarily those who migrated with their families. The stigmatising labels such as 'dormitory girls', 'girls from the cities' and 'the whores from the cities' all have the same meaning: they construct an image of young girls with no morals, who lead a life that is unacceptable by any established moral norms. They are widely believed to engage in sexual relations for money and to have 'destroyed married couples' through their relationships with married men. They can get away with unacceptable behaviour as they live far from their families who would usually exert control over them.

There seems to be no such stereotyping of young male students. In Kiara's words:

> That was the most disturbing thing. People think we do evil things while away from our families. I think of these as stupid stereotypes and as stereotypes only about girls as boys could do whatever they want, and no one would judge them. To the contrary, they would be congratulated.

The lives of male students who moved to Tirana appear to be extensions of their lives in their cities of origin and are not marked by the radical change that the young women encountered. Young men were allowed to pursue activities in public by themselves in their hometowns and continue to do so when in Tirana. They were allowed to have relationships with girls and were not judged for them, and this continues in Tirana. In contrast, young women encounter an environment that is very different from their previous lives in their native homes. In Tirana, they are freer, as they say, to do things they could not do in their cities of origin. They may have a nightlife, establish relationships with younger men or older men and go to bars, for instance.

6.2.2.1 Mobilising One's Erotic Capital

Often, young people who migrate to Tirana for educational purposes do not return to their hometown. Young migrant women invest as much as possible in their education and training (e.g., pursuing post-graduate degrees and graduating from two faculties to increase their employment chances) to find well-paid jobs in Tirana and, as they say, perhaps to leave the country. To achieve these objectives, they try to mobilise all possible resources, primarily their social networks. That is quite paradoxical: they appreciate the anonymity Tirana offers as they know very few people, but they also need to develop and maintain social networks to find a good job. As mentioned in Chap. 4, most Albanians find jobs through informal connections, not institutionalised channels. The nepotism required to access the labour market affects both men and women. They must establish and nurture relationships to find and keep jobs. Accordingly, most of the women interviewed report finding employment through their friends' network. Others found work in their field of study with the assistance of their professors. For instance, Kiara says that after she held several temporary jobs, a professor in the psychology department helped her secure work with an NGO providing psychological research and counselling. Erjona recounts a similar set-up. During her studies, she had the opportunity to work as an intern at her professor's law firm. She still works there.

A specific strategy is mobilising one's erotic capital (Hakim, 2010) to establish new social relations and achieve one's plans and objectives. As Marjola says:

> *I was in a relationship with an older man, much older. It's not the end of the world. I know that people in my close family would die if they knew, but to be honest, I am so far away from home, and in few months, I'm going even farther away and will probably never return. Why care so much about what people say? This happened during my time as a student. I was lost, and I did not want to return home. Having a relationship with this man and all the niceties that he was providing for me was a kind of work [laughs]. … It's impossible to find a job in Tirana the 'right' way. Everybody knows this. You need to have high-level connections and have some security. … He helped me to find a reasonable job, in an office. I've worked two years there, but I'll be leaving soon as I've got a scholarship for a master's in Germany. I did it; I succeeded.*

Here, we can refer to Hakim's definition of erotic capital (i.e., beauty, sexual attractiveness, flirtations, social presentation and sexuality) (2010, 512). It is a handy concept for understanding sexual relationships and social processes in public and private spheres of the individualised and sexualised cultures of modern, twenty-first-century societies. Hakim (2010) notes that like social capital - the resources, material or otherwise, that accrue to an individual or a group by possessing a durable network of more or less institutionalised relationships of mutual acquaintance and recognition (Bourdieu & Wacquant, 1992, 119) - erotic capital can be an important, hidden factor improving success in employment. The mobilisation of sexuality has been analysed mostly in the context of international migration. For example, investigating the case of Chinese migrants in Paris, Levy and Lieber (2009) show that Chinese migrant women turn sexuality into a resource that allows them to achieve their objectives.

6.2.2.2 Financial Uncertainties and Precarious Jobs

Additionally, the interviews show that these young migrant women tend to find jobs that are unrelated to their studies and are more precarious (i.e., lack collective contracts and employment protection and characterised by a generalised, permanent state of insecurity) (Bourdieu, 1998; Fredman, 2004). For instance, Erida, who has a master's in political sciences, works as a unit supervisor in a call centre:

> *I still work for the call centre. It's not well paid, and the work is quite tricky. It's not a regular workplace where you go, and you can have some friendly relations with your co-workers. We are afraid of being fired or fearful that someone will badmouth to the supervising manager. They may fire you right away, with no explanation and nobody cares to verify if you were guilty or not. But this is the best employment I could find, as opposed to becoming a salesperson.*

Find a job and an income that will allow them to continue living in Tirana after graduation becomes an essential objective for these young women. Consequently, they accept uncertain positions without social insurance as long as they bring in money. Taking low paid jobs and living in constant fear and uncertainty embodies what Bourdieu (1998) calls *precarité*, a generalised and permanent state of insecurity aimed at forcing workers into submission and acceptance of exploitation. The young women discuss how they lack regular work contracts, and most do not pay social insurance and lack employment protection.

Furthermore, being a woman and one who migrated on her own brings additional difficulties in the workplace, particularly with regards to forming professional relationships with superiors and male colleagues. Eriola summarises many of the challenges these women encounter while accessing the labour market:

> *Now I work for a private TV station. It's very tiring and frustrating as we don't get regular salaries. It pays well; there are no contracts, no contributions. But it's so difficult to find a job in Tirana, so you have to get used to this market. And the main problem is not the salary or the contract: it's the attitudes of men who are in higher positions or those of other male colleagues who treat you like a piece of garbage. And they are less educated than me. It goes like this: 'yes, you girls from the provinces, you have no morals. That is why you are working here'. 'Don't put on weight because you'll get fired'. ... OMG, I always wish to say to them: 'shut up, people, just worry about your job and your life'. But I don't say anything. I just play this role of the stupid girl, and that's all. I'm not staying there forever; it's just a temporary job. I can cover my rent and other expenses, and this is just enough.*

Stigmatisation as migrants along gendered lines—branded as girls from the provinces, with no morals, ready to do everything to keep their jobs, advance their careers or earn more money—recurs throughout these young women's lives in Tirana. Sexual objectification, or equating a woman's worth with her bodily appearance and sexual function (Szymanski et al., 2011, 6), characterises much of their situation. Several of the women interviewed mention how they have to stay thin and good-looking not to lose their jobs.

These pressures contribute to their paradoxical situation in Tirana, where new freedoms and new gender constraints intersect. Ultimately, it appears that these young women migrants have remained in the same gender order (i.e., unequal hierarchical positions and gender norms, roles and expectations for men and women) but a different constellation of gender constraints. Sexual harassment further exemplifies this dynamic.

6.2.2.3 Sexual Harassment

Sexual harassment, which seems to happen mostly in the workplace, was a concern for several participants. Kiara describes are her experience:

> *Sexual harassment happened daily. You had to be very strong to endure this. … The supervisor harassed me for about a month and a half. He gave up as he saw that it was not going anywhere. … He was profiting from our situation as he knew that we were students and needy of these jobs, so he considered himself to have the right to do this.*

Kiara shows that she is aware of sexual harassment and the factors that put her in a vulnerable situation, in particular, her financial dependency and status as a female migrant on her own. Sexual harassment happens not only in small informal businesses but also in those considered to be more prestigious. Olisa says that she had to quit her job as a secretary for a newspaper due to the harassment:

> *One day, the director of the newspaper where I was working started with this kind of words such as, 'You are so pretty. Your hair is like this. Your eyes are like that', etc. In the beginning, I was only smiling and, to be sincere, appreciating all these beautiful words. But this carried on with comments about my body, and he kept me in the office when everyone else left. It was then that I realised what was happening.*

Olisa adds that the day after she once refused to travel with her boss, he warned her that if she would not travel with him, then she was not right for the job. She says that it was then that she quit her job.

When faced with sexual harassment, these young women feel unprotected and do not know where to report it. Iris describes precisely this situation:

> *Once I had to quit my job as the owner of the shop was trying to persuade me to sleep with him. I didn't know what to do. I told him several times that I was not that kind of girl. But at a specific moment, he made it clear that I had to sleep with him if I wanted the job. I, therefore, left the job as I had no other choice. I could not complain to anyone about what was happening, so I just left the job.*

Sexual harassment in the workplace 'undercuts woman's potential for social equality in two interpenetrated ways: by using her employment position to coerce her sexually, while using her sexual position to coerce her economically' (MacKinnon, 1979, 7). MacKinnon's definition of sexual harassment (i.e., the unwanted imposition of sexual requirements in a relationship of unequal power) emphasises the exploitation of women's need to find or keep a job. Often, migrant women face sexual harassment due to their particularly precarious position, as they might need a job more than a non-migrant. Single women and single mothers are the group that are most vulnerable to sexual harassment in the workplace. And when they come from another city or village, this vulnerability increases. Life in Tirana is challenging and very expensive, and these young women give their best to secure employment, which often puts them in very unpleasant situations, especially sexual harassment.

According to the interviews and Kocaqi (2013), young migrant women in Tirana living on their own are subjected to sexual harassment more frequently than those living with their families. These interviews also show examples demonstrating that sexual harassment does not preclude the agency of these young women, as Erel (2007) also shows in her research on migrant women in Germany. Instead, these young women try to make use of their available resources, primarily their social networks, to carry on with achieving their goals.

6.2.3 Marriage and Family Formation — Discourses and Practices

This section focuses on the views of these young women, who were single at the time of the research, about marriage. It is important not only to analyse these views, but also to scrutinise the practices they deploy to postpone family formation while focusing on self-achievement and improving their career options.

Regarding family formation, since the interviews were conducted in 2012, I do not know what their practices actually wound up being and how their situation evolved. At this point, I may only analyse what they discussed, bearing in mind that sometimes their discourse may be influenced and biased by social desirability (Callegaro, 2008).

The young women interviewed for this chapter share a common perception that marriage would hinder their professional ambitions. They maintain that marriage and career advancement are mutually exclusive. Getting married would mean they would lose the "freedom" they had at the time, which for them meant living alone far from the control and scrutiny of their families and relatives. Eriola thinks that if she got married, she would lose control over her life. She adds that she doesn't want to become a servant obeying her husband's orders. The imaginary of marriage and family formation represents, for these women, a hierarchical gender regime with women in a subordinated position. Kiara also illustrates this by saying, *"Finding a husband, getting married, having children and living in harmony with a mother in law; this has never been part of my plans and my priorities"*.

Although some of these women, when talking about their families, describe their parents as being more or less equal in their roles within the household, they express a profound feeling of regret for their mothers. The women describe their mothers as having endured a lot of pressure from the community or relatives, and having had to give up on their own dreams at certain points in their lives. In their answers, they demonstrate strong reactions against the gender dynamics that are present in their parents' relationship; relations they don't wish to replicate for themselves. Their ideas on marriage are informed by the everyday experiences of their parents and the family relationships they have witnessed. Marjola and Alba illustrate this situation:

> *Marjola: I don't want to become like my mother. Not that I have anything against my father because he has been always working hard for us, but my mom too she worked and at the same time she dealt with housework. And she has had to endure a tense relationship with my father's relatives who have never loved my mother. But she never stopped supporting them in order not to spoil the relationship with my dad. I don't want to tolerate this all the time, but I remain silent about it.*

> *Alba: I remember my aunts always visiting my house to check if my mother had bought a new dress or something new for the house. They would then gossip all the time behind her back. My parents knew of this, but I don't remember them discussing this, at least I'm not been aware of it. [...] My mother told me once that she had been among the best students in engineering, but she didn't continue with her studies because she got engaged, and she had to prepare for marriage and everything. I am sure that my father's family has put its "nose" in this, by pressuring her to abandon her studies. And probably my dad urged her too, and maybe that is why he insists so much that I don't return to Rrëshen.*

One possible way of escaping marriage is to stay in Tirana and live alone, these women state. Another option appears to be that of *"leaving to marry a foreigner"* as Iris says, because, *"for sure then I will live with him and not with all his relatives, and I know that a foreigner is respectful and will respect my own freedom"*. In this imaginary, marrying a foreign man means having a more equal relationship, one in which other family members do not interfere. Eriola says she knows that abroad, relationships are formed differently. She says, *"I have friends abroad, and you see that men there are different, more respectful, they help with housework, they take care of children"*. She also says that she would prefer not to marry in Albania, and find somebody abroad who would allow her to have her job and lead her own life. On the one hand stands the image of the unequal gender relations experienced within the own family, and on the other, there is the idealised imaginary of the foreign partner which research has shown may be a deception (Riaño & Baghdadi, 2007). This idealised imaginary about abroad appear to reproduce the dichotomist discourse "tradition"/ "modernity" where modernity is associated with the destination place. For these women, first this was Tirana, and now it is the "abroad".

It is important to raise the question of what informs these narratives the women have formed about foreign partners being better and more respectful than Albanian partners, and specifically Albanian men. Unfortunately, I do not have enough material from these narratives to be able to answer adequately. I might hypothesise that it may be related to the general perception that life elsewhere, outside Albania's borders, is better than anything found within the country. These imaginary narratives may be the results of Albanian youth having had access to foreign TV channels and foreign programmes (as mentioned above).

Postponing Marriage While it is true that national data does not show significant changes in the marriage rate when comparing communist and post-communist periods, a slight and tentative transformation of the more significant patterns of family formation in Albania may be seen in the increase of the average age at the time of marriage. The interviews confirm this trend. We might formulate the hypothesis that internal educated migrant women are quite active actors in the transformation of this process:

> *Kiara: Girls know that if they return to their native home one thing is for sure: they will get married to someone their parents picked out, they will have two to three babies, as much as their husbands want because they don't have any control anymore, they will have a job, or maybe not, and that will be their life; they will be subordinated. And, knowing their fate in the small cities, girls choose to postpone this process. If they don't find ways to stay in Tirana, at least they try to delay the return as much as possible.*

The imagery of marriage as a process that leads to women losing control over their lives is one of the reasons why these young women decide not return to their native homes. It is interesting to look at their practices in the process that I call "marriage postponement," which appears to be a strategy in itself whose aim is to preserve women's current autonomy.

> *Alba says: Each time I go to Rrëshen, there is this question of marrying, and my aunts propose to me lists of young men ready to be married [...] I remember one time, quite recently, that they even had prepared an "random" meeting with one guy that they had picked out. My father was not informed about this, and I told him. We had an extended discussion on marriage, him and me, and it looked like he agreed with me that finally now that I have found a good job, and I am trying to find a scholarship abroad, it is not really the time to marry in Rrëshen. To be honest, since that discussion I've gotten no more propositions. I imagine he must have talked with his sisters.*

One tactic that Alba used to turn the situation to her advantage is by talking to her father, whom she considers her ally in her project of investing in education and career. Facing pressure from her kin to get married, she bypasses them by working out the situation with her father. Kiara also says that she has already openly discussed the issue of marriage with her father. She says that it happened when her aunts had inquired about her marriage plans. She decided to talk to her father to clarify that she had no plans to get married. She says that the father told her that he wanted her only to succeed at her job and in her life and that she could decide about the rest of her life herself. Young people in Albania consider the father to be the head of the household (Çela et al., 2012). This may bring about situations where he takes arbitrary decisions, which results in the unequal gender relations women identify within the family, a configuration that these young women are trying to escape from. At the same time, they use the tactic of instrumentalising this role of the father "as the head of the household" to reach their goals, given that if the father agrees to their decision, nobody else will oppose them. They try to win the father over for their cause.

Another practice towards postponing marriage and avoiding discussions on the topic, is to not treat it seriously for as long as it is possible. This was the case for Olisa and Eriola:

Olisa: Getting married is still an issue, because I am 28 years old and thus in the prime time for marriage. I may even be late. My parents try to bring up the issue often, and I understand because they need to be reassured that after attending school I will have a good husband, and I will settle down. It's still perturbing every time because I have to find justifications, I make jokes, such as "look at this famous actress, she had her child when she was 50 years old," etc., etc., to avoid concrete discussions about this.

During the communist period marriages under the age of 18 were legally prohibited. Nevertheless, marriages after reaching the age of 25 years old were not as common. Expressions such as "a woman who is past her marriageable age," etc., were used for those women in their 30s who were not yet married. This upper limit of the age when a woman can get married also depends on the education level. For example, those studying at the university level having a higher threshold. This perspective regarding the age at marriage may also be seen in Eriola's words. Eriola says that she jokes around with her mother regarding marriage as her mother too was considered past her "marriageable age" when she married. She adds:

Eriola: I joke with my mom because she is just driving me crazy all the time about marriage and children. [...] But I don't get angry about this because we're not going to solve anything. Every time she brings this up, I start joking that she was older than her friends when she got married, so let's wait until I turn 30 and then talk again about this (laughs).

There were even women who deployed a more explicit approach, as Marjola did:

Marjola: I have told them [my parents] that I was not going to stay in Tirana, but that I would find a way to go study abroad. Maybe I could find someone abroad too. The idea of me going abroad is very important to them, so now we're concentrating on this and are no longer talking about engagement and marriage.

Focusing on a career and preserving her independence are also key to Kiara's plans for her future: *"I don't want to depend on my husband. I want to have my job, to be good at it".* Similarly, Kalaja (2014) explains that young women are aware that as soon as they go back to their native home, the pressure from their kinship and their mother to get married and "settle" will be very strong. She adds that we are well aware of expressions such as "your age of marriage will soon be over, you need to settle". On the other hand, as Kalaja (2014) argues, marriage would reduce or lose the investment that these young women have made in their education because they would very soon be in charge of caring for their children and household, and thus would become disconnected from the aspirations of finding a good job that is appropriate to their education.

Postponing marriage may be seen as another example of these women's transgression of the boundaries of accepted femininity in Albania, manifested in this case through marriage as the hegemonic form of family formation. Marriage is considered by these women as an obstacle to their career advancement and as an institution that would make them lose the "freedom" they have newly acquired. Marriage and family formation are for them the epitome of a hierarchical gender regime, which puts women in a subordinated position, from which they have escaped by migrating to Tirana.

6.2.4   Tirana as a 'Jumping Board' to the Future

Many women who migrate for educational purposes do not return to their native cities or villages. The scope of this research does not allow assessing how their situation will evolve in the future, what will happen to them if they return to their place of origin or whether they will migrate abroad or continue to live in Tirana. Here, I focus on their plans and reasons behind their choice not to return to their native homes. Iris reports her feelings about returning to her hometown by recounting her best friend's story:

> My best friend at university went back to Librazhd. The pressure of the family was too high. They could not support her financially because of economic difficulties. She could not finding a job and had nothing to live off. ... Maybe she was right to go back; I don't know. But she told me once that she has now a boyfriend. They meet in secret, meaning that the family doesn't know about this guy. My God, it scares me to go back again to hiding things and to fear getting out of the house and lying to do so. I am not sure I could do this.

Some women return for varied reasons. Iris says her best friend faced financial difficulties and found it impossible to get a job. But Iris also emphasises the distance she feels from life in her native city. The other interviewees also say that returning to their place of origin is out of the question.

> Erjona: What is the solution? Return to the village? Erase everything I've sacrificed? ... The choice is between either bearing this disgusting environment here or to go back to what I despise. I escaped that many years ago.

> Kiara: Going back to my city has never been an alternative for me.

Tirana is not 'a field of flowers', if I may use an Albanian expression referring to having a comfortable, beautiful life. A big city like Tirana offers anonymity and opportunities that allow young women to experience new things and face new difficulties, while at the same time enabling them to explore their abilities and potential. The interviewees' narratives highlight the challenges and constraints they faced in Tirana with regards to their financial situation, job insecurity and gender and sexualised prejudices, stigmatisation and harassment. Reflecting on their life in Tirana, though, they contrast the possibilities of Tirana with the impossibilities of their hometowns. It seems that this constant comparison with their previous situation helps them manage the contradictions they encounter. Iris says:

> I am happy to be here. The things I've experienced here, I could have never had them in my city of origin. It's not easy as you are all by yourself, and we're human. We need to be with people that we love and that love us back. But this is life. You have to make some sacrifices on the one hand to gain something else on the other hand. ... So, I believe I should be here for the moment. There is no going back for sure, but there is also no permanently staying here in Tirana either.

With regards to their plans for the future, there is a frequent and recurring wish to go abroad. As Kiara declares:

> Living in Tirana is a transitory phase. I have always considered this time to be a temporary phase before going abroad. I've always wanted to go overseas.

Tirana is *'a transitory phase'*. The city does not seem to be the young women's final destination. They see it as a jumping board, another step on their journey to go abroad. Olisa also specifies that she continuously looked for new educational opportunities abroad to leave Tirana and settle somewhere else. In this case, we see that student migration is part of a broader life migration strategy, as emphasised by Findlay et al. (2012). Marjola had already applied and been accepted to a master's programme in Germany. As she made it clear throughout her interview, migrating abroad had always been her primary objective.

Although these interviews conducted in 2012 do not provide information on how the participants' situations evolved or whether they succeeded in their goals to go abroad, based on their plans for the future, migration appears as a strategy in and of itself (Dahinden, 2009). Tirana is only a step in a grand migration journey. At the time of the research, all of the interviewees had already applied to study abroad. By the time of the writing of this chapter, two of them likely had already left Albania.

6.3 Conclusions—Discussing the Findings

Here, I observed the experiences of single migrant women who moved to Tirana on their own for educational purposes. In what follows, I give some general concluding reflections and then follow with three key findings.

I begin with a general reflection on the meaning of 'moving on their own'. As a term, *women moving on their own* covers varying realities, as well explained by Schmoll (2006) in the case of Tunisian female migrants. Here, *on their own* refers to single women who moved to and lived in Tirana to attend university while their parents and siblings remained in their native home. However, women migrating on their own are not entirely alone as they are taken in by various relational networks that support them during migration, as explained later. Additionally, it is not very socially acceptable for young women to move on their own. The interviewed young women mobilise various tactics and strategies to face the stigma against them for migrating on their own. Below, I discuss this further in combination with the three key findings from the interviews.

First, the interviews show female student migrants embrace education not only as a strategy for a better career but also as a rationale for migrating to Tirana. Migrating for education also allows them to escape from gender constraints and the lack of opportunities in their hometowns. Since the communist era, education has been a significant value for Albanian families across parents of different educational levels (Danaj et al., 2005). This value appears to be highly gendered, and young women exploit it as a tool and resource for migration: migrating as students is more acceptable for single women. According to the interviews, and as also stressed by Vullnetari (2009) and Kalaja (2014), emigration by young women on their own is less gossiped about and more readily accepted by the kin and the community in the hometown when it is for educational purposes. This acceptance would hardly happen if the daughter were leaving on her own for work purposes, for instance. Parents consider their daughters' education to be an investment in a better career and social mobility, as well as a more acceptable way to migrate given the social control exerted by the community. The young women thus strategically mobilise the value placed upon education as necessary and accepted among Albanian families as a resource to achieve their migration projects. The interviews show that internal migration to Tirana may also serve as an early phase in step-wise migration. Young women sometimes first migrate internally to obtain education and skills and later migrate to other international destinations to gain more and better opportunities, as also reported by King and Skeldon (2010). To accomplish migration projects, the women rely heavily on parental support, not only to cover their financial expenses but to protect them from the reactions and gossip of the community. Even when an individual migrates alone, the family left behind still play a significant role, especially in those cultures where the family exercises influence over their daughters and sons even in adulthood.

Education is not the only motivation for moving to Tirana; these women's interviews show that internal migration is a double escape. Women escape from the social control and the gender norms of their hometowns, which constitute a driving factor. Migration as an escape from the dominant gender constraints and customs in the place of origin is stressed by other researchers, such as Kihato (2009) in the case of women's migration to Johannesburg, and Erel (2009) in the experiences of Turkish migrant women. Women's migration often provides an escape from the patriarchal structures in their hometown (Kofman et al., 2000). At the same time, the interviews reveal that women desire to escape from the lack of opportunities in their cities and villages of origin to Tirana, which appears to them to be the land of opportunities. This imaginary attracts them toward Tirana and reinforces their drive to migrate from their hometowns.

The second key finding expands upon the paradox of these women's situations in Tirana: The capital city offers liberating anonymity and autonomy compared to their places of origin. However, this freeing lack of social control in Tirana is accompanied by new gender constraints and difficulties that arise from the same mechanisms as those they escaped. The situation leaves young women in new forms of precarity and dependency.

On the one hand, the young women much appreciate their escape from the social control of their hometowns and the new freedom gained by moving to a city where they know very few, if any, people. According to the interviews, anonymity frees one from social control. The fewer people know you, the participants maintain, the freer you are as the control of others over you, primarily through gender norms and roles, diminishes. Participants describe the release from the close surveillance of family and friends and the lack of need to report one's choices and movements to anyone else as an outstanding achievement. In Tirana, they experience anonymity and indifference, similarly to what Simmel ([1903] 2002) analyses in his influential work on the city and mental life.

On the other hand, from the interviews, it appears that this liberating dimension of Tirana comes at a price. The women's paradoxical situation quickly becomes apparent upon their arrival in Tirana. As their cases show, they face gendered and sexualised prejudices as living on their own, far from their families, is perceived to transgress the borders of accepted femininity. Furthermore, sexual objectification and sexual harassment are prevalent in the workplace, and young migrant women living on their own are more vulnerable to these practices than women living with their families. Young migrant women can be coerced into having unwanted sexual relations due to their economic vulnerability. Their experiences confirm the sexual harassment framework proposed by MacKinnon (1979), according to which workplace sexual harassment arises from and reinforces a labour market characterised by sex segregation and the sexual objectification of women.

Paradoxically, while appreciating the liberating anonymity, these women need to rely heavily on well-developed social networks, especially when accessing the labour market. The interviewees mobilise various types of capital, including erotic or sexual capital, to enter the workforce. In the notion of erotic or sexual capital, sexuality is transformed into a resource to achieve one's objectives, as discussed in Levy and Lieber's (2009) work on Chinese migrants in Paris. The mobilisation of erotic capital illustrates how these women enter new gender configurations that might be different than those dominant in their hometowns but have the same underlying mechanisms of unequal gender relations.

In the third and final key finding, the interviewees articulate the gendered geographical imaginaries that shape their migration projects. They demonstrate Appadurai's (1996) suggestion that the imaginary is a powerful force driving human action. Imaginaries about Tirana as a place bursting with opportunities and freedom and lacking the social control of gender norms entice these women to migrate there. The imaginary positions Tirana as a site where women may achieve individual freedoms unavailable in their hometowns. Nevertheless, the educated women migrants discussed in this chapter consider living in Tirana to be a transitional phase and express their desire to continue their migration project abroad. Their interviews reveal a chain of geographical imaginaries in which internal migration is insufficient by itself and entangled with international migration projects. As the participants express, the idea of moving abroad is deeply related to opposition to marriage and the contrasting ideal of the foreign husband, constructed based on media representations and other emigrants' stories.

Importantly, these cases illustrate the role of gender in shaping geographical imaginaries and consequently, migratory projects. For example, Riano (2015) analyses how the imaginaries of equality of Europe inform Latin American women's migration projects, influencing their decisions on how and where to migrate. Similarly, the interviewees in this chapter ground their imaginaries on the persistent opposition of tradition and modernity. Tradition refers to the hometown, and modernity first to the imagined life in Tirana and then to that abroad. Regarding their experience in Tirana, the interviews show that the presumed opposition of tradition and modernity cannot be supported, as evidenced by the women's paradoxical situation in their new city. This paradoxical situation drives them toward further gendered geographical imaginaries and gendered idealisation of abroad.

References

Appadurai, A. (1996). *Modernity at large: Cultural dimensions of globalization*. University of Minnesota Press.

Bourdieu, P. (1998). La précarité est aujourd'hui partout. In P. Bourdieu (Ed.), *Contre-feux, Propos pour servir à la résistance contre l'invasion néo-libérale* (pp. 95–101). Éditions Raisons d'agir.

Bourdieu, P., & Wacquant, L. J. (1992). *An invitation to reflexive sociology*. Polity Press.

Callegaro, M. (2008). Social desirability. In L. Paul (Ed.), *Encyclopedia of survey research methods* (pp. 825–826). SAGE Publications.

Çela, A., Fshazi, T., Mazniku, A., Kamberi, G., & Smaja, J. (2012). *Rinia Shqiptare 2011 – Mes besimit për të ardhmen dhe dyshimit për të tashmen!* [Albanian Youth 2011 - Between the faith about the future and the doubt about the present!]. Friedtich Ebert Stiftung.

Dahinden, J. (2009). Migration and mobility: Universality and resulting tensions. *Universality - From Theory to Practice*, 359–376.

Danaj, E. (2019). Young, educated, and female: Narratives of post-1991 internal Albanian migration. In G. T. Bonifacio (Ed.), *Global youth migration and gendered modalities* (pp. 235–254). Policy Press.

Danaj, E., Festy, P., Ekonomi, M., Lika, M., Guxho, A., & Zhllima, E. (2005). *Becoming an adult: Challenges and potentials of youth in Albania*. INSTAT.

Danaj, E., Plaku, A., Ekonomi, M., & Cavo, Z. (2008). *Unpaid care work – The invisible burden of women*. ASC and UNIFEM.

Drotbohm, H. (2010). Gossip and social control across the seas: Targeting gender, resource inequalities and support in cape Verdean transnational families. *African and Black Diaspora: An International Journal, 3*(1), 51–68.

Ekonomi, M., Danaj, E., Dakli, E., Gjermeni, E., Budowski, M., & Schweizer, M. (2004). *Gender perspectives in Albania*. INSTAT.

Erel, U. (2007). Constructing meaningful lives: Biographical methods in research on migrant women. *Sociological Research Online, 12*(4).

Erel, U. (2009). *Migrant women transforming citizenship: Life-stories from Britain and Germany*. Ashgate.

Findlay, A. M., King, R., Smith, F. M., Geddes, A., & Skeldon, R. (2012). World class? An investigation of globalization, difference and international student mobility. *Transactions of the Institute of British Geographers, 37*(1), 118–131.

Fredman, S. (2004). Women at work: The broken promise of Flexicurity. *Industrial Law Journal, 33*(4), 299–319.

Gibbs, J. P. (1981). *Norms, deviance, and social control: Conceptual matters*. Elsevier-North Holland.

Hakim, C. (2010). Erotic Capital. *European Sociological Review, 26*(5), 499–518.

INSTAT. (2012). *Rezultate kryesore nga Anketa e Forcave të Punës 2011 [Main results from the LFS 2011]*. INSTAT.

Kalaja, D. (2014, January 6). *Education and marriage patterns for young women in Albania*. E. Danaj.

Kihato, C. W. (2009). *Migration*. University of South Africa.

Kim, Y. (2012). Female individualization? Transnational mobility and media consumption of Asian women. In Y. Kim (Ed.), *Women and the Media in Asia the Precarious Self* (pp. 31–53). Palgrave Macmillan.

King, R., & Skeldon, R. (2010). 'Mind the gap!' Integrating approaches to internal and international migration. *Journal of Ethnic and Migration Studies, 36*(10), 1619–1646.

Kocaqi, M. (2013, December 5). *Sexual harassment and other types of violence against women in Tirana*. E. Danaj.

Kofman, E., Phizacklea, A., Raghuram, P., & Sales, R. (2000). *Gender and international migration in Europe: Employment, welfare and politics*. Routledge.

Lévy, F., & Lieber, M. (2009). La sexualité comme ressource migratoire. *Revue Française de Sociologie, 50*(4), 719–746.

MacKinnon, C. (1979). *Sexual harassment of working women: A case of sex discrimination*. Yale University Press.

Mai, N. (2004). 'Looking for a more modern life…': The role of Italian Television in the Albanian Migration to Italy. *Westminster Papers in Communication and Culture, 1*(1), 3–22.

Moujoud, N. (2011). La tradition n'est plus ce qu'elle était… Constructions historiques des discours sur migrantes, Maghreb et vieillesse. *Ecarts d'identité, 118*, 70–76.

Musaraj, S. (2009). Passport troubles: Social tactics and places of informal transactions in postsocialist Albania. *Anthropology of East Europe Review, 27*(2), 157–175.

Riaño, Y. (2015). Latin American women who migrate for love: Imagining European men as ideal partners. In E. Begonya & J. Roca (Eds.), *Rethinking romantic love. Discussions, imaginaries and practices* (pp. 45–60). Cambridge Scholars Publishing.

Riaño, Y., & Baghdadi, N. (2007). "Je pensais que je pourrais avoir une relation plus égalitaire avec un Européen". Le rôle dugenre et de l'imaginaire géographique dans la migration des femmes. *Nouvelles Questions Féministes, 26*(1), 38–53.

Schmoll, C. (2006). *Moving "on their own"? Mobility strategies and social networks of migrant women from Maghreb in Italy.* IIIS Discussion Paper 154.

Simmel, G. ([1903] 2002). The Metropolis and mental life. In G. Bridge, & S. Watson, The Blackwell City reader (pp. 11–20). Wiley-Blackwell.

Szymanski, D. M., Moffitt, L. B., & Carr, E. R. (2011). Sexual objectification of women: Advances to theory and research. *The Counseling Psychologist, 39*(1), 6–38.

Vullnetari, J. (2012). Women and migration in Albania: A view from the village. *International Migration, 50*(5), 169–188.

Open Access This chapter is licensed under the terms of the Creative Commons Attribution 4.0 International License (http://creativecommons.org/licenses/by/4.0/), which permits use, sharing, adaptation, distribution and reproduction in any medium or format, as long as you give appropriate credit to the original author(s) and the source, provide a link to the Creative Commons license and indicate if changes were made.

The images or other third party material in this chapter are included in the chapter's Creative Commons license, unless indicated otherwise in a credit line to the material. If material is not included in the chapter's Creative Commons license and your intended use is not permitted by statutory regulation or exceeds the permitted use, you will need to obtain permission directly from the copyright holder.

Chapter 7
International Student Returnees: Nowhere at Home

In this chapter, I explore the experiences of female migrants who migrated to undertake undergraduate or graduate studies rather than specifically for economic or work reasons. I analyse a group of female student migrants who returned to Tirana after their international migratory trajectories. Unlike the other group of international migrants introduced in Chap. 5 all the women in this group migrated with regular student visas and documents, and their destination countries are not limited to Greece and Italy but encompass a wider area.

The seven women featured in this chapter come from various cities in Albania but all ended up living in Tirana upon completing their studies abroad. Again, I refer to them as having migrated on their own, or without the physical presence of their families. Among these seven women, only one was married; none of the others were in committed relationships or cohabiting at the time the fieldwork was conducted. This group is composed of the following women:

Artemisa is 30 years old and from the city of Vlorë. She has a younger brother, who is also a student migrant, in the United States. In 2000, she migrated to Germany, where she studied Political Science, obtaining a bachelor's and a master's degree. After that, she found a job as a research assistant at her alma mater. She obtained legal residency but returned to Albania in 2008. Instead of moving back to Vlore, her city of origin, she settled in Tirana, where in 2012 she worked as jousnalist at a television station and as an adjunct lecturer. In 2012, she lived on her own in a rented studio in Komuna e Parisit, before moving back to Germany in 2014.

Beti is 31 years old and from the city of Durrës. Originally from Dibër, her family migrated to Durrës during the early 1990s. She has an older sister, who is married and lives in Durrës. In 1999, Beti migrated to Italy, where she studied Communications, receiving a bachelor's and a master's degree. She then moved to France, where she earned a doctorate in communication studies. In 2010, she

A shortened and summarized version of this chapter has been published as Danaj, E. (2019) Gendered experiences of international student migration: the case of Albania, in Gender, Place & Culture, A Journal of Feminist Geography, 26:4, 607–611.

© The Author(s) 2022

E. Danaj, *Women, Migration and Gendered Experiences*, IMISCOE Research Series, https://doi.org/10.1007/978-3-030-92092-0_7

returned to Albania but, like the other young women introduced in this chapter, to Tirana rather than her hometown of Durrës. In 2012, she worked as a university lecturer.[1] She first shared an apartment with a friend and later found a small one bedroom in Don Bosko, where she lived on her own in 2012.

Fiona is 28 years old and from the town of Kukës. Fiona has two younger sisters; one lives with their parents in Kukës, while the other works in Prishtina, Kosovo. In 2002, Fiona migrated to Romania, where she studied Language and Political Studies at the undergraduate level. After 3 years of studies, Fiona moved to the United Kingdom and graduated with a degree in Political Economy. In 2010, after returning to Tirana, she worked as a university lecturer and consultant and lived on her own in a small rented apartment in Don Bosko.

Egesta is 35 years old and from the town of Lezhë. Egesta has two younger sisters; the elder is married and lives in Vlora, her husband's city of origin, while the youngest lives with their parents in Lezhë. In 1995, Egesta left for Italy, where she studied and graduated with a degree in Psychology. Upon graduating, she first worked for a travel agency and later for a centre providing support to migrants, as a psychologist and social worker. She is a legal resident of Italy. In 2005, she returned to Tirana. In 2012, she worked for a television station and as a consultant for various projects while living on her own in a rented studio apartment in Komuna e Parisit.

Monika is 28 years old and from the city of Fier. She is an only child. In 2003, Monika moved to Tirana to pursue a bachelor's in Political Science. After 2 years of undergraduate studies, she left for Italy to study Political Economics. In 2009, she returned to Tirana. In 2012, Monika was working for an NGO and living in a rented studio apartment in Don Bosko.

Lindita is 28 years old and from the city of Vlorë. She has an older brother who is married and lives in Greece. In 2009, she left for Sweden, where she obtained a master's in Business Administration. Her scholarship required that she return to Albania upon graduating. In 2011, she relocated to Tirana, and as of 2012, she was employed by an NGO and pursuing various other temporary projects. Lindita lived in a shared apartment with two young women in Komuna e Parisit.

Elida is 38 years old, is from the town of Dibër, and is an only child. She is the only married woman in this group and has a young daughter. In 1994, Elida first moved to Tirana with her partner to pursue her studies. Afterwards, in 2007, she moved to Italy on her own to obtain a doctoral degree in Public Policy. She returned to Tirana in 2010. In 2012, Elida was working as a university lecturer and lived with her husband, daughter, and parents in an owned apartment in Komuna e Parisit.

---

[1]To protect the interviewees' identities, I do not specify whether they worked for a private or a public university.

7.1 Pre-Migration Phase—Between Individual Desires and Family Support

Student migration in post-communist Albania began in the early 1990s.[2] Of the women in this chapter, Egesta was the first to migrate, in 1995, and Lindita the last to do so, in 2009. In this section, I explore their reasons for choosing to study abroad and the actors involved in the preparatory phase of the student migration project.

7.1.1 Migration Driven by a Diverse Set of Motivations

Although student migrants move for an obvious reason – to further their education – their narratives point to a wide range of motivations. Let us examine in more detail why these young women migrated abroad.

> *Artemisa: There were many reasons why I wanted to study in a European country, whether in Italy, Germany or France. First, I sought a good education and, later, a prestigious job.*

Artemisa had not thoroughly thought out her plan for migrating abroad to get her education, but she knew that she wanted to study abroad, no matter where. Investing in a better education in order to have better job opportunities was the first reason mentioned by her. Especially since 1991, a foreign university diploma has been perceived as an added value for finding a job back in Albania or abroad. Monika, too, says that finding a 'good job' abroad was what pushed her to apply persistently to study in other countries. She says that she initially migrated from Fier to study Political Science in Tirana. There, she continued to send applications to foreign universities, and after 2 years, she managed to leave for Italy. Elida and Lindita have similar stories despite their different circumstances. Elida, the only married woman in this group, left for Italy to do a three-year doctoral programme that would qualify her for a better-paid job *'in the private universities that were just about to be established'* in Tirana. Lindita, too, says that she went to Sweden for a two-year master's degree to become familiar with public institutions and to have a wider range of better employment opportunities upon return by virtue of holding a well-regarded master's degree.

Although education as a passport to a better job is chief among the reasons pushing women to migrate, other reasons also come to the fore. The words of Artemisa and Fiona point to a second one.

---

[2] Since 1992, increasing numbers of young Albanian people, mostly young and single, have gone abroad to study (Trimçev et al., 2005, 7–8). The figures for this category are complete. In 2003–2004, approximately 9000 Albanian students were studying abroad (Gërmenji & Milo, 2011, 347). According to Zenelaga and Sotirofski (2011, 5) during the 2007–2008 academic year, the highest number of foreign students in Italy was from Albania, with 11,415 Albanian students at Italian universities.

> *Artemisa: I wanted to gain more experience, to see how it was to live for a while in a developed country, to live alone and be free and independent. I wanted this because living by myself for some years would help me come back stronger to Albania*

> *Fiona: I had this strong desire to go abroad, and at the same time, I wanted to succeed in my endeavours [studies and work]. I thought that the only way to grow was to study abroad. At the same time, I wanted to leave the life of Kukës behind. It was just school and home and school and home. I knew I would go crazy were I unable to leave Kukës. ... When I left, it was mainly because of the mentality... as I wanted to leave Kukes and live a different life. ... It is so difficult for a young girl to live in a small city such as Kukës where everyone knows each other, and everyone has eyes on you all the time. ... It's like living inside the Big Brother ... I needed to go somewhere else where I could be freer.*

Migrating to study abroad is an escape from the lives they are leading in their cities of origin and from the constraining gender roles and surveillance of their hometowns. Living abroad is perceived as a gateway to the promised land of freedom and independence. Migration appears to embody the pursuit of anonymity and autonomy byputting physical distance between the migrant and her community, especially small cities where young women are subject to stricter social control.

Thirdly, education may also be an explicit strategy in the service of migration in those situations where women wanted to migrate in and of itself, and education provided the best gateway to do so. Artemisa says:

> *Moving abroad for studies was a safer way. You could get a visa and leave Albania like an average person, not through speed boats, and I know very well what that means as I come from Vlora.*

Egesta echoes a similar sentimet:

> *I wanted to leave Albania. Many people were going in different ways and, to be honest, I wanted to leave; it was like an obsession. ... But I was an excellent student, had perfect grades in high school, and sought to use them as a way to leave Albania and not go illegally. My parents would have never agreed to let me migrate by illegal means. I am just saying [laughs]. Studying abroad was the only option I was considering during that period.*

Crossing borders through legalised ways (student visas) supplies a further motivation for young women student migrants. Although we saw in the earlier chapters that young women also migrate through illegalised practices, there is a clear and dominant gender division across the different migration paths in that women generally pursue legalised pathways. In the context of constraining migration regimes, student migration serves as a valuable way for young women to leave Albania through legalised practices. As mentioned, complete data on Albanian student migration are still lacking, but existing research (Trimcev et al., 2005) shows that Albania has sent more female students and professionals abroad than male ones. Furthermore, Zenelaga and Sotirofski (2011, 5) report that during the 2007–2008 academic year, 4659 of the Albanian students in Italy were men, and 6756 women. Finally, Egesta's quotation recognizes the parents' role in the possibility (or lack thereof) of migrating abroad.

7.1.2 Making Migration Possible—Relying on 'Parental Support

In this section, we turn our attention to the parents' role in these women's migration, which is significant and manifold. Similar to the findings discussed in Chap. 6, the interviews in this chapter show that parents aim to offer their children better educational opportunities than what are available in Albania. In most cases, therefore, the young women and their parents make the decision together on a basis of mutual consent. Egesta says:

> I had made up my mind that I was going to study abroad, and if I failed in my undergraduate studies, I would try again to go overseas for a master's degree. My parents wanted me to study abroad too.

First, parents are visibly involved in the pre-migration motivation phase. Parents want their daughters to study abroad so they can secure better jobs and achieve upward social mobility. Children's education is a significant value for Albanian families, regardless of the parents' education level (Danaj et al., 2005). Beti, for example, says that her parents moved from Dibër to Durrës in the early 1990s to give her 'better opportunities for study and work. Thus, they wanted to send me abroad for my studies at any cost'. For Beti's parents, Durrës, a bigger, coastal, central city, offered more opportunities for migration abroad compared to their native town of Dibër.

Second, parents also play a central role in facilitating the migration project through financial support, mostly – though not exclusively – by covering the costs of moving abroad. Not all student migrants receive scholarships and, in many cases, their parents' savings finance their studies, at least long enough to get them settled. Egesta says:

> My parents gave me some money for the first few months, some of their savings. … I had no scholarship because I enrolled individually, not through any scholarship programme.

Beti also relied on her family's financial support during her first year of study, as they suplemented the partial scholarship she received from the Italian government. Similarly, Fiona recounts that her parents assisted her financially to supplement the partial scholarship she received from Romanian government programmes. Artemisa also says that her parents helped her financially during her first months in Germany until she found a job and could cover her own expenses. Similarly, in researching Chinese student migration, Kajanus (2014) emphasises how parents often use their life savings to finance their daughters' education.

Thirdly, as in Chaps. 5 and 6, here too the family acts as a shield protecting a daughter migrating alone from family and community gossip. Egesta describes this role when discussing the support her family gave her to migrate abroad:

> Another problem was that back in 1995, few girls, especially from small cities, were leaving the country alone. I can imagine some possibly embarrassing moments for my parents. I mean it has been a difficult situation for them in many ways. That is why I consider this a great sacrifice from my family. … They have had to endure some gossip from the neighbours

and also from the family, the usual things you know: how could you send your daughter alone? She will be doing what she wants now, etc.

Once again, the parents' role is revealed to be manifold. They emotionally motivate and support their daughters to migrate abroad for their studies and help them escape social pressures in their place of origin.

The fourth type of parental support emerges in the case of Elida, who had to leave her husband and daughter in Tirana to move to Italy for a three-year PhD programme. As mentioned, Elida says that she migrated to find a better-paid job upon returning to Albania. She explains:

> *I had already discussed this with Genti (Elida's husband). … But we had to find a solution for our daughter. It would be too much for Genti to take care of her alone during all this time. I asked my parents to move to Tirana, as at that moment my father was retired and my mother unemployed. So, they could take care of the daughter and the house. … My father was mostly doing grocery shopping. That had also been his speciality back in Diber [laughs].*

The decision to migrate abroad for studying depends upon the transference of Elida's caregiver role not to her husband but to her parents, particularly to 'her mother. This case shows another configuration of the parents' role and family solidarity in supporting a daughter's migration by assuming her caregiver role. Amid 'resistance to sharing care at home' (Hochschild, 2000, 141) between husband and wife, it was the support provided by Elida's parents that allowed her to migrate. In most cases, this very transference of the caregiver role to grandparents enables mothers to migrate, as also observed by Hondagneu-Sotelo and Avila (1997) and Olwig (1999). Grandparents' (mostly grandmothers') care for grandchildren facilitates the migration not only of single mothers but also of married ones like Elida. Parents free their daughters from their caregiver role so that they can migrate, as research on highly educated Turkish and Chinese migrants has also revealed (Erel, 2009, Kajanus, 2014). The case of Elida also highlights the fact that student migrants are not only students but also daughters and wives. Their decisions and negotiations about their migration project, therefore, reflect these other roles, as also underscored by King and Raghuram (2013) and Oluwaseun (2016).

The parents' role appears to be quite crucial for the migration of these young women. However, social network support is not limited to parents alone, but also extends to friends, relatives and other acquaintances, and is evident throughout the various phases of the migration project, as elaborated in the next section. Parents do not physically accompany their daughters on the move to the destination countries (unlike, say, in the case of the young women moving to Tirana in Chap. 6). Still, kinship and friendship networks act as substitutes for parents, taking charge of these student migrants' initial reception in their destination country.

7.1.3   Organising One's Migration: Relying on the Support of Social Networks

Boyd (1989) states that in many cases, the destination country is chosen based on the social networks migrants have available. That holds true for most of the women discussed in this chapter, as Artemisa illustrates:

> *I left Albania in 2000 for Germany. I had finished my high school studies in Vlorë and was applying to study in Italy. It was by chance that a cousin of ours who had migrated to Germany at the beginning of the 1990s told us that he could help me go to Germany instead of Italy. … He found all the necessary information about registering for a language course and everything… It made everything more comfortable than going somewhere else.*

Fiona and Egesta also stress the significance of social networks in the destination country. Egesta explicitly states *'I went to Italy as the cousins I had there helped me with the documents at the university'*. Fiona says that she went to Romania first as her family had some relatives there, and they helped her tackle the initial bureaucracy issues. Vullnetari (2007) describes Albanian migration as a process of chain migration in which people migrate to regions and countries where they have relatives or friendship networks. These cases further illustrate this pattern of Albanian migration: female student migrants often follow a chain migration pattern moving to countries where they already have established social networks, whether relatives or friends.

Elida, too, says she chose Italy as she had some relatives there who could assist her. However, she adds:

> *Italy was the best option as it is so close to Albania, I could quickly fly home if needed. I am not sure I could have borne it to be far from Albania, you know. Your mind mostly stays at home, on my daughter, so being in Italy would be more bearable.*

Elida is the only woman to mention the proximity of her family in Albania as a criterion for her migration destination. The other women in this chapter do not report similar reasons. Elida's prioritising proximity appears to be related to her role as mother and caregiver. Often, women choose to migrate to nearby countries so as to not be very far from their families, to return home more quickly and to combine their reproductive and their productive roles better.

In other cases, the destination depends on the availability of scholarships, along with the availability of social networks. Monika states that the Italian government granted her a partial scholarship after she applied with the support of a friend already living in Italy as a student migrant. Lindita is the only woman who says that she migrated to Sweden after she was accepted to a master's of business administration programme and granted a full scholarship there without having any local social network.

Aid from social networks extends from helping incoming migrants prepare documents and sharing preliminary practical information, to providing accommodations during the initial migration phase. In some cases, friends and relatives secure housing for women. Monika shared a room with a friend who went to Italy 2 years earlier. Likewise, Elida, Fiona and Egesta say that at first, their relatives hosted them. Again, similarly to Chap. 5, the roles of parents and social networks in these women's migration processes illustrate how moving on one's own is a relatively complex process involving a wide range of actors.

7.2 Transition Phase—Life Abroad

In this section, I focus on the early phases of adjustment to the destination cities and the main patterns that emerge. Again, social networks play a significant, palpable role in how the women cope with the new everyday practices and social relations, as well as the new divisions of space and time, in the destination cities to establish a smooth everyday routine (Boyd, 1989; Shu & Hawthorne, 1995, Çaro, 2011) in these novel, unknown places. I use Çaro's (2011, 82) definition of adjustment as a process by which 'individuals attempt to pursue their goals, satisfy their needs and respond to cultural differences in a new environment'. In this regard, Fiona and Egesta describe how their cousins helped them get to know their new cities and how these cities were organised, their main streets and corners and other useful information. All the women mentioned in this chapter migrated to big European cities, some during the 1990s and early 2000s. The organisation of life in their cities of origin, and sometimes even in Tirana, was quite different in terms of infrastructure, transportation, social relations, communication styles, the organisation of time and space and the functioning of institutions. Those who migrated directly from their cities of origin used to spend their lives within minimal spaces, such as school and home, and were accompanied by parents or other family members most of the time. Thus, many of these young women faced new everyday practices, from mundane everyday tasks such as buying a metro ticket to widescale communication patterns and gendered divisions of space and time. They no longer had to conform to their hometowns, and space and their timewas not confined to home and school.

In the next two sections, I expand on two elements of what that which Egesta calls the 'new world' means for most of these women: the relations of anonymity that prevail in the 'big city' and the new gendered division of space and time.

7.2.1 Facing Anonymity

In the following excerpt, Beti expresses how she struggled with the new minutiae of everyday life. She also highlights shame as a feature of the dominant culture, especially in small cities in Albania, used to control others (as also identified by Mai & Paladini, 2013). The feeling of 'shame' mentioned by Beti may be explained by a culture of control that often leads to self-censure. Nixon's (2009) analysis of how shame in Albania works as a tool for social pressure reveals that, during communism, shame served as a tool for the social control of both genders but, since 1991, it has been applied more to women's behaviour. One's behaviour seems to be controlled by an inner voyeur that projects the judgment of the community, as demonstrated by the fact that it took these women some time to get used to their newfound freedom.

> *Beti: The first year in Italy was quite tricky, but after some time, you got used to living there. It was more complicated when it came to some tiny, stupid things. I didn't know how to use various automatic machines for cards or train tickets, all these silly things that I was unfamiliar with. And I was so ashamed. I was embarrassed because I was thinking that everybody was looking at me, but nobody was looking at me. … I was used to my neighbourhood where people were checking on you: "'What is she doing? How is she doing? Who's she talking to'?"*

Similarly, Fiona states*:*

> *In the beginning, I was embarrassed to walk alone or go to the park to read a book by myself as I watched the others do. But later I got used to this as I understood that nobody was judging me there.*

These quotations show that it is not easy for such student migrants to go from a provincial city in Albania, with very few afterschool activities but strict community control exercised under the guise of tradition, to a big European city, with utterly unknown spaces and modus operandi. They become familiar with new social relations, with the anonymity that replaces the constant social control in their hometowns, with new technologies and urban facilities, and with different bodily representations. In this context, Fiona recounts while laughing, that, within a short period, she went "*from a normal long-haired young girl from Kukësto a punk, short-haired, young girl in Bucharest'*." Not only do the young women gain a new relationship to their bodies but, in the cities of destination, they also faced new gendered organisations of time and space, as I elaborate in the next section.

Finally, I want to turn to the cases of Monika and Lindita. They report fewer difficulties adjusting to living more independently and new everyday practices than the other women. They had already taken a step in the process of migration by moving internally from their cities of origin to Tirana,so migration abroad was a continuation of their independent life. It appears that they had already acquired some mobility capital (Dahinden, 2010b), which assists one not only in migration possibilities in and of themselves, but also in gaining experience in how to adapt to the new social realities of migration. By migrating to Tirana on their own, Monika and Lindita had already faced anonymity, new everyday practices, and new gendered divisions of space and time.

7.2.2 A New Gendered Division of Space and Time

Before migration, most of the interviewed women split their days and space between school and home. Once abroad, many discover a continuum between home, school, work and social life. Beti says:

> *Another challenging thing at the beginning was how to organise the day because I used to get home very early. [In Albania], after school, I went back home, had lunch, and then did some work in the house and studied. But the afternoon was mainly at my place, and very rarely did I go out alone. […] In Italy, I had an entirely different experience. We had classes late in the afternoon, people were inviting me to go out for a drink in the evening, and things like this. … These were all new things for me at the beginning.*

New spaces, different or unavailable from those in their cities of origin, were finally open to them. In the beginning, Egesta was scared of the idea of having afternoon classes; she did not know '*what to do during the free hours in the morning*'. It took her some time to get to understand the city as she was scared to walk alone '*in such a big city.*' She adds:

> *In Lezhë, the only thing I did alone was buying bread next to our building. Now imagine me having to walk alone for more than half an hour, sometimes during the evening. … The beginning was challenging.*

She adds that, initially, she spent a lot of time at home but, after a while, it served only as a place to sleep, and she spent her day at school, work, and doing other activities with friends.

As the students appropriate new spaces outside their cities of origin, they also get to know the new gendered organisations of space. Monika illustrates this:

> *It was helpful knowing the safe places where to go to. … You know, some streets are dodgy, not very suitable for women to walk, especially during the night-time, so I was careful not to go nearby these areas that I was told about by my friends.*

The cities of destination themselves have their gendered divisions of space and time that may differ from the students' hometowns and they represent new configurations where space and time are not necessarily without constraints for women, as mentioned in the previous excerpt. Women everywhere learn to avoid some areas of the city during the evening, for instance, for fear of certain risks, such as sexual assault (Rose, 1993).

The interviews illustrate the entanglement of gender with the organisation of space and time. As Massey (1994, 186) states, 'the gendering of space and place both reflects and has effects back on how gender is constructed and understood in the societies in which we live'. The interviewed women come from post-communist Albania, where the gendered configuration of space and time was transformed after the communist period. After communism, public spaces in cities became more dangerous for women and girls, and a more traditional gender division of time and labour re-emerged. (In the immediate post-communist period, women and girls were mostly confined to the domestic space and labour.) The gendered division of space is a common feature across many societies but also differs geographically and historically (McDowell, 1983). The women discussed in this chapter move from a specific gender division of time and space to new such configurations that, in turn, influence their construction and understanding of femininity. Despite the difficulties that such changes may entail initially, as Egesta mentions, they appropriate new organisations of space and time, distinct from those of their hometowns, affecting, for instance, streets, parks, bars, late-night hours, and even physical representations.

Elida's case presents another example of how gender shapes space and time. She recounts how at first, when she moved abroad, she experienced some challenging moments because she was far from her daughter and the sense of *'being a bad mother'*. Elida often declined invitations to social activities, such as dinners and other gatherings, as she felt guilty over leaving her daughter and husband behind in Tirana. She says, *'I was just going to classes and, after that, straight back home.'* She organised her time and space according to maternal guilt by distancing herself from activities in the destination city. The experience of transnational mothering may be painful due to feelings of guilt. As Erel (2009, 126) emphasises in the case of Turkish migrant women, 'mothers may also find it difficult to reconcile transnational motherhood with their ideals of good mothering'. Elida says that this feeling of guilt and anxiety over her family negatively influenced her academic results during the first year. Still, afterwards, she *'made up her mind to continue and succeed'*. Student migrants are not only students but also daughters, mothers, wives; their migratory experiences, therefore, reflect these other roles (King & Raghuram, 2013; Oluwaseun, 2016; Brooks, 2013). Given the aim of this analysis is to examine these migrant women's experiences after they migrated to Tirana, I focus less on the other phases of their migration. As in Chap. 6, I attempt to narrow in on the significant features of this group's migration abroad, and the adjustment process during their earlier migration phases appears to be such a feature. That process of adjustment entails making a new home (Ahmed, 1999) in new social realities. After the return to Albania that, for most, also means another move to Tirana, they undergo the processes of adjustment and homemaking all over again, as analysed in the next section.

7.3   Tirana as a 'Middle Ground'

This section explores the main patterns of the return experience for these women who moved to Tirana. Here, I focus on their reasons for returning and their methods for coping with the adjustment process in Tirana in their social networks and the labour market. As in Chap. 6, return migration also entails a new move (i.e., not a return to their city or town of origin), making it difficult to speak in terms of a strict return. I start by analysing their reasons for returning to Albania and for moving to Tirana instead of their hometowns. I then trace the main patterns of their adjustment to Tirana, which is a new place for most.

7.3.1 Reasons for Returning

Similar to Chap. 5, it is quite hard to delineate the motivations for returning to Tirana, as they often overlap or are due to factors attributable to both Albania and the destination country. Furthermore, the grounds for returning to Albania are, for some, intermingled with their reasons to return not to their hometowns but to Tirana. First, a distinction, albeit not entirely clear, could be made among those migrants unwilling to return and those planning to return. Only Elida and Lindita left Albania with clear, voluntary plans to return from the beginning of their migration. Elida moved to Italy for her doctoral studies while her family (husband and daughter) stayed in Tirana, and she had no plans to stay in Italy after graduation. Lindita received her scholarship on the condition that she return to Albania after studying for 2 years, and she complied with the restriction.

The other women returned to Albania for various reasons, some unexpected. Family reasons are the most prevalent. As Egesta explains it, she returned because her father became ill:

> *I didn't want to return to Albania. After so many years in Italy, I had no plans to return. But my father had some health issues, and I decided to come back for a few years, and here I am still. I came back in 2005 after ten years [of migration]. I didn't want to return as I had nothing, except my family, to attract me here. … But I had to, for my father who was ill and for my family, so that I could support them.*

In this particular case, Egesta had to return to Albania. Although her sister lived there, as Egesta says, she was married and lived with her husband's family in Vlorë, so she could not be of constant help, physically or financially, to their parents. Thus, the household gender structure influenced her return. Care is considered the responsibility of women; in this case, of the single daughter. Artemisa, too, returned from Germany in 2008 after 8 years when her mother suffered a long neurosis after her younger sister's death in a car accident. To be near her mother and father, Artemisa decided to stay in Tirana for a while:

> *I didn't plan my return. The accident just happened, and I came back as soon as possible. … My mother was not recovering from the stress and the pain, so I thought it would be better to stay a little bit longer with her. Maybe a change would help her recover soon. … I decided to live for some time in Albania to be closer to my parents. They still live in Vlorë, as they have all their life there, but being in Tirana allows me to meet them almost every weekend. … I go there, or they come to Tirana.*

Egesta and Artemisa had already obtained legal residency permits in Italy and Germany and could therefore return to their home countries or move to another country. Possession of a residency card in a foreign country facilitates the decision to return to Albania and gives a sense of comfort and flexibility if the women envisage migrating again. According to Mai and Paladini (2013, 50), having legal residency status in Italy or another country remains a priority for Albanian migrants and constitutes a safety valve, as stated in Chap. 5. In the case of Egesta and Artemisa, their Italian and German residency cards provided an additional resource allowing them to return to Albania and leave again quickly.

That brings us to the second reason why the women decided to return: the lack of residency cards or passports in the destination country. Difficulties obtaining residency permits and visas are a significant reason for returning to Albania (Zenelaga & Sotirofski, 2011, Trimçev et al., 2005). Some of the participants cite the impossibility of regularising their stay abroad as their primary reason for returning.

Fiona: I returned because of the residence permit in the UK. … I couldn't arrange the documents for work, and I could not register for doctoral studies as it was costly. I could have found some other ways, such as marrying, for example, finding someone and marrying him to stay. But I was not ready for this, to be honest. I know that many do this, but I could not, it was like stepping on my dignity. I may sound foolish...

Fiona's return story points to a combination of structural constraints, individual agency, and the difficulty of getting a residency permit in the choice to return and preserve her *'dignity'.*" Beti and Monika also report the structural constraint of obtaining a work permit as a reason for returning to Albania. Beti says that after failing to arrange for a work permit in Italy, she left for France but still had difficulties switching from a student visa to a work permit, so she *'thought it best to return to Albania for some time".* This demonstrates how the impossibility of complying with residency permit regimes drives circular migration or moving among various countries, as defined by Triandafyllidou (2013). Switching from a student permit to a work permit is a process strongly tied to the labour market structure in the destination country.

Unwillingness to do "any sort of job in the country of destination is a third reason for returning to Albania, as Monika illustrates:

It was complicated to find an appropriate job that would count towards a work permit, and I didn't want to work in a whatever position only to stay there. That is why I decided to come back, as I thought that I could find a better job in Tirana, more appropriate for my education... My roommate stayed in Italy. She is from Fier too, but she didn't want to return to Albania. We both completed bachelor's and master's studies in Bologna. … I returned. She found a job in a travel agency, nothing to do with political economy and her master's studies. But she didn't want to come back, and this was the way to stay there as she applied for a work permit.

Mai and Paladini (2013) describe the marginalisation of Albanian migrants (economic and student) in Italy and their dilemma of whether to stay in Italy or return to Albania and try their luck in finding jobs in their professions. The reasons why migrants return thus are related to structural constraints, such as the absence of regular residency permits and the structure of the labour market in the destination country(ies). As stated by Cassarino (2004), the decision-making process leading refugees to return is explained not only by individual factors but also by broader social and economic contexts influenced by the situations faced in the host or home country. Similarly to the cases presented here, Sondhi and King (2017) show that female Indian international migrants return due to visa expiry after completion of studies, the desire or obligation to stay close to their parents, and the better job prospects in their home countries. The difficulty of clearly defining the return as voluntary or involuntary arises here, too.

7.3.2 Choosing Tirana as a Middle Ground

The women in this chapter all settled in Tirana instead of their hometowns. First, Tirana appears to offer more opportunities for finding jobs related to their education and experience.

> *Egesta: I live in Tirana and go very often to Lezhë. It's a less-than-one-hour trip now. [...] I didn't think of living in Lezhë when I returned as I could not find a job related to my education. Indeed, I returned as my father was ill, but staying unemployed in Lezhë would not help him much. I needed to continue working to be more useful to them all [Egesta's family].*

Egesta preferred returning to Tirana over her place of origin due to the economic opportunities available in the capital. Although she returned for family reasons, she preferred to live in Tirana and take care of her family at the same time. She was able to do this thanks to the improved infrastructure of Albania, which has shortened the time it takes to cover distances.[3] Thus, travelling and visiting one's family can be done comfortably and quickly. Artemisa tells a similar story. She goes to Vlorë very often to stay with her parents, and they also come to Tirana more frequently than before her return.

> *I had no idea where to work in Vlorë. Tirana seemed a little different, a growing city and with a lot of international and private institutions. Nowadays, it's not such a great distance, less than two hours by car, so I can quickly go there if they need me, and I usually go at least two weekends per month, and my parents often visit as well. It is suitable for them too, to come to Tirana and have some distraction.*

Economic prospects and better job opportunities are therefore the first reason why returnees choose Tirana instead of their hometowns.

Secondly, for those whose first migration abroad was also an escape from the social control and the mentality in their cities of origin, Tirana, asa big city, may be still considered a getaway from their towns of origin. These migrants move to Tirana in an attempt to continue the lifestyle they nurtured abroad, living on their own away from their communities of origin.

> *Fiona: I returned and decided to live in Tirana, as a middle ground. Going back to Kukës was absolutely out of the question. I go there very often... but I could not live there. The pressure of the small city is unbearable. ... I could not go and live with my family after eight years of living alone. It is so difficult to go back to the comments, 'Where are you going'? 'You are coming home late', etc.*

> *Artemisa: But I never thought to stay in Vlorë, first of all as I could not get back to that way of living in a very provincial city where everybody controls everybody else, with very aggressive men, no respect for women at all, lack of safety in the streets, a lot of these things.*

Although they have not lived previously in Tirana, they imagined it to be a big city, with a different lifestyle from their hometowns and somehow similar to the cities in which they lived abroad.

---

[3]The road infrastructure has been visibly improved since the early 2010s. For example, where it once took six hours to go from Tirana to Kukës, it now takes only one and a half.

Fiona: Tirana appeared to be a more open city compared to Kukës, with more job opportu-nities, and people returning from abroad ... more of a cultural life, more activities. ... I've had not so much contact with people in Tirana. ... it's not that I'd visited Tirana so much previously. ... I was not planning to return, so that's why.

Again, as analysed in the previous chapter, Fiona's quotation shows that geographical gendered imaginaries shape migration projects, illustrating Riano's (2015, 45) descriptions of the role of gender aspirations and geographical imaginations in migratory projects. Imaginaries about Tirana as a place of opportunities and freedom, with less social control through gender norms, inform the women's plan to return to Tirana. The capital shines in the imaginary of these women, who hope to continue the life they had abroad. For instance, Artemisa says that, to her eyes, Tirana appears as a place where she can continue living on her own, with '*no unbearable gossiping around*'.

In these cases, we notice a process of estrangement from their hometowns. Ahmed (1999, 343) argues that '"the past"' becomes associated with a home impossible to inhabit and be inhabited by, in the present. ... Migration can hence be considered as a process of estrangement, a process of becoming estranged from that which was inhabited as home.' By staying in Tirana, these young women find a middle ground between their previous homes, their hometowns, and the homes they made during international migration. Living in Tirana helps them preserve the independence they gained abroad and secure good jobs while also maintaining a relationship with their hometowns and caring for their parents. Gender informs their practices, as it becomes manifest in their frequent visits to their cities of origin to look after their parents. Moreover, gender influences the women's choice of Tirana over their hometowns, which are viewed as less free with regards to gender expectations and relations and as sites of stricter social control—places to which they have become estranged.

7.3.3 Tirana: Between 'Estrangement' and 'Homemaking'

Most of the migrant women discussed in this chapter lived abroad for longer than 4 years and did not visit Albania regularly. Elida is the only one who travelled to Albania a couple of times a year as her family (daughter and husband) stayed in Tirana. The financial costs associated with frequent travel to Albania from the UK or Germany also pose an issue. Still, it is important to note that most of the women who left Albania, had no apparent plans to return. Returning to Tirana after several years or moving to Tirana upon their return entails a new process of adjustment to the city in finding housing and jobs and learning everyday practices.

Nevertheless, their interviews show that the migrants do not return out of the blue, and with no plans, but rather engage in varying amounts of preparation beforehand. A returning migrant mobilises various ways to prepare for the return. Particularly for these women who are also moving to a new and unknown place, this requires a process of adjustment to a new location (Ley & Kobayashi, 2009) that is often anticipated through previous transnational relations with people in the home country. Let us explore in detail some of the patterns of this new adjustment process.

First, mobilising existing social relations is one of the essential elements in the process of returning and adjusting to Tirana. As seen, friendships play a larger role than family relations here. Monika recalls that while in Italy, she maintained her friendship contacts in Tirana and *'knew a little bit of what I was to expect back in Tirana'*. Dahinden (2010b) argues that often migrants maintain transnational relations that turn out to be highly relevant after the return. These transnational networks might not be robust but are mobilised after the return to cope with the adjustment process. Artemisa speaks about how some of her friends from Vlora have moved to Tirana:

> *I have not had much contact with my old friends in Vlora, but with two or -three of them, I kept in touch more … They had moved to Tirana … It was good to know some people here [in Tirana], especially at the beginning after you return after many years abroad. … She [an old friend from her hometown now living in Tirana] helped me a lot to find an apartment. … You have someone with whom to have lunch sometimes or get invited to her place.*

Additionally, Beti says that she only had a few friends left in Albania, only one of whom was living in Tirana, but that friend's help was crucial upon her double return.

> *When I came back from France, I was a little bit depressed. I came to Tirana and was living at a friend's house. I wanted to start searching for a job immediately, … but I was entirely shocked by the chaos in Tirana. … Here, everything was being done through friends and acquaintances. I almost went crazy. But this friend of mine helped me a lot to adapt a little bit.*

Beti's friend acquaints her with where the locals go to have coffee or attend cultural events. The use of networks, friendship networks in this case, is crucial for everyday life and for finding employment (as I elaborate in the next section). Therefore, it is useful to understand how these social networks are built.

Here, we come to the second point of this section: the intricate weaving of new social networks. Most of these women seek out relationships with international students returning from abroad who followed similar pathways. The ways the women build their social networks seem to follow a homophilic principle, both in terms of status and value. In status homophily, similarity 'comprises the large, socio-demographic dimensions, which stratify society: i.e., attributed or acquired characteristics like ethnicity, gender, age, religion, education or occupation' (Dahinden, 2010a, 128). Status homophily can be seen in the case of female, educated, returned migrants who stay more frequently with women than men, and with both women and men who have similar education pathways and experiences. 'Value homophily, on the other hand, is based on shared values, attitudes and beliefs' (Dahinden, 2010a, 128).

> *Egesta: I have made some friends, mostly women and a few men with similar pathways to mine. They have also been abroad, and they have studied abroad and are now back in Tirana to work. It is easier to be with them as we have similar ways of thinking, of organising the day. We feel the same lack of activities here in Tirana.*

Similarly, Artemisa says that she has not made many new friends but, of the ones she has, the majority are young women, returned student migrants. Monika, in contrast, says that she has many friends of approximately the same age, young female and male return migrants who have studied abroad:

I spend a lot of time with them. We share quite the same passions and ideas. … We struggle a lot to create some new spaces for debate and exchange of ideas. … A lot of young people are returning from abroad, and sometimes they do not feel at ease in Tirana, and when we are together, it feels better.

This brings us to the third point in this section: after returning to Tirana, most young women try to maintain their previous habits, for instance, going to a particular coffeeshop which reminds them of their life abroad:

Beti: I used to go to the French bakery here in Tirana every weekend, to establish a routine that I had in France. It's not the same, I know, but just to do something I loved to do there and I was missing here.

Similarly, Fiona goes to a coffee shop doubling as an art space established by a friend who is also a return migrant. Fiona says that this coffee shop makes her feel at home, reminding her of the places she went to while abroad. Thus, the return from abroad involves adjustment processes that do not demand detachment from or abandonment of the previous migratory experience (Cassarino, 2004). The interviewees go to bookshops, cafés and cultural centres where they follow particular routines, meet with other people similar to them and keep up with certain cultural activities. This behaviour may explain the creation of new communities in Tirana that consist mostly of young people returning from abroad who try to engage in cultural and social activities and create spaces alternative to those that are managed by the state or that are entirely absent. These gatherings of young women and men returning from migratory experiences can be analysed through the processes of estrangement and homemaking (Ahmed, 1999). These particular young people may form these new communities 'through the shared experience of not being fully at home' (Ahmed, 1999, 345).

The fourth point worth noting is that adjustment and homemaking in Tirana involve both old and new Albanian networks as well as the social networks established during migration. The web of social networks is quite intricate and includes foreign connections. Women in this group maintain their social contacts and relations abroad after their return to Tirana. For Egesta and Artemisa, keeping in touch with their previous social links is relatively easy, as they both have long-term residence permits in Italy and Germany. These permits serve as a mobility resource, allowing them to visit their destination countries and maintain their contacts. However, new technologies such as the Internet and, more recently, social media also facilitate these transnational relationships. For instance, Fiona and Monika mention that they talk regularly with their friends (in the UK and Italy, respectively) through various types of online chat programmes. Fiona says:

It is good to talk with them [friends in the UK] often. … We talk about the social activities they have there, anything new and exciting I make here—movies, books, conferences, articles. I mean, the things that we talked about there, now we talk about through Google Talk or Facebook. … It's virtual, but it's okay, it's comfortable. … I think I would go crazy without this continuation of my friendship with them. … Can you imagine, starting a new life from scratch, like a tabula rasa? That would be awful.

In Fiona's case, previous social networks serve to mitigate the adjustment process upon her return. Again, as highlighted by Cassarino (2004), the return process is not merely a turning page but also includes the maintenance of existing habits and social networks. Additionally, Elida often talks to friends she made in Italy:

I keep in touch with some of my colleagues from my PhD programme. … We share information about our work, about conferences, or books and articles that could help us in our work. … Information about conferences or workshops abroad is the most valuable, as they have more connections than I do here in Tirana, so keeping these contacts helps me a lot with that.

In this case, relationships with previous social contacts continue in the context of professional life. Black and King (2004) state that returnees need to maintain their access to the broader international professional and social world in which they have worked and lived. This need creates a motivation to keep the transnational links to their social networks abroad.

7.3.4   Employment in Tirana

As previously stated, educated female return migrants live in Tirana, among people who are similar to them due to employment opportunities that are more appropriate for them given their education. It is their relation to the labour market and career advancement that I flesh out in this subsection. First, the interviews demonstrate the importance of family and friendship networks and the lack of institutional support in finding jobs. None of the interviewed women has any knowledge of governmental programmes for return migrants, and they report a lack of trust employment agencies. Four have heard of the Brain Gain programme[4] but none has ever applied to benefit from it.

Fiona illustrates the informal practices involved in looking for a job in Albania and the lack of trust in institutional channels:

One has no idea how to find a job, and there are no announcements, no employment agencies, nothing. The announcements in the newspapers are just to comply with official rules because vacancies have already been assigned. … I knew nobody. I spent about six months just going around, completely lost and also disappointed. I started to look for ways to leave again as I had absolutely no hope here. And I graduated from my MA with very high grades.

---

[4]The Brain Gain programme was implemented by the Albanian government from 2006 to 2012, with the aim of reversing brain drain through the return of qualified migrants (for more information on the Brain Gain programme, see Zeneli (2013, 9-52)). The Brain Gain officers operated until 30 June 2013 and a total of 138 individuals (50 women, 88 men) benefited from the incentive packages. The Brain Gain programme also supported legal and regulatory changes. As of June 2015, it was unknown whether the program was still operative as the official website was offline.

> *If you do not have the right connections, nobody cares for your diploma. Then, entirely by chance, I met somebody who needed a consultant for a two-year project.*

Interestingly, in this excerpt, Fiona claims that Albania has 'no employment agencies'. In fact, each of the country's twelve prefectures has employment agencies[5] but job seekers rarely resort to them since these agencies focus more on low-skilled employment (Wittberger et al., 2012; Danaj, 2014). Beti also highlights the role of social relations: *'Here everything was being done through friends and acquaintances'.* In the same context, Elida says that one of her former colleagues recommended her to a private university looking for staff with doctoral degrees. The interviewees reveal that finding a job is a process generally mediated through social relations (mostly friendship networks). Egesta, too, says that she found her first job through her friends' acquaintances. She adds that she later found complementary, part-time employment through friends she made at her primary job.

The women in this chapter work for public and private universities as lecturers and for NGOs and private television stations. These sectors hold the most appeal for international student returnees. Mai and Paladini (2013, 52) also emphasise that well-educated returnees from Italy mainly work in recently developed sectors in Albania, such as private universities, NGOs, private televisions and the public administration sector.

A second point concerning the participants' employment in Tirana is career advancement, which they stress as a significant issue for them. Therefore, it is worth exploring how they succeed in this area.

> *Monika: Here, it is like a jungle. There are no rules. Nobody knows what should be done to advance your career or to keep your job. It's just like a jungle.*

> *Egesta: It is challenging to advance in your career. I mean, the worst thing is that one day, you may have a high position, surprising even to yourself, and then tomorrow, you are out. And, you know neither why you obtained the fantastic job to start with, nor why you were thrown out.*

A lack of gradual steps to career advancement and the absence of specified regulations and competencies pertaining to job positions emerged as the main issues in the interviews. Other obstacles include corruption, nepotism and political favouritism in the labour market in Albania, as has been extensively documented (Vullnetari, 2012; Trimcev et al., 2005; Musaraj, 2009; Mai & Paladini, 2013). Beti describes this lack of clarity about career advancement:

> *There is no clear idea how the hell you can advance in your job. Yes, we all know that you have to know the right people, but I don't know if there is any other way. ... It's only a question of image.*

Beti adds:

> *You have to be good-looking, present across the media. These are the values required to progress in your career. And this is so humiliating. It's humiliating to be appreciated only*

---

[5] According to the structure of the Ministry of Welfare (formerly the Ministry of Labour, Social Affairs and Equal Opportunities), www.sociale.gov.al

*for this. It's like a violation, which is not physical, but sometimes it is even worse. I had
forgotten these 'values' entirely, and now I have to adapt to this situation. Sometimes I find
myself acting in ways I don't recognise. It's terrible.*

Here, we come to the third pattern that materialises in these women's relation to
the labour market as it emerges from their interviews: physical appearance seems to
carry much more weight than competency. As shown by Beti's quotation, prizing
appearance over competency violates her values and beliefs. Furthermore, she experiences an inner conflict as, to preserve her job, she might have to behave in a way
she does not like. In addition to Beti, Fiona also says that she hates women have to
look like "*'supermodels when they go to work, so they can be appreciated and have
a good career'.*" It is evident that women often face escalating sexual objectification. Accordingly, Egesta declares:

*I often get pissed off, especially at older men and their offensive comments about your
physical appearance and other sex-related comments. … I mean, yes, in Italy too, men are
like this, with their words and stuff, about your legs and breasts, and whatever … but not so
gross and not so persistent and offensive… Then you have to become either arrogant and
act brutally or refuse any contact and keep to yourself. … The problem is that this disgust-
ing man might be your boss or your boss's friend, so then you don't really know how to
behave since you want to keep your job.*

Interestingly, Egesta's words testify to the existence of sexual offences both in the
home and the destination country. Sexual objectification is not an Albanian-specific
problem that these returnees experience only after returning to Tirana. Additionally,
and more importantly, Egesta denounces sexual objectification and sexual offences
for adding to job uncertainty.

On a last note, insecurity about keeping their jobs preoccupies all the participants. We have seen that they criticise the lack of regulation regarding career
advancement and promotions or even the lack of official rules for a job. On the one
hand, this isa feature of the Albanian labour market where corruption, nepotism and
informality replace institutional functionality. On the other hand, job insecurity is
an issue that extends beyond Albania: the growing employment precarity among
young, educated people is a global phenomenon (Simone et al., 2015). This precarity is not exclusive to low-skilled workers but affects even highly skilled ones, as
highlighted by Pierre Bourdieu (1998). The women in this chapter are all highly
educated but in a situation of uncertain and unstable employment despite that fact.

In the wider Albanian context, these women are considered to have good, well-
paying jobs relatively in line with their professions or, at least, with the Albanian
expression 'office jobs' (*pune zyre*). However, the participants all report that they
have no trust in the contracts they maintain, and some, particularly Egesta, even
doubt whether the employer was paying their social insurance contributions.
Likewise, Fiona says that her contract is *'just a piece of paper'*, as one of her colleagues was fired within one day despite it. Elida shares that the risk of being fired
is ever-present; therefore, she tries to keep her and her husband's social networks as
stable as possible in order to keep their jobs or possibly find others in case something happens to their current positions. Most importantly, this uncertainty surrounding the 'interviewees' employment and social statuses is also reflected in their

dilemmas and projects about leaving Albania again. Migrants find it very difficult to readjust upon their return in Albania due to their home country's different work climate and culture, and that drives them to consider other migration projects (Kopliku, 2016).

7.3.5   Return Migration as a Transitional Phase

This section focuses on women's projects to migrate again, showing that for most of them, Tirana is only a phase in their migration project. Similarly, other researchers (Black & King, 2004; Ley & Kobayashi, 2009; Sondhi, 2013; Sondhi & King, 2017) see return migration not as a permanent move but as part of a broader, continuing migration process. Everyday informal practices and insecure jobs drive returnees' projects to migrate once again. Sondhi and King (2017) underline similar patterns among Indian return international students.

The state of being in between two countries is another factor in these return migrants' projects of migration. Egesta, for example, describes how some returnees to Tirana remain in limbo between their current life in Tirana, to which they have difficulties adapting, and their previous experience in the destination country.

> *I don't know how the health insurance system works because anytime you need to go to the hospital you have to deal with everything individually. … Yes, life in Tirana is indeed far more dynamic than in other Albanian cities. Still, this insecurity that you have, especially when you are alone and live alone, is becoming unbearable. … What hurts me more is that despite the life that I had built in Italy, I was not feeling at home as my family was in Albania, but here in Tirana, I don't feel at home either. It's a complicated feeling. Leaving aside the sentimentalism, I am concretely planning to go to Italy again as soon as I manage to take my parents with me.*

Egesta gives one example of what it is like to be caught in a vicious circle. She returned to Tirana since it offers more job opportunities than her hometown and allows her to live on her own. However, her employment situation and the difficulties of living alone push her to plan to re-emigrate. Here, once again, we also see how gender intersects with migration strategies. Caring for one's parents influences the decision of whether to re-emigrate and, if so, when and how.

Egesta also addresses the matter of feeling at home. Uncertainties of 'being at home' characterise the returnees' experiences in Tirana (i.e., the home is considered to be a 'physical location or 'house/apartment and, in the Albanian language, the same word, *shtëpi, also* denotes the set of feelings and ideas associated with it) (Vullnetari, 2015, 40). The returnees experience estrangement not only in their place of origin but throughout their migration experiences. In the words of Egesta, 'home' is neither in Italy nor Albania. Fiona, too, reports feeling like a stranger in Tirana:

> *I am looking to leave again. … I hope to find a job somewhere else. I've applied for some jobs in Switzerland, and the UK also—that would be great—and Germany too. … It is complicated here, I need to work very hard, and at the same time, I have nothing stable. …*

I feel like a stranger most of the time. … It's this feeling like I am here temporarily until I find something better abroad.

Artemisa explains that when she left in 2000, she expected Albania would make more progress in 8 years' time. To the contrary, she says the situation looks even worse in some ways. She stresses the feeling of uncertainty that dominates in Tirana, especially regarding employment:

If you lose your job here, you're practically lost. There is nothing there to protect you, no assistance, nothing. … Tirana is perfect as long as you don't have any problem, as long as you have a job and good money and good health. Otherwise, you're lost.

In the same vein, Lindita, who only stayed in Sweden for 2 years, is trying to leave again, probably to a Nordic country where, she says, *'women are in a far better position than in other countries'*. As Lindita recounts, the situation of women and men in Sweden, and the differences from Albania, impressed her. Configurations of gender roles and relations fuel Lindita's desire to migrate as well as her choice of destinations. Her experience abroad also informs her plans to re-migrate:

I hope I will manage to find some opportunity for a PhD programme or even a masters. … But sometimes I think, uh, I am 28 years old, and I'll have to study again, instead of having a good job and some clarity about the future. It's not a very beautiful picture. But what can I do?! But, you know, I am also thinking about applying to the Canadian lottery[6] as I have heard that it is an excellent country to live in, a very social one, and maybe it will be easier to find a job and settle.

Again, they perceive further education as a strategy to enable migration in the context of the constraining migration regime for Albanian citizens. A paradoxical situation emerges as women try to fulfil their desire for stability by re-emigrating. They build their migration project on gendered geographical imaginaries about social and gender-equal countries, as highlighted in this research.

7.4   Conclusions—Discussing the Findings

This chapter analyses the experiences of female international students who migrated on their own and settled in Tirana after returning. Similar to the cases analysed in the previous chapter, it is difficult to speak of a definite return as here, too, women returned to Albania but moved to Tirana instead of their hometowns. Thus, the process of adjustment to Tirana has particular significance for most of the women as a completely new settlement. In what follows, I start with outlining the overall findings and then emphasise four specific patterns.

I should first note that, as previously observed, the decision-making process of these international migrant students is not individual but is embedded within social relationships, particularly to their parents and friends. Again, parental support is not

---

[6] She refers to the Canadian immigration programme.

only financial but also motivational, emotional and protective in the face of the social pressure these women face in their hometowns. Parents also relieve their daughters of their caregiver role so that they can migrate, as research on Turkish and Chinese international student migrants has also found (Erel, 2009; Kajanus, 2014). The cases in this chapter show that female student migrants are daughters, wives, and mothers, as well as students, and they must juggle all these roles while making decisions about whether to migrate abroad and return to Albania.

Additionally, the women's interviews depict the multiple processes of adjustment and readjustment that they experience. Through their cases, migration manifests as a plurality of experiences and histories (as defined by Ahmed et al., 2003). Most of these women are in a constant process of 'uprooting and regrounding home and migration' (Ahmed et al., 2003, 2,10). They adjust to, among other factors, new everyday practices and new gender divisions of space and time both in the destination countries and upon their return to Albania.

The first particular pattern of this chapter is related to the motivations triggering the migration process for these international student migrants. The results of the analysis reveal these motivations are numerous and gendered. Similar to other studies on international student migration (Findlay et al., 2012; King and Ruiz-Gelices, 2003; Ichimoto, 2004; Kajanus, 2014; Oluwaseun, 2016), these women migrants are attracted by better educational opportunities which they hope will lead to better jobs. The saying 'better education means better jobs' is a general maxim in Albanian society, as it became evident in the preceding chapters. The insight that better education does not necessarily lead to better jobs and career advancement has wide-ranging repercussions for the lives of international student returnees. In many of the cases presented in this chapter, it has forced them to return to Albania or engage in countless cycles of remigration.

The female students' international migration is not only shaped by a desire for better education and job opportunities but also informed by an aim to transgress the accepted borders of femininity in their places of origin. These young women migrate to escape the social pressures borne out of gendered expectations in their hometowns. Matsui (1995) and Ichimoto (2004) relay similar accounts of Japanese female international student migrants, who explain that one of their motivations for leaving is to escape the patriarchal society in Japan.

Education provides another means of migrating with proper paperwork and not through illegalised channels. Again, education is revealed as a strategy for migration, in this case for international migration. Women in this chapter illustrate King and Raghuram's (2013) finding that international students are involved in a life migration strategy and their educational objective is part of their life-course desire for long-term migration.

In a second point, I observe one of the gendered patterns of these migrants' return to Albania in their new move to Tirana. They favour Tirana over their hometowns as the capital offers more economic opportunities and enables them to emulate the lifestyle they had abroad to a certain extent: living on their own, away from the social pressures of their communities of origin. This strategy asserts these young women's agency and resistance to the traditional gender roles and expectations dominant in their places of origin. By staying in Tirana, these young women find a middle ground between the two homes they have made. Gender informs their preference of Tirana over their cities of origin which, with their stricter gender relations and more stringent social control, are places to which they have become estranged. This pattern confirms Ghosh's (2000) claim that the initial motivations for migration heavily influence the decision to return. In this case, the initial motive was to escape the social pressure present in the interviewees' cities of origin. Again, as noted, gendered geographical imaginaries—Tirana as a place with less strict gender expectations and more freedom—inform their choice to not return to their hometowns. Settling in Tirana may be seen as a resistance to giving up their autonomous way of life and freedom. Sondhi and King (2017) similarly discuss Indian international female students who do not want to return home specifically because they want to avoid losing the sense of freedom they experienced while living abroad. Interviewed women here prevent their loss of liberty by moving to a space in the middle instead of returning to their hometowns.

The third pattern concerns the new social relations created upon the participants' return to Tirana. Their narratives show that they base their new social networks on similarities and include mostly return international students with similar migration experiences. The participants cope with the constraints experienced in Tirana by mobilising existing social networks, as well as creating new ones. These international student return migrants establish new communities and alternative spaces, confirming Tarrius's (1993) view that migrants participate in the social construction of the place of destination. Furthermore, we can analyse the gatherings of young women and men returning from migratory experiences through the lenses of estrangement and homemaking (Ahmed, 1999). 'Having come from other places', they attempt to 'come together' in this new place (Ahmed, 1999, 345). The sense of estrangement they may feel after returning to Tirana presses these young people to create new spaces and communities of exchange and interaction that, in turn, help transform the city itself. The creation of new social networks and connections is an adaptation to the new social reality in Tirana.

The chapter's fourth finding centres on the paradox that the desire for stability pushes these women to consider additional re-emigration projects. Paradoxically, re-emigration means seeking stability in migration. More concretely, the cases analysed in this chapter reveal that return migration is not a permanent move but more often is part of a continuous migration process, confirming the findings of Ley and Kobayashi (2009) and Sondhi and King (2017). Although these women have more opportunities to find better jobs than highly educated women who have migrated only internally within Albania, these groups have in common the fact that their jobs are precarious. Some aspects of the post-return experiences relate to job insecurity, precariousness, and sexual objectification. This finding is similar to the experiences of Indian female return student migrants who face a male-dominated labour market and a lack of freedom in everyday life (Sondhi & King, 2017). Thus, the cases in this chapter show how, paradoxically, these women seek job stability in instability, by planning to migrate again.

Another noteworthy point is that their return migration is not a conclusive return, since they describe themselves as in a state of in-betweenness and estrangement (see also Ahmed, 1999). As in other research (Mai & Paladini, 2013; Ghosh & Wang, 2003), some women can find that they fit culturally or economically neither abroad – where they have no work appropriate to their education – nor in Albania – where they feel culturally estranged. They report not feeling at home anywhere, similarly to what Ghosh and Wang (2003) reveal about their experiences between India, China and Canada.

Finally, like the international migrant women discussed in Chap. 5, some women analysed in this chapter engage in circular migration upon their return to Tirana to maintain contact with their networks abroad. In line with other research (Black & King, 2004; Cassarino, 2004; Dahinden, 2010a), the cases in this chapter show that return does not entail total detachment from previous migratory experiences. Instead, return migration involves the maintenance of transnational links to previous social, professional, and friendship networks and the retainment of some earlier habits. The women featured in this chapter show that what their experience upon their return, appears to be a constant state of limbo between their hometowns, Tirana and abroad.

References

Ahmed, S. (1999). Home and away. Narratives of migration and estrangement. *International Journal of Cultural Studies, 2*(3), 329–347.

Ahmed, S., Castañeda, C., Fortier, A.-M., & Sheller, M. (2003). Introduction. In S. Ahmed, C. Castañeda, A.-M. Fortier, & M. Sheller (Eds.), *Uprootings/Regroundings: Questions of Home and Migration* (pp. 1–22). Berg.

Black, R., & King, R. (2004). Editorial introduction: Migration, return and development in West Africa. *Population, Space and Place, 10*, 75–83.

Bourdieu, P. (1998). La précarité est aujourd'hui partout. In P. Bourdieu, *Contre-feux, Propos pour servir à la résistance contre l'invasion néo-libérale* (pp. 95-101). Paris : Éditions Raisons d'agir.

Boyd, M. (1989). Family and personal networks in international Migration: Recent developments and new agendas. *International Migration Review, 23*(3), 638–670.

Brooks, R. (2013). International students with dependent children: The reproduction of gender norms. *British Journal of Sociology of Education, 36*(2), 195–214.

Çaro, E. (2011). *From the village to the city: The adjustment process of internal migrants in Albania.* Rozenberg Publishers.

Cassarino, J.-P. (2004). *Theorising Return Migration: a revisited conceptual approach to return migrants* (EUI Working Paper(2004/02)).

Dahinden, J. (2010a). Are you who you know? A network perspective on ethnicity, gender and transnationalism: Albanian-speaking migrants in Switzerland and returnees in Kosovo. In C. Westin, J. Bastos, J. Dahinden, & P. Góis (Eds.), *Identity processes and dynamics in multi-ethnic Europe* (pp. 127–148). Amsterdam University Press.

Dahinden, J. (2010b). Cabaret dancers: "Settle down in order to stay Mobile?" bridging theoretical orientations within transnational migration studies. *Social Policies, 17*(3), 323–348.

Danaj, E. (2014). Family in Albania as primary solidarity network. In R. Pichler (Ed.), *Legacy and change: Albanian transformation from multidisciplinary perspectives* (pp. 117–134). LIT Verlag.

Danaj, E. (2019). Gendered experiences of international student migration: The case of Albania. *Gender, Place & Culture, 26*(4), 607–611.

Danaj, E., Festy, P., Ekonomi, M., Lika, M., Guxho, A., & Zhllima, E. (2005). *Becoming an adult: Challenges and potentials of youth in Albania.* Tirana.

Erel, U. (2009). *Migrant women transforming citizenship: Life-stories from Britain and Germany.* Ashgate.

Findlay, A. M., King, R., Smith, F. M., Geddes, A., & Skeldon, R. (2012). World class? An investigation of globalization, difference and international student mobility. *Transactions of the Institute of British Geographers, 37*(1), 118–131.

Gërmenji, E., & Milo, L. (2011). Migration of the skilled from Albania: Brain drain or brain gain? *Journal of Balkan and Near Eastern Studies, 13*(3), 339–356.

Ghosh, B. (2000). Return migration: Reshaping policy approaches. In B. Ghosh (Ed.), *Return migration: Journey of Hope or despair?* (pp. 181–226). IOM.

Ghosh, S., & Wang, L. (2003). Transnationalism and identity: A tale of two faces and multiple lives. *Canadian Geographer, 47*(3), 269–283.

Hochschild, A. R. (2000). Global care chains and emotional surplus value. In W. Hutton & A. Giddens (Eds.), *On the edge: Living with global capitalism* (pp. 130–146). Jonathan Cape.

Hondagneu-Sotelo, P., & Avila, E. (1997). "I'm here, but I'm there": The meanings of Latina transnational motherhood. *Gender and Society*, 548–571.

Ichimoto, T. (2004). Ambivalent 'selves' in transition: A case study of Japanese women in Australian universities. *Journal of Intercultural Studies, 25*, 247–269.

Kajanus, A. (2014). *Journey of the Phoenix: Overseas study and women's changing position in China.* Helsinki.

King, R., & Raghuram, P. (2013). International student migration: Mapping the field and new research agendas. *Population, Space and Place, 19*(2), 127–137.

King, R., & Ruiz-Gelices, E. (2003). International student migration and the European «year abroad»: Effects on European identity and subsequent migration behaviour. *International Journal of Population Geography, 9*(3), 229–252.

Kopliku, B. (2016). Return migration in the Shkodra region – what's the next step? In M. Zbinden, J. Dahinden, & A. Efendic (Eds.), *Diversity of migration in south East Europe* (pp. 111–134). Peter Lang.

Ley, D., & Kobayashi, A. (2009). Back to Hong Kong: Return migration or transnational sojourn? In D. Conway & R. B. Potter (Eds.), *Return migration of the next generations: 21st century transnational mobility* (pp. 119–138). Ashgate.

Mai, N., & Paladini, C. (2013). Flexible circularities: Integration, return, and socio- economic instability within Albanian migration to Italy. In A. Triandafyllidou (Ed.), *Circular migration between Europe and its neighborhood, choice or necessity?* (pp. 42–67). Oxford University Press.

Massey, D. (1994). *Space, place, and gender.* University of Minnesota Press.

Matsui, M. (1995). Gender role perceptions of Japanese and Chinese female students in American universities. *Comparative Education Review, 39*, 356–378.

McDowell, L. (1983). Towards an understanding of the gender division of urban space. *Environment and Planning D: Society and Space, 1*, 59–72.

Musaraj, S. (2009). Passport troubles: Social tactics and places of informal transactions in postsocialist Albania. *Anthropology of East Europe Review, 27*(2), 157–175.

Nixon, N. (2009). 'You can't eat shame with bread': Gender and collective shame in Albanian society. *Southeast European and Black Sea Studies, 9*(1-2), 105–121.

Oluwaseun, S. (2016). *Understanding international student migration: The case ofNigerian Christian women students engaged in postgraduate studies in UK higher education.* University of Nottingham.

Olwig, K. F. (1999). Narratives of the children left behind: Home and identity in globalised Caribbean families. *Journal of Ethnic and Migration Studies, 25*(2), 267–284.

Riaño, Y. (2015). Latin American women who migrate for love: Imagining European men as ideal partners. In E. Begonya & J. Roca (Eds.), *Rethinking romantic love. Discussions, imaginaries and practices* (pp. 45–60). Cambridge Scholars Publishing.

Rose, G. (1993). *Feminism and geography: The limits of geographical knowledge*. University of Minnesota Press.

Shu, J., & Hawthorne, L. (1995). Asian female students in Australia: Temporary movements and student Migration. *Journal of the Australian Population Association, 12*(2), 113–130.

Simone, A., Schilling, H., Dembélé, O., Febriyani, R., Irawaty, A. M., & Triantafyllopoulou, E. (2015). Practices within Precarity: Youth, Informality, and Life Making in the Contemporary City. Paper presented at the RC21 International Conference on "The Ideal City: between myth and reality. Representations, policies, contradictions and challenges for tomorrow's urban life" Urbino (Italy) 27–29 August 2015. http://www.rc21.org/en/conferences/urbino2015/

Sondhi, G. (2013). *Gendering international student mobility: An Indian case study*. University of Sussex.

Sondhi, G., & King, R. (2017). Gendering international student migration: An Indian case-study. *Journal of Ethnic and Migration Studies, 43*(8), 1308–1324.

Tarrius, A. (1993). Territoires Circulatoires et Espaces Urbaine. *Annales de la Recherche Urbain*, 59–60.

Triandafyllidou, A. (2013). Circular migration: Introductory remarks. In A. Triandafyllidou (Ed.), *Circular migration between Europe and its neighborhood: Choice or necessity?* (pp. 1–21). Oxford University Press.

Trimçev, E., Dakli, E., & Ymeri, S. (2005). *Albanian brain drain: Turning the tide*. Albanian Institute for International Studies.

Vullnetari, J. (2007). *Albanian migration and development: State of the art review* (MISCOE Working Paper 18).

Vullnetari, J. (2012). *Albania on the move: Links between internal and international migration*. Amsterdam University Press.

Vullnetari, J. (2015). 'Home to go': Albanian older parents in transnational social fields. In K. Walsh & L. Näre (Eds.), *Transnational migration and home in older age* (pp. 38–50). Routledge.

Wittberger, D., Plaku, A., Jaupllari, V., & Miluka, J. (2012). *The national report on the status of women and gender equality*. Tirana.

Zenelaga, B., & Sotirofski, K. (2011). *The 'Brain gain hypotheses' of transition countries elites and socioeconomic development in their home country (Albanian Emigrants in Italy Sample)* (AlmaLaurea Working Papers).

Zeneli, B. (2013). Brain gain program in Albania: Case study and policy guide for policymakers in Southeast Europe. In T. Pavlov, (Ed.), *Brain gain policies and practices in the Western Balkans*, Group 484 Centre for Migration.

Open Access This chapter is licensed under the terms of the Creative Commons Attribution 4.0 International License (http://creativecommons.org/licenses/by/4.0/), which permits use, sharing, adaptation, distribution and reproduction in any medium or format, as long as you give appropriate credit to the original author(s) and the source, provide a link to the Creative Commons license and indicate if changes were made.

The images or other third party material in this chapter are included in the chapter's Creative Commons license, unless indicated otherwise in a credit line to the material. If material is not included in the chapter's Creative Commons license and your intended use is not permitted by statutory regulation or exceeds the permitted use, you will need to obtain permission directly from the copyright holder.

Chapter 8
Conclusions

I began my research by asking, '*How can we understand the interrelation between gender and migration in Albania?*'. As my research progressed, three other questions emerged, which necessitated, first, investigating the tactics migrant women used during migration; second, identifying their migratory trajectories; and finally, understanding their experiences in the city of Tirana. To answer these questions, I conducted interviews with thirty-two migrant women involved in internal or multiple migratory trajectories who were all living in Tirana at the time when I conducted my fieldwork.

Using a feminist perspective, my research aimed to analyse and highlight some aspects of these migrant women's experiences to help better understand how gender and migration are entangled in Albania. The sample is separated into four groups: women who migrated only internally, female students who migrated internally on their own, women who migrated internationally for purposes other than education and female students who migrated internationally on their own. I opted for this separation to avoid homogenising Albanian female migrants, to highlight the particularities of each group's experiences and to reveal what these specific experiences can tell us about the social processes related to migration and gender. I begin the introductory section of this chapter by laying out three overall findings of my research, before turning to the two core findings of the study. The particular insights emanating from these two core findings are detailed in the next five sections.

Quantitative analysis on Albanian migration has revealed its significant scale but also contributed to forging a masculinised image of international migration and a feminised image of internal migration. During the 1990s, male international migrants certainly outnumbered female ones. Nevertheless, women, too, were present in significant numbers in this migration phase, and not only as passive migrants leaving Albania for the purpose of family reunification. The examples in this book add to this line of research by shedding light on women's migratory experiences that often remain hidden in statistical research. These examples underpin the first overall finding: *migrant women in Albania have been participating in international*

© The Author(s) 2022

E. Danaj, *Women, Migration and Gendered Experiences*, IMISCOE Research Series, https://doi.org/10.1007/978-3-030-92092-0_8

migration since the early 1990s, often crossing borders in the same risky ways typically associated only with men.

I premised my analysis on the gender and migration theoretical stream that rejects the characterization of migration as a single move from the sending country to the receiving country in favour of approaching it as a gendered process involving a multiplicity of movements. My analysis indeed captures a broader picture of the intersection of gender and migration in Albania that challenges the mainstream view that female migration is entirely internal in nature. In fact, the second overall finding of this study is that *migrant women in Albania engage in multiple migration trajectories combining internal, international, return and circular migration.*

This book repeatedly shows that migration is a complex process involving numerous decisions that cannot all be explained by a single motivation. Furthermore, these motivations are gendered, as the examples presented here illustrate, which brings us to the third overall finding: *women do not migrate solely for economic and educational purposes but also to escape from the gender constraints and the patriarchal practices and customs prevailing in their villages and cities of origin.*

Answering the main question raised at the beginning of this research required me to conduct an in-depth investigation of these female migrants' experiences. This book is situated within the research stream that highlights the complexities of the interrelation between gender and migration. Migration can challenge and transform but also reinforce gender equalities; it might lead to new opportunities and liberation or to new forms of gender inequalities and precarity. Now, at the conclusion of this research, my analysis clearly reveals the complex interplay between gender and migration as evidenced by the fact that Albanian migrant women do not automatically move from inequality to liberation. Instead, per the first core finding, *the results of the study show that migrant women encounter various gender constraints and inequalities that might be different from those in their places of origin but stem from the same underlying mechanism of unequal gender relations.* Women, however, do not passively go through the migration process but mobilise their available resources and manifest agency in various forms, primarily through the tactics they employ. The concept of tactics, or the weapons of the weak (Scott 1985) who operate within the prevailing systems and cannot effect significant change in the dominant relations, gives a nuanced understanding of these women's manifestations of agency and processes of empowerment across their migration journeys. This brings us to the second (and complementary) core finding of the study: *these migrant women manifest their empowerment not by tearing down deeply rooted gender relations and constructed gender roles but by deploying their agency and resources within the existing gendered power relations.*

The following section expands on these two main findings, elaborating on how they contribute to the existing body of literature on gender and migration. More specifically, the key results presented therein explore the case of female student migrants, the role of social networks, the experiences of return migration, the complexity of care chains, and Tirana's role as a locus of the interplay between gender and migration.

8.1 Key Results

8.1.1 The Complex Relationship Between Gender, Migration and Education

The study of student migration, particularly internal migration, from a gender perspective remains a domain open to further development. One of the aims of this book is to address this lacuna in the areas of both internal and international migration by exploring the experiences of Albanian female students who are internal and return migrants. At the international level, the number of female migrant students is growing and often exceeding that of male students, as is the case in East Asia (Kim 2012, 31). This trend has emerged in Albania, too, both internally and internationally. By focusing on individual experiences at the intersection of gender and migration rather than simply numbers, this analysis shows that *young women in Albania use education for a dual purpose: to cross physical internal and international borders and to break through the social barriers that obstruct the migration of young women migrating on their own.* Albanian families, independent of parents' education level, place significant value on education, largely due to the emphasis and work that the communist regime put on education. At the same time, I saw that kinship and communities do not widely accept migration by women on their own. However, Vullnetari (2009) and Kalaja (2014) argue that kins and hometown communities gossip less about and are more likely to accept young women who migrate on their own for educational purposes.

Education, therefore, becomes a gendered value used by young women to leave their hometowns in a way that is considered more socially acceptable. Moreover, for international student migrants, education provides a way to cross borders in legal, safe ways, endowed with appropriate visas and, often, the financial support of scholarships.

Given the significant, socially-accepted value of education, these student migrants sometimes rely heavily on financial and other forms of support from their parents. And non-financial support can take many forms. The cases show that, for instance, parents mobilise to protect their daughters from family and community gossip that attacks them for having migrated alone. A second major form of support is the parents' decision to take on their daughters' caregiving responsibilities, thereby enabling them to migrate.

Adding to the international literature on gender and student migration (Ichimoto 2004; Matsui 1995; Kim 2012), and particularly contributing to that on Albanian migration, *this analysis highlights the fact that for female students, both internal and international migration offer an escape from the gender constraints of their hometowns.* Migrating to Tirana or abroad also means fleeing from the social control and the roles and norms applied to young women that remain entrenched in their places of origin. Migration enables them to seek a freer, more independent way of life.

In this context, a new question emerges: what do these young women find in their destinations? Are they free from the gender constraints they sought to escape? This brings us to a third related finding: the paradoxical situation of student migrants. *The results show that, in their destination cities, female student migrants are granted an anonymity that stands in direct contrast to the social control experienced in their places of origin, but they also encounter new gendered prejudices and constraints.* In Chap. 6, we see how student migrants in Tirana face prejudice, stigmatisation, and even sexual harassment – especially in the workplace – as young women who migrate and live alone. To cope with these new constraints, young women mobilise their resources and capital.

More significantly, these cases provide new insights into the complexities of the relationship between gender and migration, as migrant women juggle various gender constraints throughout their migration process. As highlighted in the second core finding of this study, the complex relationship between gender and migration manifests itself, not in the form of women breaking down the deeply rooted gender relations that constrain them, but by these young women using the available resources to achieve their objectives within the existing gendered relations.

However, it is worth considering a little more how these student migrants transgress socially accepted gender expectations, as illustrated by the tactics young women employ to postpone marriage and motherhood. They see marriage as a loss of independence and a threat to their professional development, burdening them with care and housework. This dissertation is based on interviews conducted in 2012, and it is impossible to know the participants' future views on marriage. Nevertheless, the analysis shows that these women engage in numerous negotiations and tactics to postpone marriage, which continues to be the hegemonic form of family formation in Albania (Danaj et al., 2005; Lerch, 2009). Interestingly, these tactics include using the father's role as the head of the household to escape the gendered requirement of marriage. Here, the logic of not fully disturbing the unequal gender roles persists. To postpone marriage, these young women use the same unequal gender roles they want to transgress.

8.1.2 The Dynamics of Social Networks

Another noteworthy aspect of the intersection between gender and the migration process is the role of social relations and networks. These social relations and networks are crucial to understanding the patterns of migration, settlement, employment and links with home the women interviewed for this research describe. When it comes to Albanian internal and international migration, they present key factors that play a role in determining migration decisions, selecting a destination, and organising the migration project. Unsurprisingly, my research results show that preexisting networks often appear to make both internal and international migration a feasible option. Various existing social relations and networks are mobilised to accomplish the migration project and to figure out the logistics of crossing internal and international borders and securing accommodations, employment, and dealing with a number of other challenges.

Let us focus our attention on the further insights this study offers into the dynamic nature of social networks and the establishment of new ties once one reaches their destination. Regarding the dynamics of social networks throughout the migration process, *the findings evidence Albanian migrant women's ability to extensively use their resources to establish new ties and networks in order to adapt to unfamiliar social realities.* These results add to the existing literature (e.g., Boyd 1989; Hagan 1998; Schmoll 2006; Ryan 2007; Dahinden 2010) on the dynamics of social networks during the migration process by highlighting new gendered configurations of the role of these networks. Such studies reveal that gender plays a critical role in the creation of social relations, sometimes hindering the process. For instance, Hagan (1998) shows that because of their confinement to domestic care jobs, Guatemalan female migrants suffered from lack of information regarding residence permit procedures, compared to their male counterparts who had a more extensive social network. Examples illustrating how gender influences social networking structures are present in this book too, as demonstrated below.

First, to adapt to a new life in Tirana and to find sustainable jobs, internal student migrants need to rely heavily on well-developed social networks, particularly so as to access the labour market. In Tirana, nepotism and corruption run rampant in the labour market, and for the women, it appears quite impossible to find jobs without the right informal connections. To build the new connections they need in Tirana, these female students mobilise their existing social capital and their erotic capital, defined by Hakim (2010) as beauty, sexual attractiveness, flirtations, social presentation, and sexuality. Taken together, these types of capital appear to be significant resources that female student mobilise in their quest for good employment and additional income. For instance, a case in Chap. 6 illustrates how a young student migrant engages in a sexual relationship with a wealthy, married man to create new connections and find a well-paying office job.

Second, I consider the networks created among the internal migrants working as domestic workers. Domestic work is an emerging sector and employs many migrant women in Tirana. However, domestic work also remains an invisible sector in the formal labour market. Most domestic workers do not have formal contracts but only verbal arrangements outlining their pay, work schedule, holidays and other job rules. Lacking institutional information and networks, migrant domestic workers have set up solidarity networks of mutual support, sharing information about job openings and the average pay to seek.

Third, international migrants in Greece mobilise their (in)formal employers to overcome administrative and everyday obstacles and to build new social networks. We see that migrant women in Greece, engaged mostly in informal work, use their employers to build the new connections they need to handle the various issues they encounter in their destination. For example, these illegal migrant women in Greece use their employers' important connections when it comes to regularising their residency permits. They also utilise their primary employers' connections to find additional part-time jobs and boost their financial capital.

Fourth, international students who have returned to Tirana present an interesting example that reveals migrant women's ability to adapt to new social realities. They construct new social networks that include mostly highly educated return migrants with similar experiences. They set up new communities and alternative art and cultural spaces in attempts to "'come together"'in this new place (i.e., Tirana), "'having come from other places"'(Ahmed 1999, 345). The estrangement they feel from both Tirana and their hometowns pushes these young women to create new networks and join these new spaces of exchange and interaction.

Taken together, these examples demonstrate the women's capacity to adapt to the new social realities in their destination and to increase their social capital by establishing new relations and networks. Gender informs these social relations and networks, often by limiting them, as we saw in the case of domestic workers in Tirana, for example. The mobilisation of one's erotic capital for the purpose of expanding their social relations and finding a job is an additional example of how gender influences the creation and structure of social relations.

These cases advance our understanding of the complex intersection of gender and migration, and the equally complex role that social networks play at this intersection. Second, these participants show how women attempt to achieve their objectives by working within the existing systems of unequal gender relations and often-hostile institutional structures, including but not limited to nepotism in the labour market and 'the strict Greek immigration policies and informal employment structures.

8.1.3   Gendered Return Experiences

We now turn our attention to the return migration phase and returnees' experiences. As existing research has shown (Cassarino 2004; Sri Tharan 2010), no single factor can fully explain return migration and no single motivation drives it. Moreover, the motivations that do are undeniably gendered. This section explains how the return experiences analysed in this study improve our understanding of the intersection of gender and migration.

First, the analysis shows that a major reason for returning to Albania is to care for and be close to one's parents. *Gender affects the return project because caring for parents is considered to be women's responsibility.* This holds true for both student and non-student international migrants who return to care for their aging or sick parents. Furthermore, these cases add to the exploration of dynamic complex care chains detailed in Sect. 8.1.4, showing that the caregiver role remains exclusively feminised.

Second, this study reveals that another reason for returning to Albania is to invest in one's own business or find a job more appropriate for one's education and skills. Migrant women use the money they have saved and the professional knowledge they have gained while abroad to open their own businesses, such as hair salons, bakeries, and dry-cleaning shops. This pattern further illustrates the migrant status paradox (Nieswand 2011). In Greece and Italy, these migrant women see their social status decline, accepting jobs in the low-income and the informal segments of the labour market. Upon their return to Tirana, however, their economic and social statuses increase due to their financial capital and knowledge, which they invest in entrepreneurial projects and self-employment. The study brings to the fore the ambiguity of women's upgraded status. In Albania, they gain status relative to their jobs in Greece but are hindered by the masculine state manifested in the *bureaucratic institutions that discriminate against female entrepreneurs.* To cope with these obstacles, women employ various tactics, such as being accompanied by male relatives and mimicking masculine behaviour. Paradoxically, they instrumentalise the same power of those whose dominance they try to challenge. This, too, perfectly encompasses the study's two main findings: during the entire migration process, women encounter old and new gender constraints and, to cope with them, employ various tactics present within the existing unequal gender configurations.

8.1.4   From Care Chains to Care Webs: Women's Caregiver Role

Research on gender and migration has extensively analysed caregiving, mostly in global care chains. Understood as a series of personal links between people based on paid or unpaid care work, care chains may be local, national or global. They might start in poor countries and end in rich ones or move from rural to urban areas within the same poor country (Hochschild 2000). In this vein, Albanian studies scholars highlight the complex, post-1991 dynamics of care, provided to both children and aging parents, including intra-familial support and the employment of domestic care workers (Vullnetari and King 2016). Situated within this rich body of literature on care chains, the present analysis brings to the fore further configurations that expose the complexity of care chains and the entanglements of gender and migration.

One notable example of care chains involves internal migrants to Tirana who are employed as domestic and care workers. This first configuration shows how Tirana-based women who enter the labour market pass on their caregiving duties to internal migrants. Women who employ internal migrants as domestic care workers may be non-migrants, internal migrants or return international migrants themselves. In turn, internal migrants employed as domestic care workers by women in Tirana transfer their mothering and caregiving roles to female relatives. This analysis thus points to the complexity of the intersections of internal and international care chains in the particular setting of Tirana.

Second, internal and international migration by women is often possible only because women pass their caregiving duties on to their parents or their daughters. Women become free to migrate thanks to intra-familial care chains, or family solidarity, in which female migrants' caregiver role is assumed by their mothers or daughters. This occurs with both economic and student migration. For instance, grandparents look after their grandchildren, enabling the mother to migrate internationally for educational purposes or economic reasons. Several participants utilise this strategy - which I call intra-familial care chains - so that they can engage in paid employment or migrate internally and internationally.

Another example of intra-familial care chains is the case of migrant women returning to care for their parents. The cases analysed in Chap. 7 show how international student migrants return to care for their parents who are sick or face other difficulties. Another case explored in this Chapter is that of an economic international migrant who was able to migrate and work as a domestic care worker in Greece as her parents-in-law assumed her caregiver role. After several years of pendular migration, she returns to take care of them. In addition to an intra-familial care chain, this particular case illustrates how one migrant woman can take different places in the entrenched local and global caregiving configurations and participate in multiple migration trajectories.

Finally, we come to the third case that further depicts the complexity of care chains: that of return female migrants. While in Greece, these women fill the caregiving gap left by Greek women entering the productive workforce. These cases add to the body of literature demonstrating that the employment of international female migrants as domestic and care workers is framed, first by the inadequacy of welfare regimes and second by the absence of legal immigration channels, sometimes compensated by the toleration of illegal migration and informal employment. The analysis reveals that after returning to Albania, these female migrants who worked as domestic care workers in Greece remain part of care chains but now in the opposite position: as employers, not employees. To fill the caregiving gap in Albania and to engage in productive work, especially entrepreneurial initiatives, these same women hire internal migrants as domestic and care workers. This example illustrates how the city of Tirana emerges as part of entrenched global and local care configurations that, given their multiple entanglements, look more like care webs than care chains.

The notion of a care web should matter for the emotional, psychological and social relations that it entails. Going beyond the labour and financial chains, domestic care work and the intra and interfamilial care transfers also include a substantial emotional and social element. We saw the significance of the psychological aspect in the case of transnational mothers' guilt and suffering at having left her children behind or that of return migrants who hire other internal migrants to pay forward the support and solidarity they have previously received. Hence, when I refer to care webs, I am referring to the complexity of such relations, including the economic transactions as well as the emotional and social dimensions.

To conclude, the multi-layered care chains and webs described in this research account also for men's persistent lack of engagement in the caregiver role. The study results emphasise that these migrant women do not share their constructed caregiver role with their male partners but transfer it to other women who are relatives or employees. This pattern again reinforces the study's core conclusion that migration does not fundamentally change gender relations or produce new gender arrangements. Instead, these migrant women operate mostly by deploying tactics aimed at handling different variations of the same unequal gender arrangements.

8.1.5   Tirana as a Site of Paradoxical Gendered Migratory Experiences

The women at the focus of my research had various experiences and followed multiple migratory trajectories, but they all lived in Tirana at the time of my research. However, none of them considered Tirana their hometown. Tirana may be seen as a site where people, whether married or single, male or female, and from all over Albania come to live, study, and work and where different lifestyles and points of view intersect. Moreover, there is a continuous, both ongoing and incoming, stream of migrants whose trajectories, experiences, and histories continuously intersect. Tirana can be described as a site balancing multiple worlds—the global and the local, the modern and the traditional, the sedentary (non-migrant) and the migrant. In the cases explored in this study, the city of Tirana seems to represent more of a 'crossroads of mobilities' than a place of 'sedentariness'/*sedentarité*, in the words of Tarrius (1993, 1, 52). Internal and return migrant women living in Tirana are keen to engage in further international migration projects and maintain relationships in their destinations through circular migration. Where the intersection of gender and migration is concerned, Tirana is the space where women find new opportunities and new configurations of gender relations together with the same underlying unequal mechanisms, as the following cases reveal.

A first case exploring migrant women in Tirana, as detailed in Chap. 4, is that of internal migrants who moved to the city with their families for multiple reasons. Among the potential internal migration projects under the families' consideration, Tirana offers the best economic, social, and educational opportunities and is the most feasible option for a family migration project, balancing the needs of all family members and containing already-established social networks that serve as a source of support. At the same time, Tirana also provides these women only low-paying job opportunities in the informal labour market, without regular contracts or social insurance.

The analysis further shows that moving to Tirana contributes to the nucleation process for those previously living as part of extended families, thus affecting gender relations within the family. The physical separation of housing is followed by the reorganisation of economic responsibilities, giving women more power and leading to new negotiations of gender relations within the extended household. Despite that, nucleation does not contribute to the reorganisation of gender hierarchies: the husband remains the head of the household, with the most decision-making power. The new negotiations of gender relations take place within the existing unequal gender hierarchies. As shown in Chap. 4, in the context of the nuclear household, men, even when laid off and outside the realm of productive work, do not engage in domestic work. Furthermore, in cases when women become the primary breadwinners in the family, they still go to great pains to maintain for their children the façade that the man is the head of the household. Again, the transformation wrought by negotiating gender does not threaten rooted hierarchical gender relations; to the contrary, migrant women seek to preserve them.

The second case examines the experiences of internal student migrants. To them, Tirana offers not only better educational opportunities but also a more autonomous life, far from their hometowns' stringent gender norms and resulting social control. Such imaginaries of Tirana inform these women's migration projects. This is in accordance with the literature on imaginaries as a powerful force shaping human action (Appadurai 1996) and imaginaries of equality as a driving force behind women's migration projects and actions (Riano 2015). The literature further shows that, typically, one source of this imaginary is the media's positive portrayal of such places (Mai 2004; Kim 2012). However, Tirana does not live up to the gendered imaginaries of a more equal, liberating place. The study results show that, paradoxically, Tirana's lack of social control and liberating dimension are accompanied by new gender constraints and difficulties arising from the same underlying mechanisms as those from which the women escaped. These gender norms place them under new forms of precarity and gendered constraints, such as gender discrimination, job precariousness and sexual objectification and harassment in the workplace. This paradoxical situation appears to inspire in female student internal migrants further gendered geographical imaginaries reflecting a gendered idealisation of abroad and turning Tirana into just a phase in their migratory project.

The third case is that of female international return migrants. Not surprisingly, the analysis shows that better economic and job opportunities are the primary reasons return migrants choose Tirana over their hometowns. However, and more to the point within the scope of this investigation, the results contribute new insights into the intersections of gender and return migration. In particular, the analysis laid down in Chaps. 5 and 7 shows that, for the women whose first migration abroad brought an escape from the gender constraints experienced in their hometowns, Tirana represents the 'big city' that may serve a similar purpose. By staying in Tirana, they find a middle ground between their previous homes in their hometowns and the homes they made while abroad. Gender informs their choice of staying in Tirana over moving back to the hometowns that they consider to be less flexible in gender expectations and relations and spaces that exert stronger social control over these women —places from which they have become estranged.

A fourth case, already discussed in Sect. 8.1.3 on return migration but worth briefly mentioning here too, consists of migrant women who return to invest their financial and know-how capital in Tirana. As previously mentioned, once in Tirana, they are hindered by masculine bureaucratic institutions during the process of opening their businesses.

To conclude, this study shows that Tirana embodies a paradox: *for migrant women, it is a city that offers new and additional avenues for further education, employment and entrepreneurship opportunities; a city for anonymity and independence. At the same time, it is also a city of precarious jobs, sexual prejudice and harassment and the masculine state*. Tirana thus appears to exemplify what the migration process is to these female migrants—a site where new opportunities coexist with both new and old gender constraints, a site where the complex interplay of gender and migration continuously manifests.

8.2   Dilemmas, Limitations and Some Self-Critical Reflections on Further Research Avenues

With this research, I wanted to contribute to further understanding the experiences of Albanian migrant women in particular and the intersections of gender and migration in general.

First, the results of my work emphasise the importance of exploring migration through an integrative approach combining multiple migratory trajectories. It was this approach that helped me uncover and understand the complexity of female migration and the multitude of experiences contained within their various migration trajectories. Secondly, examining female migrants' experiences helped showcase the entrenchment of gender and migration through women's voices and perspectives. I wanted to put their voices centre stage. Analysing their experiences allowed me to identify and explore the possible transformations that gender roles and relations undergo throughout the migration process, the experiences that make migrant women's agency tangible, and the opportunities and the constraints they encounter during their various migration trajectories. Thirdly, this study examines female internal and international student migrants, an under-researched group both within and beyond Albanian migration studies. Analysing their experiences enables us to tease out how gender intersects with this specific type of migration, whether internal or international.

This research focusses on the experiences of migrant women living in the city of Tirana. Although Tirana is Albania's most populated city with the highest percentage of incoming migrants, restricting the analysis to only the city of Tirana limits the scope of the research. I often ask myself, what could this analysis have brought to light if I had used a comparative approach between Tirana and another city? Although the research participants come from across Albania, the experiences of return, student, and internal migrant women could be different in cities other than Tirana. Hence, many other voices and angles could have come to the fore. But I had to decide on my approach and site of analysis, so I opted to focus on those women having relocated to Tirana. That means that the analysis of female migrants' experiences in various regions of Albania remains open to future research on gender and migration in Albania. Such a more comprehensive and comparative approach could also break down the privilege granted to Tirana in this field.

Another point of inner discussion is that the sample could have been narrower, for instance, including only student migrants. In making such a choice, I could have then deepened the analysis of this domain of migration studies. That would have run the risk of limiting the picture of the complexities of female migration trajectories and their intersections with gender. Again, the findings of my analysis open the way for further, in-depth research on internal and international student migration. Such research could offer insights into academic and policy contexts, both domestic and international, and highlight the interplay of structures, institutions and individuals throughout the process of female student migration. Narrowing the focus to student migrants alone could allow for the comparison of the experiences of, for example, internal and international female student migrants; between students remaining in Tirana after their studies and those returning to their hometowns, etc. Issues such as sexual harassment or job precariousness could (and need to) be analysed more in-depth and contribute not only to the academic research but also to policy-making.

Another topic scholars, myself included, need to scrutinise further is the intersection of care, gender and migration. A significant body of international research on this topic provides a solid frame for further work on how local and global care chains manifest in a small, developing country such as Albania. Scholars could also contribute a comparative perspective to this domain of research. Such an analysis could provide new insights into Albanian and foreign domestic workers in Tirana, the role of ethnicity and citizenship in the intersection of gender and migration, the relationship between Albanian emigration and immigration and policy related to domestic workers, both Albanian and foreign. Again, the utility would not be limited to academic research but would be of significant benefit to policy-makers.

While working on my doctoral dissertation in Lisbon, I met a young Albanian gay residing in Italy but coming to Portugal to get married. Same-sex marriage has yet to be legalised in Italy. The interaction made me realize that, in my work, I was missing the experiences of LGBTIQ+ in migration. At that point, I couldn't change my research. But I need to mention this element now because Albanian studies entirely miss LGBTIQ+ migration. My work too is mostly focussed on a gender binary relation, limiting the broad spectrum of experiences in the migration processes. This is as much self-criticism as it is a call to other scholars to further research in this direction.

Finally, Albanian migration needs to be further analysed through an integrative approach as a gendered process that includes various migratory trajectories. Following the work of Juli Vullnetari and Zana Vathi (and here I apologise to other scholars that I am not mentioning only because of my ignorance), this study offers some insights into how gender and the migration process influence each other. It also shed some more light on how the gendered experiences of Albanian migrant women inform and are in turn shaped by their various migration trajectories: internal, international, circular and return migration. These complex entrenchments of gender and migration trajectories await further investigation that may deepen our understanding of how gender influences social processes.

References

Ahmed, S. (1999). Home and away. Narratives of migration and estrangement. *International Journal of Cultural Studies, 2*(3), 329–347.

Appadurai, A. (1996). *Modernity at large: Cultural dimensions of globalization*. University of Minnesota Press.

Boyd, M. (1989). Family and personal networks in international migration: Recent developments and new agendas. *International Migration Review, 23*(3), 638–670.

Cassarino, J.-P. (2004). Theorising Return Migration: a revisited conceptual approach to return migrants. *EUI Working Paper*(2004/02).

Dahinden, J. (2010). Are you who you know? A network perspective on ethnicity, gender and transnationalism: Albanian-speaking migrants in Switzerland and returnees in Kosovo. In C. Westin, J. Bastos, J. Dahinden, & P. Góis (Eds.), *Identity processes and dynamics in multi-ethnic Europe* (pp. 127–148). Amsterdam University Press.

Danaj, E., Festy, P., Ekonomi, M., Lika, M., Guxho, A., & Zhllima, E. (2005). *Becoming an adult: Challenges and potentials of youth in Albania*. INSTAT.

Hagan, J. M. (1998). Social networks, gender, and immigrant incorporation: Resources and constraints. *American Sociological Review, 63*(1), 55–67.

Hakim, C. (2010). Erotic Capital. *European Sociological Review, 26*(5), 499–518.

Hochschild, A. R. (2000). Global care chains and emotional surplus value. In W. Hutton & A. Giddens (Eds.), *On the edge: Living with global capitalism* (pp. 130–146). Jonathan Cape.

Ichimoto, T. (2004). Ambivalent 'selves' in transition: A case study of Japanese women in Australian universities. *Journal of Intercultural Studies, 25*, 247–269.

Kalaja, D. (2014, January 6). Education and marriage patterns for young women in Albania. (E. Danaj, Interviewer).

Kim, Y. (2012). Female individualization? Transnational mobility and media consumption of Asian women. In Y. Kim (Ed.), *Women and the Media in Asia the Precarious Self* (pp. 31–53). Palgrave Macmillan.

Lerch, M. (2009). The impact of migration on fertility in post-communist Albania. *Southeast European and Black Sea Studies, 9*(4), 519–537. https://doi.org/10.1080/14683850903315003

Mai, N. (2004). 'Looking for a more modern life…': The role of Italian Television in the Albanian Migration to Italy. *Westminster Papers in Communication and Culture, 1*(1), 3–22.

Matsui, M. (1995). Gender role perceptions of Japanese and Chinese female students in American universities. *Comparative Education Review, 39*, 356–378.

Nieswand, B. (2011). *Theorising transnational migration: The status paradox of migration*. Routledge.

Riaño, Y. (2015). Latin American women who migrate for love: Imagining European men as ideal partners. In E. Begonya & J. Roca (Eds.), *Rethinking romantic love. Discussions, imaginaries and practices* (pp. 45–60). Cambridge Scholars Publishing.

Ryan, L. (2007). Migrant women, social networks and motherhood: The experiences of Irish nurses in Britain. *Sociology, 41*(2), 295–312.

Schmoll, C. (2006). *Moving "on their own"? Mobility strategies and social networks of migrant women from Maghreb in Italy*. IIIS Discussion Paper 154.

Scott, J. (1985). *Weapons of the weak: Everyday forms of peasant resistance*. Yale University Press.

Sri Tharan, C. T. (2010). *Gender, migration, and social change: The return of Filipino women migrant workers*. University of Sussex.

Tarrius, A. (1993). Territoires Circulatoires et Espaces Urbaine. *Annales de la Recherche Urbain*, 59–60.

Vullnetari, J. (2009). Women and migration in Albania: A view from the village. *International Migration, 50*(5), 169–188.

Vullnetari, J., & King, R. (2016). 'Washing men's feet': Gender, care and migration in Albania during and after communism. *Gender, Place & Culture: A Journal of Feminist Geography, 23*(2), 198–215.

Open Access This chapter is licensed under the terms of the Creative Commons Attribution 4.0 International License (http://creativecommons.org/licenses/by/4.0/), which permits use, sharing, adaptation, distribution and reproduction in any medium or format, as long as you give appropriate credit to the original author(s) and the source, provide a link to the Creative Commons license and indicate if changes were made.

The images or other third party material in this chapter are included in the chapter's Creative Commons license, unless indicated otherwise in a credit line to the material. If material is not included in the chapter's Creative Commons license and your intended use is not permitted by statutory regulation or exceeds the permitted use, you will need to obtain permission directly from the copyright holder.

Printed by Printforce, United Kingdom